HURRICANE
MANUAL
1940

This book is dedicated in memory of Merchant Ship Fighter Unit 'Hurri-cat' pilot and Battle of Britain Spitfire veteran Flying Officer John Kendall, whose last selfless act before bailing out into the Atlantic was to report the position of the enemy Focke-Wulf Condor crew he had just shot down. The enemy airmen were rescued but Kendall remains missing. He was twenty-one.

HURRICANE MANUAL

1940

Edited by Dilip Sarkar
MBE FRHistS

AMBERLEY

First published 2013

Amberley Publishing
The Hill, Stroud
Gloucestershire, GL5 4EP

www.amberley-books.com

British Library Cataloguing in Publication Data.
A catalogue record for this book is available from the British Library.

ISBN 978-1-4456-2120-3
ISBN 978-1-4456-2129-6 (ebook)

Typesetting and Origination by Amberley Publishing.
Printed in Great Britain.

CONTENTS

ABOUT THE EDITOR

Dilip Sarkar is an internationally recognised expert on the Battle of Britain and Fighter Command, on which subjects he has now produced thirty-five well-received books. Made an MBE in 2003 for services to aviation history, Dilip was elected to the Fellowship of the Royal Historical Society in 2006; he achieved a First in History when a mature student upon retirement from the police service. In addition to pursuing historical interests, Dilip has combined his life-long passion for angling and policing experience by leading on the Angling Trust's Fisheries Enforcement Campaign. The author's personal website can be found at www.dilipsarkarmbe.co.uk - and he is a keen Facebook user!

1

THE HAWKER HURRICANE STORY

'This is the story of the greatest aeroplane that has ever flown. It is the story of a machine which embodies the characteristics of the British people – adaptability, reliability, pugnacity when aroused, and the ability to "take it" even when loaded beyond endurance.' So wrote F. H. M. Lloyd in 1945. The Hawker Hurricane monoplane fighter was not, in fact, 'the greatest aeroplane that has ever flown', but Lloyd's parallel with the tenacity of Britain during the Second World War and the Hurricane's faithful service definitely has a ring of truth to it. Indeed, the Hurricane was the RAF's first modern monoplane fighter, the first available in numbers, and the machine flew and fought in all theatres of war in ways unimagined by its creator, Sydney Camm. So, while demonstrably not the 'greatest aeroplane', the Hurricane was certainly a remarkable and essential one.

The potential of military aviation was first demonstrated during the First World War. The 'reach' of air power was confirmed on Christmas Eve 1914, when a German aircraft dropped a bomb on Dover – indicating that island Britain was no longer secure and was thus vulnerable to air attack. As the war ground on, enemy Zeppelins and twin-engined bombers continued their primitive raids, culminating in a 1-ton bomb being dropped on London in 1918. By the Armistice, Britain had suffered over 100 air attacks, killing 1,413 people. This experience generated an awe and fear of air power. Indeed, the doctrinal thinking of the day was that 'the bomber will always get through', to deliver a 'knock-out blow'. After the war, the victorious Allies sought to massively restrict Germany's military capacity in order to prevent the jingoistic Teutons rising again, and set about disarming themselves. The Wall Street Crash in 1922 then plunged the Western world into the Great Depression – meaning that cash for defence was limited. In 1933, however, the Nazis came to power in Germany, determined to redress the hated Versailles *Diktat* and forge

9

a new Germanic Empire. While the 'doves' still cooed for peace, the 'hawks' warned of the perils ahead while Nazi Germany re-armed.

Between the wars an exciting air race, the Schneider Trophy, took place, which Britain ultimately won in 1931. The victorious aircraft was the Supermarine S.6B, designed by Reginald Joseph Mitchell. This machine achieved a record speed of 379.05 mph. Significantly the S.6B was a monoplane – at a time when biplanes almost exclusively dominated military and civil aviation. The RAF's Bristol Bulldog biplane fighter, however, had a top speed of 174 mph. The Hawker Hart biplane light bomber, designed by Sydney Camm, entered service in 1929 but was 10 mph faster than the Bulldog! The Air Member for Supply & Research, Air Marshal Hugh Dowding, immediately recognised the enormous potential of monoplanes as fighters; they were fast and highly manoeuvrable. On 1 October 1931, the Air Ministry issued a specification for a new single-engine, single-seat monoplane fighter. Inspired by Mitchell's S.6B, and also recognising that the monoplane was undoubtedly the future, Sydney Camm got to work on designing the 'Hawker Interceptor Monoplane'. A one-tenth-scale model of Camm's fighter was built and withstood speeds of up to 350 mph in wind tunnel trials. The fuselages of Camm's previous biplane designs were of fabric-covered tubular framework. The 'Interceptor Monoplane' was identical but had retractable undercarriage, an enclosed cockpit, and metal – not fabric – covering the wings, due to the weight of eight Browning machine-guns. Significantly, the aircraft was powered by a Rolls-Royce Merlin engine. Having studied Camm's detailed performance calculations, on 21 February 1935, the Air Ministry ordered a prototype: K5083.

In April 1935, the Air Ministry updated its requirement for the new day-and-night fighter:

1. Had to be at least 40 mph faster than contemporary bombers at 15,000 feet.
2. 'Have a number of forward firing machine-guns that can produce the maximum hitting power possible in the shortest space of time available for one attack.' The Air Ministry 'considered that eight guns should be provided'.
3. Had to achieve 'the maximum possible and not less than 310 mph at 15,000 feet at maximum power with the highest speed possible between 5,000 and 15,000 feet'.
4. Have the best possible climbing performance to 20,000 feet, although this was considered of secondary importance to 'speed and hitting power'.
5. Be armed with at least six but preferably eight machine-guns, all forward firing and wing mounted outside the propeller arc. These were to be fired by 'electrical means'. In the event of six guns being used, 400 rounds per gun was necessary, 300 if eight were fitted.
6. Had to be 'a steady firing platform'.

7. Had to include the following 'special features' and equipment:

a) Enclosed cockpit.

b) Cockpit heating.

c) Night flying equipment.

d) Radio Telephony (R/T).

e) Oxygen for two-and-a-half hours.

f) Easily accessed and maintained guns.

g) Retractable undercarriage and tail wheel.

h) Wheel brakes.

Watched by an anxious Sydney Camm, Hawker's response to the Air Ministry requirement soared aloft on its maiden flight from Brooklands on 6 November 1935. The company's chief test pilot, P. W. S. 'George' Bulman, complete with trilby, subsequently declared the Hurricane to reveal 'no major deficiency'. Following this historic flight, Bulman initiated minor improvements leading to his assertion on 7 February 1936 that Hawker Hurricane K5083 was ready for evaluation at Martlesham Heath by the RAF Aircraft & Armament Experimental Establishment. These trials largely concerned performance and handling, the Hurricane reaching a top speed of 315 mph at 16,000 feet, 2,960 rpm and 6 pounds boost. The all-silver fighter reached 15,000 feet in just 5.7 minutes. The enclosed cockpit and retractable undercarriage were commended, although heavy aileron and rudder controls at high speed caused concern. Having passed these initial service trials, Camm's fighter returned to Brooklands for further development.

On 3 June 1936, the Air Ministry issued Contract 527112/36 for 600 aircraft – later that month officially approving the name 'Hurricane'. As Mason wrote, 'This was the largest production order ever placed at a single time for a military aircraft in Britain during peacetime and undoubtedly reflected the growing anxiety now being felt at Air Ministry for the re-equipment and expansion of the RAF.' It was just in the nick of time, as future events would confirm. In November 1937, 111 Squadron at Northolt received the first production Hurricane, L1547. By Christmas the squadron boasted four of the new monoplanes. One by one the squadron's Gloster Gauntlet biplanes were replaced and, under the command of Squadron Leader John Gillan, 111's pilots converted to the Hurricane. They found the Hurricane extremely fast – nearly 100 mph faster than the Gauntlet. The monoplane increased visibility enormously without compromising manoeuvrability. In sum, the Hurricane was a revelation. Nonetheless the conversion was sadly not without incident: during the first few weeks there were several accidents, one of them fatal.

On 14 January 1938, by which time 111 Squadron had been equipped with the Hurricane for four weeks, Gillan reported comprehensively on the new fighter's 'operational characteristics':

(i) The Hurricane is completely manoeuvrable throughout its whole range, though slow at speeds between 65 mph and 200 mph controls feel a bit slack.

Owing to its weight and speed, some-time is taken in coming out of a dive and at high speed the turning circle is large.

On the ground the Hurricane is as manoeuvrable as is possible and has the additional advantage of feeling secure across wind or a strong wind due to its high wing loading.

(ii) Cross-wind landings are particularly easy in the Hurricane. Simplicity in cross-wind landings is a characteristic of aircraft with a high wing loading.

(iii)

(a) Taxying with the seat full up and the hood back is exceptionally good all round, far better in front and above than the fighter aircraft before in the service, and just as good in all other directions.

(b) Taking-off. The view is considerably better than the Gauntlet and better than the Demon, both individually and in formation.

(c) Landing. The view is considerably better than the Gauntlet and better than the Demon both individually and in formation.

(d) Flying in Formation. The view is better than the Gauntlet or Demon with the hood open or closed, though at present no experience is available of flying in formation, in bad rain or damp cloud when it is thought the hood may fog or ice up.

(e) The view is better than the Gauntlet or Demon.

(iv) Formation flying at height at speeds in excess of 200 mph is very simple. It is thought the reason being that air resistance at this speed is considerable and that the power used by the engine at this speed the pilot can slow his aeroplane up or accelerate it very quickly indeed.

At slow speeds in the neighbourhood of 100 mph when only a small proportion of the engine power is in use and the resistance to the air of this clean aeroplane is comparatively small, some difficulty is found in decelerating the aircraft, though no difficulty is found in accelerating.

Landing in formation is similar to landing in formation in any other type of aircraft.

Taking off in formation is simple, but immediately after leaving the ground when pilots retract their undercarriages and flaps aircraft cannot keep good formation as undercarriage and flaps retract at different speeds in each aircraft. It is recommended, therefore, that take-off should be done individually, in succession.

(v) The Hurricane is a simple aircraft to fly at night. There is no glare in the cockpit, either open or closed, from the cockpit lamps or luminous instruments.

The steady steep glide at slow speed, which is characteristic of this type, makes landing extremely simple.

The take-off run being longer than has been experienced in the past, it is recommended that the landing light should be at least 600 yards away from the beginning of the run, instead of the normal 250 yards on ordinary flare paths.

(vi) The minimum size of aerodrome from which the Hurricane can be operated in still air in England must depend on obstructions surrounding the aerodrome. With good approaches and inexperienced pilots the Hurricane could be operated from an aerodrome 800 x 800 yards and with experience could probably be reduced to 600 yards.

(vii) The Hurricane without its engine running has a very steep glide and to the pilot inexperienced on this type judging the flattening may be difficult. Therefore it is recommended for initial training that pilots should come in with their engines running. After they have become accustomed to an aeroplane of high wing loading and steep glide they should be able to land efficiently off the glide in the Hurricane as in any other aircraft. It follows that landing with an engine lengthens the period of holding off, making landing easier, and in the event of flattening out too high gives the pilot time to stop the aeroplane falling heavily on the ground as speed falls off.

(viii) The cockpit is large and comfortable and there is room for the largest man inside with the hood shut and by using the adaptable seat the smallest man can see everything comfortably.

It is thought that from an operational point of view that the system of having a selector box and a lever which must be operated to move either the undercarriage or the flaps is unsatisfactory and furthermore it occupies for a period of perhaps half a minute the right hand of the pilot whilst he flies with his left and neglects the throttle. Should it be essential to take-off in formation or as in conditions of bad visibility the difficulties of the system are obvious, and it is recommended that two simple controls, one which moves the flaps to full up and full down position, and the other which would move the undercarriage from full down to full up and vice versa could well be substituted.

All other controls are easily accessible and efficient and the instrument layout is good and not complicated.

Operational Characteristics

With more experience on this type of aeroplane further figures will be submitted, but as far as can be seen at present the indicated airspeed at 2,000 feet is 270 mph, at 10,000 feet indicated airspeed 260 mph and at 15,000 feet indicated airspeed 240 mph.

The petrol consumption at 15,000 feet and economical cruising speed of 160 mph indicated correcting to 200 mph is 25.08 gallons per hour. At + 2½ lbs boost is the maximum permissible cruising speed-petrol consumption approaches 60 gallons per hour.

At 2,000 feet an indicated air speed of 200 mph petrol consumption is 30 gallons per hour at an indicated boost of +1lb.

The remaining operational characteristics have yet to be investigated, but as yet the windscreen has shown no sign of oiling up and the cockpit is weather-proof so far as can be seen at present.

It was a good start, Gillan's report revealing no major problems.

On 10 February 1938 Gillan took off from Northolt, bound for Turnhouse near Edinburgh. Having experienced high winds while outward bound, after re-fuelling the pilot decided to use those 80 mph winds to his advantage and return south at maximum speed. He took off shortly after 5 p.m., climbed to 17,000 feet – the altitude most favourable to the performance of his machine. Forty-eight minutes later he landed at Northolt – having covered 327 miles with an average ground speed of 408.75 mph. The feat was publicised, it being conveniently forgotten that a considerable downwind had significantly assisted Gillan achieve his colossal speed. Nonetheless, in Air Force circles Gillan was forever after known as 'Downwind'. On 3 May 1938 the Hurricane was displayed to a delighted public for the first time at the Hendon Air Pageant. *The Times* subsequently described the aircraft as 'the fastest plane in service anywhere in the world ... outstanding in its class in respect of duration as well as speed'. This was an impressive reaction, and one with which Camm and Hawker were no doubt well pleased.

Understandably re-armament in Britain accelerated after the Munich crisis over Czechoslovakia in September 1938. On 5 October Churchill told the House of Commons, 'We are in the presence of a disaster of the first magnitude. And do not suppose that this is the end. It is only the beginning of the reckoning.' Top priority was at last given to producing defensive fighters. Peter Townsend had flown Hawker Fury biplanes with 43 Squadron at Tangmere; in November 1939 he found himself converting to the new Hurricane:

By mid-December we had our full initial equipment of sixteen aircraft. The Fury had been a delightful play-thing; the Hurricane was a thoroughly war-like machine, rock solid as a platform for its eight Browning machine-guns, highly manoeuvrable despite its large proportions and with an excellent view from the cockpit ... At first the Hurricane earned a bad reputation. The change from the light and agile Fury caught some pilots unaware. The Hurricane was far less tolerant of faulty handling, and a mistake at low altitude could be fatal. One day a sergeant pilot glided back to Tangmere with a faulty engine. We watched him as with plenty of height he turned in – too slowly – to land. The Hurricane fell out of his hands and before our eyes he dived headlong into the ground. The unfortunate pilot died as the ambulance arrived.

Nonetheless conversion from biplane to the new monoplane continued apace. Townsend wrote, 'And so we came to know ourselves and our Hurricanes better. There grew in us a trust and an affection for them and their splendid Merlin engines, thoroughbreds and stayers which changed our fearful doubts of the Munich period into the certainty that it would beat all comers.' Peter Brothers was another experienced pre-war fighter pilot who found himself flying Hurricanes in 1938:

> We were shown over the aircraft. We then familiarised ourselves with the controls and instruments – no Pilot's Notes were available at that time! Then it was start-up and taxi over the grass to the boundary fence and take off. These Mk I Hurricanes had a fixed-pitch two-bladed propeller which gave rapid acceleration. It was the first type I had ever flown with a retractable undercart and closed canopy – both great improvements. On my first flight I performed a few aerobatics and was impressed by the aircraft's immediate and smooth response. I knew straightaway that going to war in this machine was preferable to doing so in a biplane which – as the record of the Polish Air Force in 1939 would show – would have been suicidal.

The fixed-pitch Watts Z33 propeller, however, required improvement. This did not just concern the Hurricane but applied to every service aircraft. German aircraft designers had recognised the benefits of the variable-pitch propeller the previous year. The pilot had a control with which he could change the pitch – or angle at which the blade bit into the air – while in flight. The effect was similar, in fact, to changing gear in a car and therefore provided more power for certain situations – including take-off and combat. In August 1938 trials began on the de Havilland two-pitch propeller. This was constructed of duralumin and had three blades. Fitted with the new variable-pitch airscrew a marked improvement was recorded in tests on Hurricane L1582. Fine pitch, which is to say 30.5°, was used for take-off, and coarse pitch, 42.5°, in flight. Even given a weight increase of 300 lbs, L1582 reduced the time climbing to rated altitude by one minute. From January 1939 onwards, therefore, production Hurricanes were fitted with the new two-pitch propeller. This was, however, only a half-way house. Rotol Ltd had been developing a constant-speed (CS) propeller. Also three-bladed and made of duralumin, the pilot could rotate the blades through 360° and therefore fly in the optimum pitch for any given circumstance. On 24 January 1939, Hurricane L1606, fitted with the experimental CS propeller, achieved 328 mph – 13 mph faster than Bulman's maiden flight in K5083 – and took 6.2 minutes to reach 15,000 feet. These improvements would soon be desperately needed on all operational RAF fighters.

Speed was all-important and the most notable difference for pilots converting to the new fighter. Douglas Grice converted from the Gloster Gauntlet biplane to Hurricanes with Peter Brothers on 32 Squadron:

It meant flying an aircraft which at cruising speed did about 240 mph – about 100 mph faster than you were used to flying. The flaps did not worry me but what was rather worrying was the Merlin engine. It was so powerful that it took a bit of getting used to ... What a thrill to be flying so fast. There were no vices with the Hurricane at all. And it was so rugged. You could virtually fly it into the ground and it would just bounce up and land by itself.

In 1938 it became known that German fighters were armed not just with machine-guns but also with the heavier 20 mm cannon. This led to the fitting of more armour plate to British fighters, protecting the pilot and fuel-tank. These improvements included a thick armoured glass windscreen. Of course this increased weight decreased performance slightly, but such modifications were essential. Although metal stressed-skin wings for the Hurricane had been mooted back in 1935, they did not become a reality until 1940. The process to address this deficiency began in April 1939. Existing Hurricanes in service were slowly fitted with new metal wings, but the factories were still producing fabric-covered wings until March 1940. Eventually all Hurricanes enjoyed the benefits of metal wings, bringing the Hurricane in line with both the Supermarine Spitfire (see the *Spitfire Manual* by this author, Amberley, 2010) and German Messerschmitt 109. It has often been argued that because the Hurricane relied upon traditional construction techniques with which the Hawker workforce was familiar, it was easy to produce and that this is why the Air Ministry initially ordered Camm's fighter in larger numbers than the Spitfire. That may be so, but the lack of a metal-covered wing was a design deficiency. Moreover, the reason that it took so long to rectify was because construction of all-metal wings required the workforce to learn new construction techniques. This slowed production, in fact. Fortunately, by the time shooting began, all operational Hurricanes enjoyed the benefits of metal-skinned wings. This is an early indication, however, that the Hurricane was technically inferior to the other two principal single-engine, single-seat fighters of the day.

By the outbreak of war on 3 September 1939, though, 400 Hurricanes had been delivered to the RAF, equipping eighteen fighter squadrons. At the time of Munich, just a year before, Fighter Command mustered a total of 759 fighters – only ninety-three of which were Hurricanes. Although the RAF received its first production Spitfire one month before Munich, the first Spitfire squadron would not be fully operational for another three months. Had Britain gone to war over Czechoslovakia in 1938, therefore, the outcome would have been disastrous. The British Prime Minister of the day, Neville Chamberlain, is often condemned by history for his policy of appeasing Hitler during the late 1930s. But had Chamberlain not bought time for Britain to prepare for war, the country's weak aerial defences of 1938 would have been exposed. One year later – largely thanks to the Hawker Hurricane – the situation was rapidly changing – albeit at the eleventh hour. Unfortunately the enemy also had two new monoplane fighters: the single-engined Me 109 and the twin-engined Me 110; both were faster than the Hurricane, the 109 by nearly 50 mph. Significantly the Hurricane's maximum service ceiling was at least 2,000 feet lower than the 109's 36,000 feet – and in aerial combat height is everything.

Hitler's first conquest – Poland – fell in a matter of weeks, Warsaw becoming the latest Guernica and further evidence of the bomber's destructive power. Anticipating an attack on the West, on 2 September 1939 the Advanced Air Striking Force (AASF) began moving from England to bases in France, the first four squadrons of Hawker Hurricanes arriving on 8/9 September. By this time, Hurricanes were far more numerous than the Supermarine Spitfire. Legend has it that this was due to the all-metal-covered Spitfire requiring Supermarine's workforce to learn new skills, thus slowing production, while the Hurricane, relying upon tried and tested production techniques, was easier to produce in numbers. This is a myth. While the Spitfire was a more advanced design than the Hurricane, the reality was that it had not made its first flight until 6 March 1936, did not begin reaching 19 Squadron until August 1938, and, more importantly, Supermarine's small Southampton factory was simply not geared up for mass production. The Air Officer Commander-in-Chief of Fighter Command, Air Chief Marshal Sir Hugh Dowding, knew full well that his more numerous Hurricanes were inferior to his precious Spitfires. Both fighters were designed to fight the defensive battle for Britain's survival, which Dowding felt certain was not far away. Consequently Dowding sent no Spitfires to France, only Hurricanes.

It was in the defence of Britain, as it happened, that the Hurricane recorded its first kill: on 21 October 1939, 46 Squadron sent three He 115 seaplanes plunging into the North Sea off Yorkshire. Nine days later, Pilot Officer 'Boy' Mould of 1 Squadron scored the Hurricane's first kill over France when he destroyed a Do 17 bomber over Toul. On 6 November, though, the Hurricane-equipped 73 Squadron's Pilot Officer Peter Ayerst was the first RAF fighter pilot to come face-to-face with the lethal Me 109:

It was a bit of a long story. I was doing what we call 'Aerodrome Defence'. We used to take it in turns. You sat in the aircraft already strapped in, and waited for an early warning that there was an aircraft approaching. Our early warning system was produced by some French soldiers in a big ditch down the side of our grass airfield. A place called Rouve, between Verdun and Metz, South of Luxembourg.

And I was sitting there in my Hurricane. The chaps in the flight office, which was a 12-foot ridge tent, shouted excitedly, 'THE RED FLAG'S

WAVING! THE RED FLAG'S WAVING!' The French soldiers had a powerful pair of binoculars, looking to the East. And if they saw an aircraft, which they couldn't identify, or they could identify as being German, then they would wave a red flag. And that was the early warning system! And as it so happened, this particular day of 6 November 1939, there was lots of blue sky, no clouds. And I could see an aircraft at about 25,000 feet over our airfield. He was obviously doing some overhead photography. So I took off. Of course, being on these two-bladed airscrews, the climbing performance wasn't very great, even at full throttle. So I was only gradually getting up. I'd been chasing in an Easterly direction for a long time trying to get him. And he was way ahead. And we had no radio aids. No navigational assistance from the ground whatsoever.

We had intercommunication between aircraft but we didn't have communication with the ground in France for navigational assistance. Nothing like that. We used to patrol up and down the French/German border, 25,000 feet for an hour at a time. Three of us used to go, but we didn't fly bunched up, in fact.

Then another three would come up, and we'd go back. And this, weather permitting, went on all day. Various of the Squadron go up. It was quite busy.

After I'd been flying far longer than I'd realised, we were going down and I saw the Me 109. I'd never have got closer than two miles, but I could see him because it was good visibility that day. And he went down in some cloud, lower level over Germany. And he went down into that and I lost him. Didn't even get a shot at him. So I said, 'Oh well … time for me to get back.' I'd been airborne a long time so I thought I'd better start finding somewhere to land. I just slowly carried on in a Westerly direction and saw some aircraft circling. So I thought, 'Ah! There must be an airfield there.' So I went over and there was. And I landed there. It was Nancy. That particular day, our Squadron and 1 Squadron were going to put up the first offensive fighter patrol of the war. And as I was sort of turning round, coming back towards France, underneath me I saw nine aircraft in line astern, turning inside me, one behind the other. And I thought, 'Here come our boys!' I hadn't been in the air all that long so thought I might as well join on to this formation. So I tacked on the end.

Then I saw bloody great black crosses! So I pulled up and gave a quick squirt at the end one and went down. Unbeknown to me, there were another eighteen of them – twenty-seven all together! Also unbeknown to me as I was crossing Germany back into France, there was a French fighter patrol up of nine aircraft. And the Germans were so concentrating on me, twenty-seven of the bastards, can't think why, they weren't taking any notice of their own backs. They must have thought, 'We've got superiority and everything here!' And the French waded into them – Shot nine of them down! It was classified as the first big air battle of the war.

I was thereafter dubbed 'Decoy'!

Then, on 29 November, Squadron Leader Harry Broadhurst, the CO of 111 Squadron, destroyed a lone He 111 off the Northumbrian coast. Fighter Command was not to claim its first 109s, however, until 26 March 1940. On that day, 73 Squadron's Hurricanes engaged enemy fighters over Saarlautern and Trier, claiming four destroyed and two unconfirmed.

After the defeat of Poland, the Wehrmacht rested and prepared for its next campaign: the securing of Germany's northern flank by the invasion of Denmark and Norway. This operation required harmonious co-operation between the German navy, air force and army. It was the first combined operation of its kind of the Second World War and successfully executed. The invasion began on 9 April 1940. Britain sent a task force to Narvik, but the campaign highlighted the problems ahead caused by the lack of a long-range fighter. Flying from aircraft carriers, air cover was provided by a handful of obsolete Gladiator biplanes and one squadron of Hurricanes. The small Norwegian air force was shocked and rapidly defeated. By 10 June it was all over. Once again the superiority of the Wehrmacht had been demonstrated to great effect.

On 2 May 1940, a section of 1 Squadron Hurricanes flew to Orleans. The unit's CO, Squadron Leader 'Bull' Halahan, subsequently reported that

…a trial took place to discover the fighting qualities of the Me 109 as compared with the Hurricane.

2. Owing to the absence of oxygen apparatus in the Me 109 the trial was carried out between 10,000 and 15,000 feet.

3. The comparison consisted of (a) take-off and climb to 15,000 feet, (b) a dog-fight, and (c) line astern formation.

4. Both aircraft took off together. Both the take-off and initial climb of the Me 109 was better than that of the Hurricane, in spite of the fact that the Hurricane was fitted with a Constant Speed airscrew, and full-throttle and revs were used.

5. At 15,000 feet the aircraft separated and approached one another head-on for the dog-fight. The Hurricane did a quick stall turn followed by a quick vertical turn and found himself on the 109's tail. The pilot of the 109 was unable to prevent this manoeuvre succeeding. From that point the Hurricane pilot had no difficulty in remaining on the tail of the Me 109. The pilot of the Me 109 tried all possible manoeuvres and finally the one most usually employed by the German pilots, namely a half-roll and vertical dive. The Hurricane followed this manoeuvre, but the Me drew away at the commencement of the dive, and it was felt that had the pilot continued this dive he might have got away. However, in the pull-out the pilot of the Me 109 found that it was all he could do to pull the machine out of the dive at all, as fore and aft it became very heavy. In fact the pilot was of the opinion that had he not used the tail adjusting gear, which itself was extremely heavy, he would not have got out of the dive at all.

The pilot of the Hurricane found that he had no difficulty in pulling out of his dive inside the 109, but that he had a tendency to black-out, which was not experienced by the pilot of the 109. This tendency to black-out in the Hurricane when pulling out of high speed dives is in my opinion largely due to the rather vertical position in which the pilot sits. It is very noticeable that in the 109 the position of the pilot is reclining, with his legs well up in front of him. It has been noticed that German pilots do not pull their aircraft out of dives at very high speeds, and as I think the position in which the pilot sits is the main reason that black out is avoided, I feel that this is a point which should be duly considered when in the future a fighter is designed to meet other fighters.

6. After the dog-fight the 109 took position in line astern on the Hurricane and the Hurricane carried out a series of climbing turns and diving turns at high speeds. In the ordinary turns the Hurricane lapped the 109 after four complete circuits, and at no time was the pilot of the 109 able to get his sights on the Hurricane. In the climbing turns, though the 109 could climb faster he could not turn as fast, which enabled the Hurricane again to get round on his tail. In climbing turns after diving, the weight of the elevators and ailerons of the 109 was so great that the pilot was unable to complete the manoeuvre, and in the diving turns he was unable to follow the Hurricane for the same reason.

7. During these tests one point became abundantly clear, namely that the 109, owing to its better camouflage, was very difficult to spot from underneath than was the Hurricane. This difference gives the 109 a definite tactical advantage, namely when they are below us they can spot us at long distance, which we when below them find most difficult. As in all our combats at the moment initial surprise is the ideal at which we aim, I strongly recommend that the underside of Hurricanes should be painted duck-egg blue, the roundels remaining the same, as it is the contrast between black and white only which is so noticeable from below.

8. The Me 109 is faster than the Hurricane by some 30 to 40 m.p.h. on the straight and level. It can out-climb and initially out-dive the Hurricane. On the other hand it has not the manoeuvrability of the Hurricane, which can turn inside without difficulty. After this clear-cut demonstration of superior manoeuvrability there is no doubt in my mind that provided Hurricanes are not surprised by 109s that the odds are more than two-to-one, and that if pilots use their heads, the balance will always be in favour of our aircraft, once the 109s have committed themselves to combat.

9. In this connection, judging by the tactics at present being employed by the 109s, namely sitting above us when they can surprise a straggler, and then only completing a dive attack then climb away, I am fairly certain that the conclusion of the German pilots is the same as our own, and I cannot help feeling that until all Hurricane aircraft have Constant Speed airscrews, to enable them to get up to the height at present adopted by the 109s, we shall have few further chances of combat with this particular type of German aircraft.

Halahan's report is as illuminating in certain respects as it is naive. Firstly, the Me 109 concerned was an E-3 of 1/JG 76, that forced-landed in France on 22 November 1939 and was captured. The comparison trials with 1 Squadron's operational Hurricanes were not flown until nearly six months later. It is hard to understand why more urgency was not attached to this. Secondly, already the German tactical experience was apparent. The 109 pilots had recognised the crucial importance of height, and how to use their machine in manoeuvres best suited to its performance – most notably high-speed dives to both attack and evade. Indeed, many years later Wing Commander David Cox, recalling the fighter combats over France in 1941, described the 109 pilots attacking from high above with what he called 'dirty darts'. This is an early indication that the 'dirty dart' – a quick 'in and out' hit – had long been practised by pilots who had probably flown in Poland, if not Spain. The only real advantage enjoyed by the Hurricane was its tighter turning circle. The statement that, 'providing Hurricanes are not surprised by 109s ... the balance will always be in favour of our aircraft, once the 109s had committed themselves to combat' almost beggars belief. By Halahan's own admission the 109 pilots' tactics already relied upon height as prerequisite – a height unachievable by Hurricanes without CS propellers, which at that time they did not have. Halahan would soon be rudely awoken; the enemy pilots would do everything possible to 'surprise' Hurricanes. In just three days, in fact, they would begin doing so.

Abruptly, on 10 May 1940 the great storm finally broke when Hitler invaded Belgium, Holland, Luxembourg and France. Two days later Liege fell, and panzers crossed the Meuse at Dinant and Sedan. Hitherto, in the naive hope of remaining neutral, the Belgians had refused Lord Gort's British Expeditionary Force (BEF) permission to fortify their border with Germany. Now the Belgian king called for help, the BEF pivoting forward from its prepared defences on the Belgian–French border. The British advanced for 60 miles over unfamiliar ground expecting to meet the German Schwerpunkt – point of main effort – which was expected to follow same route as in the Great War. It did not. Holland was certainly attacked – the Dutch Air Force being wiped out on the first day – but the main enemy thrust was cleverly disguised. As Allied eyes were firmly focussed on the Belgian–Dutch border, Panzergruppe von Kleist achieved the supposedly impossible and successfully negotiated the Ardennes, much further south. German armour then poured out of the forest, by-passing the Maginot Line, rendering its concrete forts useless. The panzers then punched upwards, towards the Channel coast – ten days later the Germans had reached Laon, Cambrai, Arras, Amiens and even Abbeville. Indeed, Erwin Rommel's 7th Panzer covered ground so quickly that it became known as the 'Ghost Division'. The effect on the Allies was virtual paralysis, so shocking was the assault, unprecedented in speed and fury. Civilians in Britain were equally shocked – not least after the bombing of Rotterdam on 14 May reportedly caused 30,000 civilian fatalities (although post-war estimates put the death toll at nearer 3,000). Hard on the heels of Guernica and Warsaw, Rotterdam's fate was terrifying news indeed.

On 10 May 1940, though, there were six squadrons of Hurricanes in France. One week later the equivalent of six more had crossed the Channel, and another four were operating from bases on the south-east coast of England, hopping over the Channel on a daily basis but returning to England – if they could – at the end of each day. Losses in France rapidly stacked up. Dowding's problem was that the more fighters he sent to France, the further he weakened Britain's defences. By 19 May the situation on the Continent had deteriorated further still. On that day the War Office and Admiralty began facing the possibility of evacuating the BEF from France, and Churchill finally authorised Dowding not to send any further fighters across the Channel. By the following day, only three of Dowding's Hurricane squadrons remained in France. Among them was Squadron Leader 'Teddy' Donaldson:

> The French bolted, including their air force. I have never seen so many people running so fast anywhere, as long as it were west. The British Tommies were marvellous, however, and fought their way to the sand dunes of Dunkirk. I was in command of 151 Squadron, and our Hurricanes were sent to reinforce the AASF, flying from Manston to France on a daily basis.
>
> In some respects the Germans were grossly over confident in the air, and so didn't have it all their own way. But every day we had damaged Hurricanes and no ground crews to mend them, dictating that we had to return to Manston every evening. In any event, our airfields in France were being heavily bombed, so had we stayed, although pilots could have got off the airfield to sleep, our aircraft would have taken a beating. 151 Squadron would fly up to seven sorties a day, against overwhelming odds, and on one occasion even stayed on patrol after expending our ammunition so as to prevent the Luftwaffe attacking defenceless British troops on the ground.

Among Donaldson's pilots was Pilot Officer Jack Hamar; on 18 May he was patrolling in a Hurricane, 3 miles north-west of Vitry:

> I climbed to 7,000 feet and attacked two Me 110s, succeeding in getting onto the tail of one enemy aircraft (E/A). I opened fire at 300 yards with a burst of five seconds. Whilst closing in I noticed tracer passing over my head, from behind, and looking around discovered the other E/A on my tail. I immediately half-rolled away and noticed two Hurricanes chasing another E/A, which was diving to ground level. I followed down after the Hurricanes, and, as they broke away, I continued the chase, hedge-

hopping, but did not seem to gain on the E/A. I got within 500 yards and put in a five second burst. I saw my tracer entering both wings, but did not observe any damage. As my windscreen was by this time covered in oil from my own airscrew, making sighting impossible, I broke away and returned to Vitry.

Hamar's combat report is interesting. A Spitfire, with a top speed of 355 mph, would have caught that Me 110.

Flight Lieutenant Gerry Edge:

> During the Fall of France I flew Hurricanes over there with 605 Squadron. After the German offensive began, the roads below were full of columns of civilians and soldiers, all progressing westwards. Once we came upon a Stuka that was strafing a column of refugees. It was plain to anyone, especially from that low altitude, that this was a civilian, as opposed to a military column. I am pleased to say that I shot this Boche down. There were no survivors. Does that concern me? Not at all. Of all the enemy aircraft I shot down, that one gave me great pleasure.

Flight Lieutenant Peter Brothers:

> Whilst operating over France as a flight commander in 32 Squadron, I naturally took our latest replacement under my wing to fly as my Number Two. Suddenly I had that feeling we all experience at some time that I was being watched. Glancing in my rear-view mirror I was startled to see, immediately behind me and between my Number Two and me, the biggest and fattest Me 109 – ever! As I instantly took evasive action his front end lit up as he fired. I escaped unscathed, the 109 climbed and vanished as I did a tight turn, looking for my Number Two. There he was, good man, cutting the corner to get back in position, as I thought, until he opened fire on me! Suggesting on the radio that his action was unpopular, as there were no other aircraft in sight we wended our way home. Not only had he not warned me of the 109's presence or fired at it, he had had such an easy shot but missed. I dealt a blow to his jauntiness by removing him from operations for two days' intensive gunnery training; sadly it did not help him survive.

John Terraine made clear the importance of fighters to German air operations during the Battle of France. He also argued that a powerful Allied fighter force could have prevented the Germans achieving aerial supremacy over the battlefield and with it devastating results on the ground. The fact of the matter, though, was that the Allies did not have 'a powerful fighter force'. As Terraine stated, while on paper, for example, the French fielded 790 operational fighters, the truth was that nineteen out of the twenty-six French fighter squadrons were equipped with the woefully obsolete Morane-Saulnier 406 – which was no match for the 109. Only 'Hurricane pilots,' wrote Terraine, 'had the satisfaction of meeting the enemy with adequate equipment and the ability to use it.' Those few Hurricanes were insufficient to stem the tide, however. Terraine continued:

> The German fighters – over 1,200 of them, but above all the Me 109s – ruled the sky, and in doing so they achieved, for the first time against a major enemy, the saturation of a battle area by air power, and that is what won the Battle of France. It was, in fact, won in six days … The Allies had lost the battle … to the achievement of complete air superiority by the German Air Force, enabling the Stukas to perform, the panzers to roam where they willed; this was an achievement above all of the fighter arm, in particular the Messerschmitt 109.

By 26 May it was clear that the Battle for France was lost. On that day the decision was taken for the BEF to retire upon and be evacuated from Dunkirk. From then on the whole nature of air operations over northern France changed. The RAF now had to provide a protective umbrella for the retreating BEF in addition to covering the actual evacuation in due course. It was now that Dowding committed his Spitfire force to battle over the French coast for the first time. The performance of the Spitfire Mk I and Me 109E was similar, although the 109 enjoyed certain technical advantages over both the Spitfire and Hurricane. Firstly, all 109s in service were fitted with a CS propeller, whereas the Spitfire and Hurricanes were still using the inferior two-pitch airscrew (and would not all be converted to the CS propeller until the forthcoming Battle of Britain); secondly the 109 had a fuel-injected engine, meaning that unlike the British fighter's gravity-fed Merlin, it did not cut out from fuel starvation in a dive; thirdly, the 109 was armed with both machine-guns and a pair of hard-hitting 20 mm Oerlikon cannons.

The German pilots, however, had a distinct edge, having not only learned their craft in the Spanish Civil War but possessing recent and extensive combat experience. Over Spain, during the mid-1930s, the loose, line-abreast formation of four aircraft had been worked out, comprising two pairs of leader and wingman. Being spread out there was no risk of collision, so the enemy pilots could concentrate of searching for the enemy. When battle was joined the two pairs broke, the leader doing the killing protected by his wingman. The RAF, however, persisted in flying ridiculous tactics worked out before the war. Then it was anticipated that Britain would only be attacked by slow-moving bombers, German bases putting England well beyond the Me 109's limited range. The catastrophic fall of France, throughout which 109s had ruled the battlefield airspace, was simply unanticipated – as was, therefore, fighter-

versus-fighter combat. The RAF tacticians simply foresaw orderly lines of slow bombers which fighters could destroy at their leisure. Indeed, it was decided that RAF fighter squadrons should be sub-divided into four sections of three, each operating in a 'V' formation and thus simultaneously bringing twenty-four machine-guns to bear. In reality, this was disastrous. Flying so close to each other, unlike their enemy counterparts, the RAF fighter pilots concentrated more on formation flying than looking for the enemy – leading to them being repeatedly 'bounced' or ambushed by high-flying 109s. Moreover, the high speeds of fighter combat require instant, instinctive, responses between hand and eye. In this cut and thrust, formation flying of any kind would be found suicidal. The problem was that monoplanes were still new, and apart from the Germans no-one had previously experienced combat in them. The RAF, therefore, was learning on the job – at the cost of many fine young pilots' lives – and reacting to an unprecedented situation.

Operation DYNAMO, otherwise known as the Dunkirk evacuation, was complete by 3 June 1940. By that time, over 300,000 Allied troops had been rescued from the catastrophe in France – but the BEF had left behind 40,000 prisoners of war, 18,000 dead, and all its armour and artillery. Fifty-five Hurricanes had been lost in France, reducing the number of fighters available to Dowding for home defence to 331. A further 106 RAF fighters were lost during the Dunkirk operation. This experience, however, highlighted the strengths and weaknesses of both the Hurricane and Spitfire, as recorded by the New Zealand ace Alan Deere, who flew Mitchell's fighter during both DYNAMO and the subsequent Battle of Britain:

> I stated that in my opinion the Spitfire was superior overall to the Me 109, except in the initial climb and dive; however this was an opinion contrary to the belief of the so-called experts. Their judgement was of course based on intelligence assessments and the performance of the 109 in combat with the Hurricane in France. In fact, the Hurricane, though vastly more manoeuvrable than either the Spitfire or the Me 109, was so sadly lacking in speed and rate of climb, that its too-short combat experience against the 109 was not a valid yardstick for comparison. The Spitfire, however, possessed these two attributes to such a degree that, coupled with a better rate of turn than the Me 109, it had the edge overall in combat. There may have been scepticism by some about my claim for the Spitfire, but I had no doubts on the score; nor did my fellow pilots in 54 Squadron. Later events, particularly in the Battle of Britain, were to prove me right.

Superior though the Spitfire overall was to the Hurricane, the fact was that there were simply not enough of them. That being so, the Hurricane, of which Dowding had twenty-five squadrons (soon fortunately increased to thirty-three) compared to just nineteen of Spitfires, was absolutely essential to the defence of Britain and Dowding knew full well that the defensive battle he had long warned of and prepared for was coming. The unanticipated collapse of France provided Hitler with an equally unexpected opportunity to attempt a seaborne invasion of southern England – prerequisite to such an ambitious combined operation, however, was aerial superiority. The British Prime Minister, Winston Churchill, told the House of Commons on 18 June that 'what General Weygand called the Battle of France is over. I expect that the Battle of Britain is about to begin.'

The historiography and popular history of the Battle of Britain has generated a vast bibliography, and it is not intended to re-tell the now well-known story in detail here (but see *The Few: The Battle of Britain in the Words of the Pilots*, Amberley, 2009, and *The Last of the Few: Eighteen Battle of Britain Fighter Pilots Tell Their Remarkable Stories*, Amberley, 2010, both by this author). The fighting began on 10 July 1940, and until 12 August featured skirmishes over Channel-bound convoys and coastal radar stations. Among the Hurricane pilots engaged on 14 July was Pilot Officer Jack Hamar of 151 Squadron:

At 1500 hours the Squadron was ordered off from Rochford to intercept E/As south of Dover. At approximately 1520 hours, when the Squadron was almost over Dover, a bunch of Me 109s were sighted about 5,000 feet above our formation, in which I was flying Red Two. As it looked as though the E/A were about to attack us, the leader ordered our defensive line astern tactics. As we turned sharply to port, two Me 109s were seen diving to attack the last aircraft in our formation. 'Milna Leader' attacked the leading Me 109 and I the second. I turned inside the E/A, which had pulled up into a steep left hand climbing turn. I closed rapidly and opened fire at about 250 yards with a 45° deflection shot. The E/A seemed to falter and straightened out into a dive. I placed myself dead astern at about 50 yards. I opened fire, closing to almost no distance. I saw a large explosion just in front of the pilot and a large amount of white smoke poured from the E/A, which by this time was climbing steeply. I was then forced to break away quickly due to fire from the rear, lost sight of the E/A and therefore did not see it crash. This action was also witnessed by Flying Officer Forster.

Between 13 and 18 August, the enemy mounted heavy attacks on radar stations and airfields. On 16 August, Flight Lieutenant James Brindley Nicolson took 249 Squadron up from Boscombe Down to patrol the Poole–Romsey line at 15,000 feet. Sighting enemy activity over Gosport, Nicolson led Red Section's Hurricanes to investigate, but the three fighters were beaten to it by a squadron of Spitfires. Turning about to re-join their squadron, Red Section climbed with the sun dangerously behind them.

Suddenly, Me 110s attacked out of the glare, hitting all three Hurricanes. Nicolson's aircraft was hit by four cannon shells, one of which set the gravity fuel tank ablaze. His cockpit an inferno, the pilot was preparing to bail out when a 110 – possibly his assailant – suddenly presented itself as a sitting duck right in front of the blazing Hurricane. Without hesitation, 'Nick' climbed back into the flames and gave chase. His left foot already wounded by shrapnel, he watched in horror as the skin on his throttle hand incinerated and his instrument panel was reduced to molten metal. Satisfied that his attack had been successfully pressed home, the wounded pilot, by now very badly burned about the hands, face, neck and legs, bailed out. As he descended, the RAF pilot played dead, hanging limply in his parachute harness so as not to attract the attention of any murderous enemy pilots, before narrowly missing high-tension cables in Southampton. Landing in Burrowdale Road, Millbrook, Nicolson was then fired at by a Home Guard sergeant, his right side being peppered by shotgun pellets. Suffering third-degree burns from the waist down and bleeding from the shotgun wound, before morphine was administered he managed to dictate a telegram to his pregnant wife, Muriel.

Flight Lieutenant Nicolson's road to recovery began at the Royal Southampton Hospital. By the autumn of 1940 he was convalescing with other wounded RAF officers at the Palace Hotel, Torquay, when a telegram arrived informing the astonished pilot that he had been awarded his country's highest award for bravery: the Victoria Cross. The citation published in the *London Gazette* stated that 'Flight Lieutenant Nicolson has always displayed great enthusiasm for air fighting and this incident shows that he possesses courage and determination of a high order by continuing to engage the enemy after he had been wounded and his aircraft set on fire. He displayed exceptional gallantry and disregard for the safety of his own life.' On 25 November, 'Nick' and his proud family attended an investiture at Buckingham Palace where he received his Victoria Cross from King George VI. This was, in fact, the only such award to a fighter pilot during the Second World War. This was not, though, because there were no further signal acts of valour performed by fighter pilots, but because due to the often high altitude and speed at which combats are fought, such things are rarely witnessed. Nicolson's well-deserved Victoria Cross he accepted on behalf of all fighter pilots – and he was a *Hurricane*, not a Spitfire, pilot. Sadly, 'Nick', who was later awarded a Distinguished Flying Cross, would not survive the war: on 2 May 1945 he was reported missing over the Bay of Bengal while flying as a passenger on a B-24 Liberator bombing Japanese installations at Rangoon; he has no known grave.

Returning to the Battle of Britain, between 19 August and 6 September was fought the most critical phase, during which the enemy pounded the all-important Sector Stations of South East England. Repeatedly Fighter Command's aerodromes at Biggin Hill, Kenley, Hornchurch and Manston were heavily bombed. Just when it appeared impossible for the defenders to continue operations from these crucial bases for much longer, *Reichsmarschall* Göring changed tack: on 7 September began the round-the-clock bombing of London. Among the RAF fighter pilots engaged was another remarkable but unique individual: Squadron Leader Douglas Bader, Commanding Officer of the Canadian 242 Squadron (see *Douglas Bader* by this author, Amberley, 2013). Bader had, in fact, lost both legs in a blameworthy pre-war flying accident. Although he mastered artificial limbs and subsequently passed a flying test, he was unable to continue flying because King's Regulations unsurprisingly failed to provide for limbless aircrew. Consequently he left the service but later argued his way back into the cockpit when war broke out. Bader first flew Spitfires with 19 Squadron at Duxford before commanding a flight of 222 Squadron 'Spits' during DYNAMO, when he scored his first combat victory. During the Battle of France, the Canadians of 242 had been badly knocked about and subsequently suffered from poor morale caused by weak leadership. Bader was considered just the chap to restore good order – which he rapidly did. Scoring his first Hurricane victory on 11 July 1940 when he shot a Do 17 down into the sea off Cromer, Bader wrote of the Hurricane:

> The Hurricane was slower than the Spitfire ... The Hurricane was less elegant to the eye, but then there has never been such a beautiful aeroplane as the Spitfire ... the Hurricane was a thoroughbred and looked like it. Like all pilots who flew the Hurricane I came to love it. It was strong, highly manoeuvrable, could turn inside the Spitfire and, of course, the Me 109. Best of all, it was a marvellous gun platform. The sloping nose gave you a splendid forward view, while the eight guns were set in blocks of four in each wing, close to the fuselage. The aeroplane remained rock steady when you fired. Unlike the Spitfire with its lovely elliptical wing which sloped upwards to the tip, the Hurricane wing was thicker and straight. The Spitfire was less steady when the guns were firing because, I have always thought, they were spread further along the wing, and the recoil effect was noticeable. The Hurricane was, in fact, a larger aeroplane than the Spitfire.

In an effort to preserve their finite fighter force, Air Chief Marshal Dowding and the commander of 11 Group, covering London and South East England, attacked the enemy formations using 'penny packet' numbers of defending fighters. With this, Squadron Leader Bader disagreed. Supported by his 12 Group commander, Air Vice-Marshal Trafford Leigh-Mallory, and the Duxford Station Commander and Sector Controller Wing Commander 'Woody' Woodhall, Bader believed in engaging the enemy en masse – with a 'wing' of at least three squadrons of fighters. On 7 September, Bader led his 'Big Wing' of two Hurricane and one Spitfire squadrons into action over London. Soon, the Wing was increased to five squadrons – three of Hurricanes, two of Spitfires. In 11 Group Air Vice-Marshal Park was using his Spitfire squadrons in pairs as a high altitude protective screen for the Hurricanes, which performed better at medium altitude – where, protected by Spitfires, they could destroy bombers unmolested by high-flying 109s. 12 Group's tactics were identical: the Spitfires fended off the 109s, whenever possible, while the Hurricanes attacked the enemy bomber formations. The Wing's combat claims were impressive, immediately generating various congratulatory signals. The impression provided from these figures was that the mass fighter formation was executing far greater damage on the Germans than Dowding and Park's penny packets. The record confirms, however, that the Big Wing's claims were accepted with little scrutiny – and due to the nature of air combat there is a gulf of difference between a claim and a confirmed kill. Indeed, the more fighters engaged the greater the confusion, with one enemy machine, for example, frequently featuring in the combat reports of various pilots. Thus one casualty could be inadvertently multiplied several times on the balance sheet, providing a completely inaccurate picture. Such was the case, we now know, with Bader's Wing – which consistently over-claimed, sometimes by as much as 7:1. Nonetheless, when the Battle of Britain's climax came on 15 September, 11 Group's hard-pressed pilots were astonished to see Squadron Leader Bader's Hurricane heave into view at the head of some sixty Hurricanes and Spitfires. It was a crushing sight to the German bomber crews, who had been told that Fighter Command was finished.

Bombing London was the mistake that cost the Germans victory in the Battle of Britain. Fighting over their very homeland and within sight of the beleaguered population, the RAF fighter pilots – immortalised by Churchill as 'The Few' – bravely resisted this aerial Goliath. By the autumn, aerial supremacy was nothing more than a pipe dream, forcing Hitler to postpone his lashed-up invasion plans. The Luftwaffe may not have been destroyed, but by having denied the Germans aerial supremacy victory undoubtedly belonged to Fighter Command. If this was Britain's 'Finest Hour', it was likewise that of the Hawker Hurricane. As Air Commodore Alan Deere wrote, 'There can be no doubt that victory in the Battle of Britain was made possible by the Spitfire. Although there were more Hurricanes than Spitfires in the Battle, the Spitfire was the RAF's primary weapon because of its better all-round capability. The Hurricane alone could not have won this great air battle, but the Spitfire could have done so.' There is no question that this extremely experienced Spitfire pilot and fighter leader was absolutely right. As has been explained, the Spitfire was able to perform at all altitudes, even as high as 30,000 feet, whereas the Hurricane could not. Had Fighter Command only been equipped with Hurricanes, therefore, it would have been decimated by the high-flying 109s. In the event, the Hurricane was able to attack bombers because the Spitfire engaged the high-flying enemy fighter screens. The Spitfire, though, could do both – but there were not enough of them. That being so, the Hurricane was absolutely essential to the defence of Britain in 1940 – and contributed enormously to victory in the Battle of Britain.

Due to the predominance of Hurricanes, Hurricane pilots claimed 1,109 German aircraft destroyed in the Battle of Britain, Spitfire pilots 942 (the Germans actually lost 1,273 – and not all of those to combat with Hurricanes and Spitfires). At the time, these claims gave currency to the belief that the Hurricane executed more damage to the enemy than all other defences combined – while the more charismatic Spitfire became the undeserved icon of Fighter Command's victory. More recent research (see *How the Spitfire Won the Battle of Britain* by this author, Amberley, 2010) by the American John Alcorn, cross-referencing combat claims with actual German losses, suggests, however, that the Hurricanes actually destroyed 655 enemy aircraft, the Spitfires 521 – representing an average over-claiming ratio of 2:1. Given the numbers of these fighters involved – thirty-three squadrons of Hurricanes but just nineteen of Spitfires, the latter were therefore actually 1.25 times per aircraft more successful than the Hurricane. Moreover, figures confirm that the Hurricane was twice more likely to be shot down than the Spitfire. Publication of this research is in no way intended to be disrespectful to the essential contribution made by and bravery of the Hurricane force – it simply more accurately contextualises the respective achievement of both fighters involved, putting flight to the long-accepted myth concerning the Hurricane.

There is no doubt that the Spitfire emerged supreme from the Battle of Britain. In July 1940 the problems of mass production were addressed when the huge shadow factory was opened at Castle Bromwich, rapidly manufacturing the improved Spitfire Mk II. The decision was made to equip all Fighter Command's front-line squadrons in England with Spitfires – a process largely complete by the summer of 1941, when Fighter Command went on the offensive, 'reaching out into France'. By then the Hurricane may well have enjoyed its 'Finest Hour' – but the story of Camm's fighter was far from over.

As Group Captain Sir Douglas Bader once wrote of Hurricanes, 'they fought on every battlefront, from the Arctic wastes of northern Russia to the tropical jungles of the Far East; from the green of Europe to the brown of North Africa. They flew high, they flew low.' They also flew at night. Unable to sustain such heavy losses during daylight in 1940, the Luftwaffe switched to night attacks. Britain's night defences, however, were in their infancy, Bristol Blenheims, Boulton Paul Defiants – and Hurricanes and Spitfires – holding the fort until the radar-equipped Bristol Beaufighters and De Havilland Mosquitos arrived. Neither the Hurricane or Spitfire, however, had been intended by their designers as night-fighters – but desperate was the hour. The single-engined fighter types were sent up into the black nights over Britain's cities on so-called 'Fighter Nights', hoping to chance across a raider. Rarely did this happen, though, but the

Hurricane emerged as the better night-flier, mainly due to its wider track undercarriage and better forward visibility. Indeed, flying the improved Hurricane Mk IIC, armed with four 20 mm cannons, in 1942 Squadron Leader James MacLachlan DFC – who had lost an arm when shot down over Malta – and the Czech Flight Lieutenant Karel Kuttlewascher DFC of 1 Squadron flew frequent night intruder operations over northern France. The pair chalked up numerous successes as they hammered the German bombers over their own bases and attacked targets of opportunity.

In October 1940, Italy attacked Greece, but by early 1941 it was clear that Mussolini's campaign was stagnating and required German intervention. Initially three obsolete Gloster Gladiator squadrons were deployed to Greece, which were rapidly re-equipped with Hurricanes. Commanding 33 Squadron was one Squadron Leader Marmaduke St John Pattle DFC – a spirited South African who had already destroyed a dozen enemy aircraft over the Middle East and earned a DFC for his efforts in Greece. Pattle was a phenomenally gifted natural fighter pilot who drove himself hard. In April 1941 he should have been grounded suffering from influenza, but continued flying. On 19 April his formation of twelve Hurricanes were attacked by Me 110s of ZG 26 over Athens, who shot down two RAF fighters. One of these casualties was Pattle, who crashed into Eleusis Bay; he remains missing in action to this day. Just how many enemy aircraft Pattle destroyed will never be known for certain, because RAF records were destroyed when Greece fell, and the likely figure is still debated. His claims amounted to fifty aerial victories, which modern researchers have narrowed down to between twenty-seven and forty-four. It is possible, therefore, that Pattle – a biplane turned Hurricane pilot – could actually be the RAF's top-scoring fighter pilot of the Second World War. As things stand, by the war's end Wing Commander James Edgar Johnnie Johnson – a Spitfire pilot – was recognised as the RAF's official top-scorer with 38½ enemy aircraft to his credit. Whether Pattle actually deserves Johnson's mantle will never be known, but either way, unofficially or otherwise, Pattle was among the top-scoring RAF fighter pilots of the conflict. Indeed, twenty-four of his victories are believed to have been achieved while flying Hurricanes over Greece.

Being an island, Britain was dependent upon the provision of certain essential supplies from overseas – but by 1941 the U-boat menace posed a very serious problem indeed. Long-range Focke-Wulf Condor reconnaissance aircraft prowled the North Atlantic, seeking convoys for the so-called 'Wolf Packs' to attack. Once again it was the Hurricane that was called upon to help with this desperate scenario. The Merchant Ship Fighter Unit (MSFU) was created, based at Speke near Liverpool, to supply Catapult Aircraft Merchant (CAM) ships with one Hurricane each – known as 'Hurri-cats'. The CAM ships were 7,000-ton cargo-carrying vessels of the Merchant Navy, sailing on trade routes to North America, Russia and Gibraltar. The Hurricane was loaded on a trolley fitted to a 70-

foot-long steel runway mounted beyond the forecastle. The trolley was propelled by rockets fired electrically by the Catapult Directing Officer (CDO) from his blast shelter situated adjacent. Unfortunately, once the Hurri-cat had been launched it could not be recovered, or even replaced until the CAM ship safely reached port. These aircraft were consequently only launched operationally and upon visual identification of a hostile aircraft. If the Hurri-cat pilot was within range of land, he could alight safely. If not, his only option was to bail out close to his ship and hope to be rescued quickly. As Air Vice-Marshal Michael Lyne remembered:

All MSFU pilots were volunteers. We tended to be rather wild individualists who had already seen action. There could be no excuse for failing to take off if a Condor showed up. Certainly in storms I would ponder on that fact as I watched the spume being torn off giant waves: no place to be on a parachute! The alert against Condors, however, only lasted to mid-Atlantic – but the expectation of torpedoes was perpetual. The MSFU's last battle was fought far out in the Bay of Biscay. The pilot had not been in action before, his target the formidably armed four-engined Condor. Paddy Flynn, our pilot, had to tackle the Condor at just 200 feet above the sea. As he concentrated fire on the enemy, heavy cannon fire blew away his cockpit hood. His Hurri-cat was also badly hit elsewhere, so ammunition expended Paddy turned to look for the convoy – anxious work with a shot up radio set. After ten minutes flying on an estimated heading he was relieved to see the convoy but before baling out had to see off another Condor. At last it was quiet enough for him to bail out and await rescue by the sailors – who never failed us once. His first target had been well hit and did not return to base. John Kendall, who had flown Spitfires with 66 Squadron during the Battle of Britain, also downed his target. He then patrolled to guard the convoy, despite worsening weather, and even broadcast the location of the unfortunate German crew who were safely picked up. When he at last bailed out in low cloud his parachute failed to open and he was killed.

The Battle of the Atlantic had been won by 1943, the MSFU being disbanded on 8 June that year – the Hawker Hurricane had won another battle honour.

On 22 June 1941, Hitler invaded the Soviet Union. Initially it appeared as though Mother Russia would suffer the same fate as France. Stalin requested aid from the Western Allies – and on 1 September RAF Hurricanes of 81 and 134 Squadrons landed at Vayhenga, near Murmansk. Hundreds of Hurricanes were subsequently delivered in crates, the RAF pilots providing air defence while training the Russians to fly Camm's machine. Operational on 12 September, 81 Squadron destroyed over a dozen enemy aircraft during the first fortnight of their Russian deployment. On 17 December, 81 Squadron arrived back in England, leaving the Russians to operate Hurricanes, and re-equipped with the Spitfire Mk V.

The Hurricane also fought with distinction over the Mediterranean – not least from Malta, the desperate air battles over which were described by one veteran as so intense as to make the Battle of Britain 'look like child's play'. Situated between German-occupied Sicily and the coast of North Africa – where Allied forces were locked in mortal combat with Rommel's esteemed *Afrika Korps* – Malta was a crucial base in that theatre and an constant thorn in the enemy's side. The Germans and Italians, therefore, threw everything at the tiny island, first defended by three obsolete Gloster Gladiators – 'Faith', 'Hope' and 'Charity' – which were reinforced first by two Hurricanes on 21 June 1940, then by two more the next day. On 2 August 1940, twelve Hurricane Mk Is took off from the aircraft carrier HMS *Argus* and flew 380 miles to Luqa. In January 1941 a convoy got through with essential supplies – including crated Hurricanes. Six more arrived a month later, but once more, in spite of their pilots' bravery and sacrifices, the Hurricane was no match for the Me 109. Hurricane Mk IIs then began arriving and equipped Malta's night-fighter unit. In September, a small number of Hurricanes were fitted with racks carrying 40lb General Purpose and 25lb incendiary bombs – these 'Hurribombers' immediately went on the offensive, raiding enemy bases in Sicily. Although an increasing number of Hurricanes managed to get through, it was Spitfires that Malta really needed. At last, on 7 March 1942, fifteen Spitfire Mk VBs reached Malta via HMS *Eagle*. Again, as in the Battle of Britain, the Hurricane had proved its worth simply by being available. This was because as the Spitfire was replacing the Hurricane in England, those obsolete fighters could be deployed in other theatres – until once more the Spitfire was available in sufficient numbers to relieve them. Ultimately Malta held out, resisting every privation and assault – earning the George Cross, in no small part due to the courage of the island's Hurricane pilots.

On 30 October 1941, Hurribombers of 607 Squadron were used from bases in England to attack enemy targets in northern France for the first time. An Air Ministry Communiqué concerning a subsequent sortie read, 'Aircraft of Fighter Command this afternoon carried out a number of offensive patrols and sweeps over northern France and the coasts of Holland and Belgium. Hurricanes carrying bombs took part in one of those operations.' One of the Hurribomber pilots involved in that operation anonymously broadcast his experiences on the BBC:

Whoever thought of fitting bombs to the Hurricane is to be thanked for giving the squadron which I command some of the most thrilling days' work that has ever fallen to the luck of Fighter Command pilots.

Low-level bombing of ground targets by fighters which it makes possible is, of course, something quite new to the RAF pilots. In our Hurricane bombers we don't have to dive on to our targets. We come down almost to ground level before we reach them, and drop our bombs in level flight, with greater accuracy than can be achieved generally in dive-bombing.

The whole thrill of the Hurribomber is in the ground-level flying over the target. There we are like a close formation of cars sweeping along the 'railway straight' at Brooklands, only, instead of fast car speeds, we are batting along at between 200 and 250 mph. At times we may exceed 300 mph.

The impression and thrill of speed near the ground has to be experienced to be believed. Even though we are travelling so fast, there would be a risk of being hurt by the blast of our own bombs if they were of the ordinary type which burst on contact. Consequently our bombs are fitted with delayed-action fuses, so that they do not explode until we have got well outside their blast range.

It might seem that, flying on to the target at only a few feet altitude, we would be easy prey for Bofors or machine-gun posts. We would be if the gunners could see us coming. But generally they cannot see the low-flying fighter until it is almost overhead, and then they have to be remarkably quick to train their gun on a fleeting aircraft. Moreover, they have little time to calculate what deflections to allow in their aim. On the other hand, of course, the pilot would have precious little chance of bailing out if his aircraft was hit. Indeed, he would have practically no space in which to regain control of his aircraft if a hit threw him temporarily out of gear.

So far, however, the advantage seems to be on our side, and not on the side of the ground defences. I have seen 'flak' and machine-gun fire pelting at my aircraft from all angles, but none of it has hit me. We get intimate, if lightning pictures, of the countryside: people on the road, soldiers scrambling for cover, bombs bursting and throwing debris all around us.

Our first big day out recently was typical of the work of this new weapon of ours. We went over in half a gale. The target we were looking for eluded us on this particular occasion. I think we passed it only a mile to one side. We did a circuit, and not seeing our main target, began to look for our alternative.

I found myself flying down a river with a main line railway running alongside. Ahead was a bridge, carrying the railway over the river. I called to my companion that I would bomb the bridge, and together we swept over it, barely skimming the structure, and let our bombs go. Another pair in the squadron coming on behind saw the bombs explode in the river and the whole bridge slump to one side. As they passed over it, they saw the bridge looking as crooked as an eel.

I looked back to see the effect of our bombs, but all I saw was a string of tracer bullets going up behind my port wing. As I turned again, I saw it coming from a gun-post on an aerodrome which my companion and I were already traversing. I was half-way across it before I recognised it as an aerodrome, but was in time to give some huts on the far edge a good burst from my guns. After this I made for the coast again, flying slap over a town and straight down one of its main streets. The squadron reassembled just off the coast, and we beat it back to base.

Altogether, it was what you'd call a party – or a rough house, according to whether you were on the receiving or the delivery end. And the only damage we sustained was a hole in a tailplane – and that was caused by a seagull!

Such raids, exhilarating though they could clearly be, were of only nuisance value. In late 1941, however, General Sir Alan Brooke, Chief of the Imperial General Staff, watched a demonstration of cannon-armed Hurricanes attacking ground targets on a range. He was convinced by this that harnessing air power to closely support ground troops would become increasingly important. Following the first use of Hurribombers from bases in England, in November 1941 such fighter-bombers became operational in North Africa. There the Hurricane Mk Is of 80 Squadron were adapted to carry eight 40lb bombs in preparation for Operation CRUSADER – aimed at relieving Tobruk. During this operation, these Hurricanes attacked Rommel's mechanised columns. Strafing was found particularly effective but 80 Squadron suffered disproportionately high losses to flak. The Hurricane was superseded in this embryonic close support role by the US-built P-40 Kittyhawk – which inevitably became known as the 'Kittybomber'. Once more, however, it was the Hurricane that had paved the way and held the fort.

In June 1942, nine Hurricane Mk IIDs – each armed with a pair of 40 mm Vickers 'S' cannons – arrived in North Africa to pulverise Rommel's armour. These Hurricanes, swiftly dubbed 'Tank Busters' or 'Can Openers', were very effective against the panzers but once more losses were prohibitive. Attacking at low level, the cannons' weight reduced speed so much that armour plate was sacrificed to compensate. Losses were so high that these aircraft were withdrawn after the Second Battle of El Alamein in October 1942. They reappeared in theatre early the following year, but between 21 and 25 March, 6 Squadron lost sixteen 'Can Openers' to ground fire – six on one sortie – and were again withdrawn. Nonetheless, the Hurricane Mk IV was developed, with a clever wing capable of carrying 40 mm cannons, 500lb bombs, or 3-inch rockets – or any combination of those weapons. Indeed, home-based Hurricanes of 137 Squadron, operating from Manston, made the first 40 mm attack on 23 July 1943 – busting trains in Belgium.

Over the desert, however, Air Vice-Marshal Coningham and General Montgomery had worked out the basics of close air support – which both knew would be essential to the success of any Allied landing in enemy-occupied France. They also knew that impressive though the Hurricane Mk IID's 40 mm cannon was, the aircraft lacked the necessary power to operate this weapon safely. Unfortunately there was no other aircraft available that had sufficient power to cope with this extra weight and retain a high level of speed and agility. Instead, what would become the RAF's close-support workhorse emerged: the Hawker Typhoon, armed with 3-inch rockets.

Hurricanes also fought over the steamy jungles of the Far East in a similarly diverse range of roles. This adventure began on 3 January 1942, when fifty-one Hurricanes arrived at Singapore, bolstering Air Vice-Marshal PC Maltby's confidence to such an extent that he 'confidently expected that the Hurricanes would sweep the Japanese from the sky'. This appeared justified when on 20 January Singapore was attacked by twenty-seven Japanese bombers – the Hurricanes destroyed eight without loss. It was a different story the following day, however: learning from their mistake, the Japanese bombers returned – escorted by Mitsubushi Zero fighters; five Hurricanes were destroyed while the nimble Zeros were unscathed. It soon became apparent that the Hurricane was superior to the Zero above 20,000 feet – for which reason the Japanese fighter pilots remained beneath that altitude, luring the RAF pilots to fight on their terms. By 28 January, of the fifty-one Hurricanes only twenty remained serviceable. A few days later, Singapore, an essential port, fell. The Hurricanes had already been withdrawn to nearby Sumatra. Continued resistance, however, was hopeless. By 7 March just two Hurricanes were still operational. These were destroyed and the RAF withdrew to Australia. Afterwards, Hurricanes originally intended for Singapore were diverted to Burma, supporting Brewster Buffalos and Curtis P-40s defending Rangoon. This time, the Japanese failed to achieve aerial superiority – losing at least sixty aircraft in combat with Hurricanes. Rangoon, however, fell on 8 March 1942, after which the Hurricanes operated from airstrips cut into the jungle between there and Mandalay. By mid-1942, many RAF aircraft, including more Hurricanes, arrived in Ceylon and India, this build-up continuing into 1943. By then, the Japanese were on the Indian border, poised to attack Calcutta. Enemy bombers raided the sprawling Bengali city, but so effective was the resistance by the Hurricane squadrons operating from 'Red Road' in Calcutta that these attacks were soon abandoned. As time went on, the Hurricanes of the 'Forgotten Air Force' slogging away in the Far East were reinforced by Spitfires and other types, including the excellent P-47 Thunderbolt. Nonetheless, it was the Hurricane which provided most close support during the crucial operations around Kohima and Imphal, and likewise cooperated with the army during the long advance south through Burma. Once more, the Hurricane fired cannon, dropped bombs and fired rockets and enemy positions, hammering the enemy wherever he could be found.

In August 1944, its duty largely done, Hawker Aircraft Ltd built its last Hurricane, a Mk IIC, PZ865. Since 1941 it had been replaced as the RAF's front-line fighter at home by the Spitfire, and had been relegated to other roles, as we have seen, and sent urgently to other theatres of war; in all of those the Hurricane did sterling service in difficult circumstances until Spitfires and other more advanced types arrived to move things forward. The Hurricane had also led directly to creation of the Hawker Typhoon. The solidly built and powerful 'Tiffie' was also designed by Sydney Camm – who began work on his new fighter as early as 1937, when the first Hurricanes started roiling off the production lines. This is significant. Although R. J. Mitchell sadly died prematurely of cancer, aged forty-two, coincidentally in 1937, Supermarine designer Joe Smith assumed responsibility for developing the Spitfire, which he did through twenty-four different marques. Like the Hurricane, the Spitfire had been pressed into roles never envisaged by its creator, from high-flying photographic reconnaissance machine to long-range bomber-escort fighter; from carrier fighter to dive-bomber – and much more. The Spitfire was remodelled around a new engine, the Rolls-Royce Griffon, providing impressive performance but producing an aircraft with little semblance to Mitchell's prototype K5054. That it was possible to develop the Spitfire in this way speaks volumes for the potential of Mitchell's original design, however. That Camm abandoned the Hurricane in favour of creating a new machine around the twenty-four-cylinder Napier Sabre engine, as opposed to continuing work around the twelve-cylinder Rolls-Royce Merlin, speaks volumes for his recognition that the Hurricane was not an advanced design capable of any significant development. Moreover, Camm's original intention was that the Typhoon would be a medium–high-altitude fighter, indicating his acceptance that the Hurricane was deficient at high altitude. Nonetheless, the Hurricane had provided Camm with essential monoplane design experience – without which there would have been no Typhoon to batter German tanks in Normandy, or, indeed, the even more potent Tempest. This, together with the undeniable fact that the Hurricane was available in numbers long before the Spitfire and made an essential contribution to victory in the Battle of Britain, is the Hurricane's lasting legacy.

The war in Europe was finally over on 8 May 1945, the fight against the Japanese continuing until 14 August. Between 3 September 1939 and both those dates, as Douglas Bader rightly said, the Hurricane had flown in every theatre, at every altitude and attitude, and provided an incredible workhorse. This brief account confirms that superior though the Spitfire may have been there just were not enough of them, making the Hurricane absolutely essential. The Spitfire's performance and the quantity of Hurricanes available is what made victory in the Battle of Britain possible – and without that, there would have been no other victories. If those dramatic sixteen weeks of high drama have gone down in history as Britain's 'Finest Hour', so too is it that of Sydney Camm and his Hawker Hurricane. Without it, history would have had a very different outcome.

Dilip Sarkar MBE FRHistS BA(Hons)

2

FLYING THE HURRICANE: PILOT'S NOTES

All aircrew were volunteers, their routes to the cockpit various. In the peacetime RAF, before the Air Expansion Scheme of 1934, pilots were almost exclusively officers – all of whom were graduates of the elite RAF College Cranwell. The Expansion Scheme, however, reacting to events in Germany, sought to increase the number of officers available by introducing the Short Service Commission (SSC) of three years' duration. Ten years before, the Auxiliary Air Force (AAF) had been formed, this being a similar concept to the Territorial Army. AAF squadrons were locally raised. At this time virtually all officers were public school boys, meaning that pre-war pilots in both the RAF and AAF were of a particular social class. In 1936 the RAF Volunteer Reserve (VR) was formed, recruiting men who remained in their civilian occupations full-time but learned to fly at weekends. Unlike the AAF, there were no locally raised VR squadrons, simply trained pilots available to join the RAF in time of emergency. Interestingly, VR recruits were mostly grammar school boys – and were sergeants; again, those commissioned had a public school background. University Air Squadrons (UAS) also trained pilots, who, in time of war, could enter the service via the regular RAF, AAF or VR. There were, however, a small number of regular RAF non-commissioned officers (NCO) who were able to become pilots – that was a good job, because all pilots, regardless of their social background, were badly needed once war was declared on 3 September 1939. SSC officers immediately had their engagements extended 'for the duration of hostilities' and both auxiliaries and reservists were called to full-time service.

Those who learned to fly either before or very early in the war did so at Flying Training Schools (FTS) in Britain, before being posted to their squadron. There new pilots would receive instruction and experience on the type of aircraft they would fly operationally. Losses during the catastrophic Fall of France, however, meant that fighter squadrons were too busy to train replacement pilots themselves. Consequently Operational Training Units (OTU) were created to provide conversion to and experience on type before replacements were posted to squadrons. In 1940, Spitfire pilots, for example, were trained at Aston Down and Hawarden, Hurricane pilots at St Athan. This operational training involved dogfight practice, altitude climbs, aerobatics, navigation exercises and formation flying but, during the early war years, surprisingly little air-to-air and air-to-ground firing practice – so short was ammunition in supply. Nor were pilots provided practical parachute training; Warrant Officer Peter Fox:

> The first time I pulled a ripcord was when I was shot down over the Dorset coast during the Battle of Britain. No-one had really explained the procedure in detail, so when clear of my Hurricane I counted to ten and pulled for all I was worth! There was then one hell of a jolt and there I was floating gently earthwards under a parachute.

Instructors at OTUs were combat veterans who strove to pass on their hard-won experience. During the Battle of Britain, so urgent was the need for replacements that students were lucky to complete ten hours on type before posting. If they were lucky these fledgling fighter pilots would be posted to a squadron recuperating in the North, where further essential experience could be gained in relative safety – otherwise it was a posting to a squadron in the front line, southern England, where the chances of survival were slim. Some were lucky and learned quickly – others died bewildered and disorientated fighting a skilful enemy.

Flying training was conducted in the western half of the British Isles, away from marauding German fighters, but many pilots were killed in flying accidents due to technical malfunction or bad weather. Later, the Empire Air Training Scheme saw pilots provided with elementary, service and operational training in America and Canada.

Every RAF aircraft was subject to an instructional booklet known as 'Pilot's Notes', an Air Ministry publication identifying and explaining the flying controls, surfaces and instruments, and exactly how to safely take off, fly and land the machine. The Hawker Hurricane was no exception. Before flying in this aircraft the pilot would study these notes carefully – and sign to say that he had done so. Reproduced here are Pilot's Notes for the Hurricane Mk I, powered by the Rolls-Royce Merlin II engine, published in March 1939.

A.P.1564A, Vol.I   Frontispiece
The Hurricane I Aeroplane - Merlin II engine.

FS/1

40

AIR PUBLICATION 1564A
Volume I

THE HURRICANE I

AEROPLANE

MERLIN II ENGINE

This handbook is promulgated for the information
and guidance of all concerned.

By Command of the Air Council,

DONALD BANKS

March, 1939

AIR MINISTRY

C 117

FS/2

AMENDMENT CERTIFICATE

Incorporation of an amendment list in this publication should be certified by inserting the amendment list number, initialling in the appropriate column and inserting the date of incorporation.

Holders of the Pilot's Notes will receive only those amendment lists applicable to the preliminary matter, introduction and sections 1 and 2.

INCORPORATING

Amendt. List No.	1			,	5	6				
Prelimy. matter					1					
Leading Partics.										
Introducn.										
Section 1										
Section 2	1									
Section 3										
Section 4										
Section 5										
Section 6										
Section 7						1				
Section 8										
Section 9										
Section 10										
Section 11										
Section 12										
Date of incorpn.					3.2.40	3.2.40				

R.A.F. Form 2804

Continued overleaf

Amendt. List No.										21.
Prelimy. matter										
Leading Partics.										
Introducn.										
Section 1										
Section 2										
Section 3										
Section 4										
Section 5										
Section 6										
Section 7										all
Section 8										
Section 9										
Section 10										
Section 11										
Section 12										
Date of incorpn.										1/9/40

AMENDMENT CERTIFICATE

Incorporation of an amendment list in this publication should be certified by inserting the amendment list number, initialling in the appropriate column and inserting the date of incorporation.

Holders of the Pilot's Notes will receive only those amendment lists applicable to the preliminary matter, introduction and sections 1 and 2.

Amendt. List No.	2									
Prelimy. matter	Eall									
Leading Partics.										
Introdum.										
Section 1										
Section 2										
Section 3										
Section 4										
Section 5										
Section 6										
Section 7										
Section 8										
Section 9										
Section 10										
Section 11										
Section 12										
Date of incorpn.	4/40									

Amendt. **List No.**									
Prelimy. **matter**									
Leading **Partice.**									
Introducn.									
Section 1									
Section 2									
Section 3									
Section 4									
Section 5									
Section 6									
Section 7									
Section 8									
Section 9									
Section 10									
Section 11									
Section 12									
Date of **incorpn.**									

Note to official users

Air Ministry Orders and Volume II leaflets as issued from time to time will affect the subject matter of this publication. It should be understood that amendment lists are not always issued to bring the publication into line with the orders or leaflets and it is for holders of this book to arrange the necessary linking-up.

Where an order or leaflet contradicts any portion of this publication, an amendment list will generally be issued, but when this is not done the order or leaflet must be taken as the overriding authority.

LIST OF SECTIONS

(A detailed List of Contents appears at
the beginning of each Section or Chapter)

Note.- Additional Sections will be issued as and when they
are prepared.

LEADING PARTICULARS

Name	Hurricane I
Duty	Day and night fighting
Type	Single-seater, single-engined, low wing land monoplane

Main dimensions

Datum line horizontal unless otherwise stated

Span	40 ft.
Length, overall	31 ft. 5 in.
Height, overall, airscrew vertical	12 ft. 2 in.
Height, overall, airscrew horizontal	11 ft. 10 in.
Height, overall, airscrew vertical, tail down	13 ft. 3 in.
Height, overall, airscrew horizontal, tail down	8 ft. 10 in.
Ground angle, tail down	$11\frac{1}{2}^{0}$

Fuselage

Length, overall	28 ft. $6\frac{1}{2}$ in.
Height, maximum	6 ft. $7\frac{1}{2}$ in.
Width, maximum	3 ft. $3\frac{1}{4}$ in.

Outer planes

Aerofoil section - at root	Clark Y.H.19% modified
Aerofoil section - at tip	Clark Y.H.12.2%
Chord at root	8 ft. $0\frac{1}{4}$ in.
Chord at tip, ignoring washout	3 ft. $11\frac{1}{4}$ in.
Incidence (aerofoil to fuselage datum lines)	2^{0} 0' ±30'

R.T.P./126
FS/1

Outer planes (contd.)

Dihedral (outer plane datum lines)	3^0 $30'$ $\pm$ $30'$
Sweepback on front spar	3^0 $0'$
Sweepback on leading edge	5^0 $6'$

Centre section

Span (joint pin centres)	9 ft. $1\frac{1}{2}$ in.
Chord	8 ft. $0\frac{1}{4}$ in.
Incidence (aerofoil to fuselage datum lines)	2^0 $0'$ $\pm$ $30'$
Dihedral	Nil
Sweepback	Nil

Tail plane

Span	11 ft. 0 in.
Chord (maximum) including elevator	4 ft. $2\frac{1}{2}$ in.
Incidence (aerofoil to fuselage datum lines)	1^0 $30'$ $\pm$ $15'$
Dihedral	Nil
Sweepback	Nil

Areas

Main plane, with ailerons and flaps	257.6 sq.ft.
Ailerons, total	20.4 sq.ft.
Flaps, total	25.11 sq.ft.
Tail plane, with elevator and trimming flaps	33.26 sq.ft.
Elevator and trimming flaps	13.46 sq.ft.
Tail trimming flaps (two)	0.38 sq.ft. each
Fin	8.83 sq.ft.
Rudder, with balance flap	13.06 sq.ft.
Balance flap	0.36 sq.ft.

Control surfaces, settings and range of movement

Tail plane	Fixed
Fin - leading edge offset to port	1° 30'
Aileron droop	Nil
Aileron movement (from main plane datum line)	22° up 21° down
Elevator	27° up 26° down
Tail trimming flaps	23° up 23° down
Tail trimming flaps, fixed	15° up
Rudder	28° port 28° starboard
Rudder balance flap -	
Inner hole (port and starboard)	28°
Middle hole (port and starboard)	23° 30'
Outer hole (port and starboard)	19° 30'
Flap, centre section	80° 0' down
Flaps, outer planes	80° 0' down
Tolerances on all ranges of movement	$\pm 2^{\circ}$ 30'

Alighting gear

Undercarriage

Type	Two separate compression legs and pneumatic wheel units retracting inwards and backwards.
Track	7 ft. 10 in.
Compression legs	
Type	Vickers oleo-pneumatic
Air pressure	See Sect.3, para.22
Wheels -	
Type	Dunlop A.H.2061
Tyres	8 in. for 10 in. wheels
Air pressure	42 lb. per sq.in.

F.S./2

50

Alighting gear (contd.)

Undercarriage (contd.) -

    Brakes -

        Type   Dunlop pneumatic

Tail wheel unit -

        Type   Compression leg (fixed) with fully castoring pneumatic wheel.

    Compression leg -

        Type   Dowty compression coil spring.

    Wheel -

        Type   Dunlop A.H.O.5000/IX

        Tyre   "Ecta" W.J.11, 4 in. for 3½ in. wheels.

        Air pressure   42 lb. per sq.in.

Engine

Name   Merlin II

Type   Supercharged, geared, glycol-cooled, 60°-V engine.

Fuel   Specification D.T.D.230.

Oil   Specification D.T.D.109.

Coolant   Ethylene-glycol (treated) Specification D.T.D.344.

Airscrew

Type   2-bladed wood tractor Drg. No. Z.3895

Diameter   11 ft. 3 in.

Pitch   20 ft. 3 in. (fixed)

Direction of rotation   Right hand, i.e. clockwise when viewed from cockpit.

Tank capacities

Fuel tanks -

Main tanks (two)	Actual 34½ gallons each. Effective 33 gallons each.
Reserve tank (one)	Effective 28 gallons.
Total effective fuel capacity	94 gallons.
Normal quantity of fuel carried	75 gallons.
Oil tank	Actual 10½ gallons. Effective 7¼ gallons.

Optimum climbing speeds (A.S.I. reading)

For aeroplanes fitted with 2-bladed wood airscrews to
Drg. No. Z.3895 and with kidney type exhaust manifolds, the
optimum full throttle indicated climbing speed at sea level and
up to 10,000 ft. is constant at 157 m.p.h., A.S.I. reading with
a reduction of 1 m.p.h. for each additional 1,000 ft. of altitude.

Note.- The all-up weight of the aeroplane during the tests
upon which the above climbing speeds are based was
6,000 lb.

Correction of A.S.I. reading for Position Error

At	80 m.p.h.	A.S.I.	reading	add	6.0 m.p.h.
"	100 "	"	"	"	3.2 "
"	120 "	"	"	"	0.5 "
"	140 "	"	"	subtract	1.7 "
"	160 "	"	"	"	4.0 "
"	180 "	"	"	"	6.0 "
"	200 "	"	"	"	7.5 "
"	220 "	"	"	"	8.7 "
"	240 "	"	"	"	9.5 "
"	260 "	"	"	"	9.7 "

Position of pressure head

The pressure head is situated below the port outer plane,
the static tube being parallel to the outer plane chord line.
The tip of the static tube is 9.55 in. from the underside of
the plane and 35.1 in. from the leading edge, the latter
dimension being measured parallel to the chord line; on both
dimensions there is a tolerance of ± ½ in.

INTRODUCTION

<u>Note.</u>   This Introduction and Sections 1 and 2 are also issued separately as 'Pilots Notes'.

1.   The Hurricane I is a single-seater low-wing cantilever land monoplane with retractable undercarriage and enclosed cockpit, designed as a day and night fighter; it is powered with a Merlin II engine which drives a R.H. two-bladed fixed-pitch tractor airscrew. The following are the main dimensions: span, 40 ft.; overall length, 31 ft. 5 in.; overall height with airscrew horizontal and tail down, 8 ft. 10 in.

2.   The cockpit is heated indirectly from the radiator circuit and is totally enclosed under a transparent hood which slides towards the rear for entry and exit purposes; the seat is adjustable vertically at any time. An emergency exit panel is provided in the starboard side of the decking and a break-out panel is incorporated in the sliding hood at its port front bottom corner to provide a clear view when landing should the windscreen be covered with ice. Flying controls are of the conventional stick type with a rudder bar which is adjustable horizontally for leg reach; the cockpit is fitted with a normal set of instruments as well as those necessary for instrument flying. A combined oil and coolant radiator is hung beneath the fuselage behind the undercarriage well; it is contained in a low-velocity cowling with a flap shutter hand-operated from the cockpit. Above the longerons, a reserve fuel tank is carried between the fireproof bulkhead and the instrument panel.

3.   The main plane is built in three sections, port and starboard outer planes and centre section, the fuselage being recessed to take the centre section so that its underside is flush with the bottom of the fuselage; the centre section is faired into the fuselage. The centre section is of the same construction on all aeroplanes but the outer planes may be either of the fabric-covered or of the skin-stressed type; each type are interchangeable cantilevered units.

4.   The main fuel tanks are housed within the centre section between the spars, one tank being fitted on each side of the fuselage; the oil tank forms the port leading edge of the centre section. The mass-balanced ailerons have a differential action and hydraulically-operated split flaps are fitted to the trailing edges of the outer planes and centre section; the flaps extend between the inner ends of the ailerons except in the way of the radiator fairing. Eight Browning guns, together with the necessary ammunition, are housed four aside at the inner ends of the outer planes; the guns fire through the leading edge and are pneumatically controlled from a single button on the control column spade grip. Landing lamps are also mounted in the leading edges of the outer planes, one on each side just outboard of the guns, their positions being controllable from the cockpit.

R.T.P./126
FS/1

5. A non-adjustable cantilever tail plane is carried over the rear end of the fuselage; fore-and-aft trimming is obtained by small flaps operated from the cockpit through an irreversible gear mounted within each horn-balanced elevator. The rudder has a small horn balance, which houses the mass-balance weight, and it is fitted with an adjustable balance flap operated automatically from the rudder hinge; the fin is slightly offset to counteract engine and airscrew torque. The tail unit surfaces are faired into the fuselage and into one another, external bracing not being employed.

6. The undercarriage consists of two oleo-pneumatic compression legs which retract inwards and backwards into a well between the centre section spars, the legs being hydraulically-operated and fitted with mechanical locking and electrical indicating devices; an audible warning signal operates when the undercarriage is retracted if the throttle lever is less than one-third open. Each compression leg carries a stub axle with a medium-pressure pneumatic wheel fitted with a pneumatically-operated brake controlled by a lever on the control column; differential action is provided for the brakes and operates in conjunction with the rudder bar. When on the ground, the tail is supported by a non-retractable spring-loaded compression leg which is fully-castoring and self-centering; the leg carries a wheel fitted with a self-earthing tyre.

7. A remotely-controlled transmitter-receiver is situated behind the pilot's seat and behind this instrument, two parachute flares are carried in their launching tubes. Oxygen equipment is also installed and a camera gun (pneumatically-operated from the gun-firing button on the control column) may be mounted on or in, the leading edge of the starboard outer plane. The electrical installation provides for navigation, identification, landing and cockpit lamps, for which power is derived from an engine-driven generator.

SECTION 1

CONTROLS AND EQUIPMENT
IN COCKPIT

R.T.P. /126
FS/1

SECTION 1

LIST OF CONTENTS

R.T.P./126
FS/2

SECTION 1

LIST OF ILLUSTRATIONS

SECTION 1

CONTROLS AND EQUIPMENT
IN COCKPIT

General

1. The lay-out of the flying and other controls and equipment is illustrated and annotated in figs. 1 to 4. Each item is given an individual number and where items are referred to in the text the item number is quoted in brackets, e.g. "Mixture control lever (1)". In the majority of instances the controls etc. are of conventional type and these notes are intended only to explain the function and use of those controls and items of equipment the operation of which may not immediately be apparent.

Fuel, oil and coolant

2. The fuel, oil and coolant to be used with the Merlin II engine are:-

Fuel	..	..	..	..	..	Specification D.T.D.230
Oil	..	..	..	..	..	Specification D.T.D.109
Coolant..	..	..	..	..	Ethylene-glycol (treated) Specification D.T.D.344

Aeroplane controls

3. <u>Control column</u>.- The spade grip and upper portion of the control column (34) hinges sideways to give aileron control; elevator control is obtained in the normal manner. The spade grip incorporates a gun pneumatic firing button (37) accessible to the left thumb and a bowden brake operating lever (35) accessible to the right hand. For parking, the brakes are applied by gripping the lever with the right hand and operating a retaining catch near the lever pivot with the left hand.

4. <u>Rudder bar</u>.- The rudder bar (31) is of the normal pivoted type, and is adjustable for leg reach by means of a starwheel (70) which may be operated in flight. Long heel rests are provided.

5. <u>Elevator trimming tabs control</u>.- The trimming tabs are controlled by a handwheel (65) on the left of the seat. An indicator on the left of the handwheel shows the necessary direction of rotation, i.e. rotate forward to correct tail heaviness and vice versa.

6. <u>Undercarriage and flap (hydraulic) controls</u>.- These consist of a selector lever (72), an engine pump control lever (73) and a hand pump lever (77). The selector lever is situated to the right front of the seat and works in a gate. It has a central neutral position and four working positions, i.e. "Up" and "Down" for both undercarriage units and flaps, the flap positions being outboard. The engine pump lever is situated outboard of the selector. The hand pump lever is on the right of the seat; it is cranked and fitted with a rubber grip.

R.T.P./126
FS/3

7.   The method of operation is to move the selector to the position required and then either depress the engine pump lever until the selected operation is completed, or work the hand pump lever until the same result is obtained. To obviate inadvertent selection on the ground of undercarriage "Up", a safety catch is provided. The catch is a swinging plate which, when in use, covers the slot of the gate and prevents entry of the lever.

8.   <u>Undercarriage indicator</u>.- The up and down positions of the undercarriage units are indicated separately by red and green lamps respectively. The lamps are duplicated and contained in an indicator (13) on the port side of the instrument panel. Two switches (12) on the left of the indicator control the lamps, that on the left being the main switch and that on the right the change-over switch for the duplicate set of lamps. The duplicate lamps are for use should it be suspected that any of the lamps normally used have failed.

9.   <u>Undercarriage warning buzzer</u>.- Should the undercarriage units not be locked "Down" at any time when the throttle lever is less than one-third open, the pilot will immediately be warned by the sounding of a buzzer (6) situated close to his head on the port side of the cockpit. This device may be tested on the ground by raising by hand one of the undercarriage side stay latch locks whilst the throttle is less than one-third open.

10.   <u>EMERGENCY CONTROL - Undercarriage releases</u>.- A separate foot-operated button release (71) painted red, situated outboard of each heel rest, is provided to unlock each of the undercarriage units in the event of the failure or stretching of the snap lock operating cable coupled to the hydraulic selector lever.

11.   <u>Flap indicator</u>.- A mechanical indicator (75) situated to the right-hand side of the seat, directly below the hydraulic selector, shows the setting of the flaps. The indicator pointer moves along a graduated scale marked "Up" and "Down" at its extremities.

Engine controls

12.   <u>Mixture control lever</u>.- The automatic mixture control lever (1) has two positions only i.e. "Rich" and "Weak"; there are no intermediate positions. The adjustment of the mixture strength to meet the varying conditions of altitude is effected by the automatic unit on the engine. The mixture control lever is returned to the "Rich" position by the closing movement of the throttle control lever.

13.   <u>Engine controls friction adjustment</u>.- In order to prevent movement due to vibration the mixture and throttle levers are separately governed by friction adjusters (39 and 40) on the inboard side of the lever spindles. The knurled wheel controls the mixture lever and the larger serrated wheel the throttle.

14.   <u>Radiator flap control</u>.- The flap controlling the air-flow through the coolant and oil radiators is governed by a long hand lever (67) on the left side of the seat. The lever is released for movement by pressure on a thumb button in the end. A mechanical indicator (64) showing the radiator flap setting is situated on a structure tube just forward of the elevator trimming tab handwheel.

15. <u>EMERGENCY CONTROL - Cut-out for automatic boost.</u>-
This is situated on the port side of the instrument panel. It
consists of a red-painted knob (5) and is pulled out to operate
and locked by a clockwise turn. It is intended for use should
the automatic boost control fail in flight or should it be
necessary in an emergency to override the automatic control for
increase of boost.

Seating and exits

16. <u>Seat control.</u>- The seat is adjusted for height by
movement of a long lever (74) on the right of the seat. The
locking device is released by depressing a thumb pressbutton
in the end of the lever.

17. <u>Safety belt release control.</u>- A bowden control
lever similar to that for locking the cockpit hood is provided
on the starboard longeron to release and relock the safety belt
shoulder straps. To relock the straps the pilot should lean
fully back before operating the lever.

18. <u>Cockpit hood locking control.</u>- The cockpit hood
slides fore and aft and can be locked in either the closed or
open position by means of a bowden control lever (58) on the
port longeron just aft of the engine controls. The hood is
unlocked when the control lever is in the down position.

19. <u>EMERGENCY CONTROL - Exit panel.</u>- A large detachable
panel on the starboard side, dowelled at the bottom to the
decking shelf and held fore and aft at the top by spring-loaded
plungers, is controlled by a single lever on the inside of the
panel. The panel is instantly freed by moving the lever
backwards and upwards to the "Open" position, BUT THE LEVER
CANNOT BE OPERATED UNLESS THE COCKPIT HOOD IS MOVED TO ITS
FULLY-OPEN POSITION.

Operational equipment

20. <u>Fuel contents gauge.</u>- A single gauge (42) on the
starboard side of the instrument panel indicates selectively
the contents of each of the three tanks - two main and one
reserve. A selector arm and pushbutton switch unit (43) is
located above the gauge. The gauge is operated by moving the
selector arm to the required position and then pushing the switch
button. The gauge scale has upper and lower graduations, the
former indicating for the reserve tank and the latter for either
of the main tanks.

21. It should be noted that when the aeroplane is on the
ground the gauge readings are not correct. A conversion table
showing the actual contents of the reserve and main tanks in
relation to tail-down readings is fixed to the exit panel on the
starboard side of the cockpit.

22. <u>Oxygen equipment.</u>- A single oxygen cylinder is
stowed behind the seat. A standard regulator unit (10) is fitted
on the port side of the instrument panel and a bayonet union
socket (59) for the low-pressure supply to the mask is located
on the decking shelf alongside the port longeron.

R.T.P./126
FS/4

23. **R/T remote controls.-** A standard controller (60) is fitted on the port side of the cockpit hooding above the engine controls. The upper lever of the controller, which operates the change-over switch of the transmitter-receiver, is pushed forward for "Receive" and pulled back for "Send"; the wireless unit is switched off by moving the lever to the vertical or "Off" position. The lower lever, which operates the tuning circuit of the receiver is pre-set before taking off but can subsequently be used for any fine tuning adjustments that may be necessary. The serrated central knob on the controller is a remote volume-control; it is turned clockwise to increase the volume and vice versa. A switch unit clipped to a diagonal structure member, just forward of the trimmer control handwheel, is provided for the purpose of connecting a time switch to the wireless unit. The combined microphone and telephone socket (66) is fixed to the front edge of the seat.

24. **Parachute flares release controls.-** A toggle release (76) for each of the port and starboard parachute flares is located outboard and below the flap setting indicator. The toggle pulls work through an indicator plate and are pulled upwards to release the flares.

25. **Landing lamp control.-** A two-way switch (3) on the decking shelf at the extreme port corner of the instrument panel enables either the port or the starboard landing lamp to be used as required; both lamps are off when the switch knob is upright. A bowden dipping control (61) is situated immediately aft of the engine control levers; the lamps are dipped by pushing the lever forward and the lever can be held in any position by tightening the knurled wheel provided. When the knurled wheel is unscrewed the lever is pulled aft into the "Up" position by a return spring in each of the lamp units.

Flying control locking gear and picketing rings

26. **Flying control locking gear.-** This gear is contained in a canvas bag stowed in a locker behind the pilot's head. The locking gear comprises a hinged bracket for attachment to the control column, a pair of tubes which lock the rudder bar to the column bracket and a telescopic interference tube connected to the column bracket and passed through the slot in the back of the seat. The bracket is fastened round the top of the lower portion of the column by a toggle screw and is positioned with its projecting lugs embracing the aileron actuating tie-rods and in contact with the tie-rod fork-end nuts; thus, movement of the hinged top portion of the column, and hence the ailerons, is prevented.

27. The rudder bar locking tubes are pinned to the column bracket and provided with quick-attachment ends for connection to spigot bolts clipped to the rudder bar. The telescopic interference tube prevents occupation of the seat whilst the controls are locked.

28. **Picketing rings.-** A pair of picketing rings, contained in a pocket of the locking gear bag, are provided for attachment to screwed sockets on the under-surface of the wing spars just inboard of the wing tip.

Miscellaneous equipment

29. **First-aid outfit.**- This is attached by means of
elastic cords to the inside of a detachable fairing panel on
the port side aft of the cockpit. In case of emergency this
panel must be kicked in, breaking the stringers and tearing
the fabric. The position of the outfit is clearly indicated
on the fuselage covering.

30. **Map case.**- A metal case for maps, books, etc. is
fixed to the front of the exit panel on the starboard side of
the cockpit. A canvas stowage case for the course and height
indicator is fixed to the face of the map case.

31. **Engine starting handles.**- Two starting handles are
stowed in the undercarriage wheel recess beneath the centre
section, one on each side wall. To remove a handle, unscrew
the wing nut on the securing bracket and swing the bolt
downwards; then lift the clip, disengage the starting handle
and withdraw it forwards.

Instrument panel, port side. A.P.1664A, Vol.1, Sect.1, Fig.1.

63

Index to items on fig.1

1 Mixture control lever.
2 Throttle control lever.
3 Landing lamp switch and instruction plate.
4 Electric starter push button
5 Automatic boost EMERGENCY cut-out control.
    PULL to operate.
6 Undercarriage warning buzzer.
7 Dimmer switch for (8).
8 Cockpit floodlamp.
9 Dimmer switch for (30).
10 Oxygen regulator.
11 Undercarriage buzzer warning plate.
12 Undercarriage indicator lamps switches
13 Undercarriage indicator lamps.
14 Head protector pad mounting.
15 Compass correction card holder.
16 A.S.I.
17 Reflector sight dazzle screen.
18 Artificial horizon.
19 Rate of climb indicator.
20 Engine speed indicator.
21 Boost pressure gauge.
22 Oil pressure gauge.
23 Fuel pressure gauge.
24 Radiator temperature gauge.
25 Oil temperature gauge.
26 Turn indicator.
27 Direction indicator.
28 Compass.
29 Altimeter.
30 Cockpit floodlamp.
31 Rudder pedal.
32 Clock.
33 Navigation lamps switches.
34 Control column.
35 Brake control lever.
36 Main magneto switches.
37 Gun firing button.
38 Fuel control cock.
39 Mixture lever friction adjuster.
40 Throttle lever friction adjuster

Instrument panel, starboard side. A.P.1564A, Vol.I, Sect.1, Fig.2.

65

Index to items on fig.2

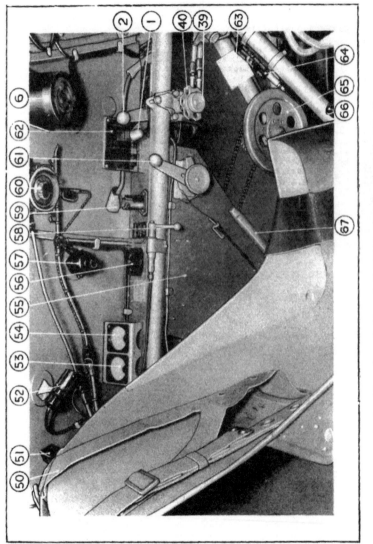

Port side of cockpit. A.P.1564A, Vol.I, Sect.1, Fig.3.

Index to items on fig.3

Starboard side of cockpit. A.P.1564A, Vol.I, Sect.1, Fig.4.

Index to items on fig.4

SECTION 2

HANDLING NOTES FOR PILOT

R.T.P./126
FS/1

SECTION 2

LIST OF CONTENTS

R.T.P. /126
FS/2

SECTION 2

LIST OF ILLUSTRATIONS

SECTION 2

HANDLING NOTES FOR PILOT

Preparation for flight

1.   The Hurricane may be flown with or without guns, ammunition or R/T equipment.

Preliminaries

2.   On entering the cockpit proceed as follows:-

(i) Switch on the undercarriage indicator lamps (port switch) when two green lights should show.

(ii) Ascertain that the safety catch of the hydraulic selector is covering the chassis "Up" position.

(iii) Open radiator flap; during cold weather the flap should be kept closed until the coolant temperature commences to rise.

(iv) Check movement of flying controls.

(v) Check throttle lever friction adjustment. The larger serrated hand adjuster should be set to hold the lever firmly to prevent it working back during "take-off".

Starting the engine

Note.- For full particulars of the Merlin II engine see A.P.1590B, Volume I, 2nd Edition.

3.   For starting purposes the engine must always be supplied from the reserve tank as this provides a gravity feed, and the main or wing tanks, being below the level of the engine, deliver fuel only when the engine is running. It is important to note that the run-up and take-off must be made on reserve supply if the main tanks are less than half full. Therefore a decision must be made, prior to running-up, as to which supply is to be used for the take-off. The supply having been chosen, the fuel distributor cock must not again be moved until the take-off has been accomplished, as such movement may disturb the flow and cause a stoppage.

IMPORTANT. To obviate any danger of air locks in the fuel system, with consequent engine failure, the reserve (gravity) tank must not be exhausted completely before switching over to the main tanks. To prevent temporary stoppage of the engine, it is preferable not to empty completely the main tanks before switching over to the reserve tank.

F.S./3

To start the engine proceed as follows:-

(i) Check contents of fuel tanks and decide which supply is to be used for run-up and take-off.

(ii) Turn the fuel distributer cock to "Reserve".

(iii) Move the throttle lever forward about ½ in. on the quadrant.

(iv) With a cold engine give four to five strokes of the primer pump. It is most important to avoid over-priming when the engine is hot; in this instance a start should be tried without priming at all, then if the engine fails to start give one or two strokes only of the primer pump.

(v) Ensure that all personnel are clear of the airscrew.

(vi) Switch on main and starting magneto switches.

(vii) Press starting switch or commence hand starting. The electric starter should not be used continuously for periods of more than 30 seconds.

(viii) If the engine fails to start immediately, one or two additional strokes of the primer pump should be given; this number should not be exceeded.

(ix) As soon as the engine has started, switch off the starting magneto. Turn the fuel distributor cock to the "Main Tanks" position and so test the engine fuel pumps for satisfactory working. If the run-up and take-off are to be made on the reserve tank supply, turn the fuel cock to "Reserve" and leave in this position until the take-off has been completed.

(x) Warm up the engine until the inlet oil temperature is at least 15°C, and the coolant temperature is not less than 70°C, before opening up to full throttle. Care should be taken whilst warming up to find a throttle position where the engine will not be running rich and will be firing as evenly as possible. For the first three minutes the engine should be warmed up at a fast tick-over and then opened up to about 1,100 r.p.m. until the above temperatures are obtained.

Checking engine and installation

4.   The throttle may be opened fully only for the shortest periods necessary for the checks to be made.

Check the following:-

During warming-up

(i) Check fuel pressures:-

Main tanks	..	..	1½ - 2 lb./sq.in.
Reserve tank	..	..	2½ - 3 lb./sq.in.

(ii) Check operation of hydraulic engine pump.
This can be done by operating the flaps; select
"Flaps down" and depress the operating lever.

(iii) Check the hydraulic handpump by returning the
flaps to the "Up" position by means of the
handpump; afterwards select neutral.

During running-up

(iv) Static r.p.m: 2,100 - 2,200

(v) Static boost: + 6 lb./sq.in. (approx.)

(vi) Oil pressure: a pressure of 70 - 95 lb./sq.in.
will be obtained initially and will fall to the
normal pressure of 60 lb./sq.in. as the oil
temperature rises to its normal value.

(vii) Check magnetos: normal drop 80 r.p.m.

(viii) Check pressure in air cylinder of brakes system;
minimum for taxying 100 lb./sq.in.

Preparation before take-off

5. Prior to taxying out for take-off proceed as follows:-

(i) Set the elevator trimming tab for take-off, i.e.
with indicator in the central position.

(ii) Depress flaps 28° (two divisions on indicator).

(iii) Move the safety catch of hydraulic selector gate
to uncover the "Up" position for undercarriage lever.

(iv) See that the pilot's cockpit hood is fully opened
(A.M.O.A.250/37) and locked in this position.

Taxying-out

6. Before opening up the engine for taxying see that the
brake parking catch is released. Taxying is normal and the
brakes can be used with confidence. During prolonged taxying
check air pressure for brakes.

Delay prior to take-off

7. If the take-off has been delayed for any reason, the
engine should be cleared by opening it up against the brakes.
Whilst doing this the wheels or brakes may slip slightly, but
the tail will not lift if the elevator control is held back fully.

R.T.P./126
FS/4

8. The flaps should be positioned down two divisions (28° approximately.) If there is ample room for the take-off the flaps may be left in the "Up" position, in which case a further run of 90 to 120 yards on the ground may be expected. The aeroplane should be taken off at full throttle with the mixture control at "Rich"; the throttle is not gated. For the take-off the following points should be noted:-

(i) A firm push on the control column is required to raise the tail; the tail should be well lifted.

(ii) Attempts must not be made to pull the aeroplane off the ground until an A.S.I. reading of 80 m.p.h. has been attained.

(iii) As soon as the aeroplane is well clear of the ground, raise the undercarriage. Select wheels "Up" and press the operating lever firmly until both red lights appear.

(iv) If the take-off has been made with flaps down, select flaps "Up" and again press the operating lever until the flap indicator shows fully "Up". The flaps should not be raised until a safe altitude is reached and not below 90 m.p.h. A.S.I. reading.

(v) If the take-off has been made with the fuel supply from the reserve tank, the fuel distributor cock should be moved to the "Main tanks" position as soon as a safe height has been attained.

Precaution after take-off

9. As a safeguard in the event of the engine failing following the take-off, a steep angle of climb should not be attempted. It is preferable to aim at clearing the aerodrome boundary by a small margin.

Climbing

10. For aeroplanes fitted with 2-bladed wood airscrews to Drg. No.Z.3895 and with kidney type exhaust manifolds, the optimum full throttle indicated climbing speed at sea level and up to 10,000 ft. is constant at 157 m.p.h. A.S.I. reading with a reduction of 1 m.p.h. for each additional 1,000 ft. of altitude. The radiator flap should be set in the fully open position for climbing, except at high altitudes or when the coolant temperature falls below 70°C.

Note.- The all-up weight of the aeroplane during the tests upon which the above climbing speeds are based was 6,000 lb.

Cruising

11. For continuous cruising the boost pressure must not exceed + 4¼ lb./sq.in. at 2,600 r.p.m. The mixture control must be in the "Rich" position at all boost pressures in excess of + 2¼ lb./sq.in. and the r.p.m. must not exceed 2,600.

Economical cruising with the mixture control in the "Weak"
position can be employed at any altitude with a boost pressure
of less than + 2¼ lb./sq.in. The mixture control must be
returned to the "Rich" position when the boost exceeds + 2¼ lb./
sq.in. It should be noted that under economical cruising
conditions the engine does not respond readily to the throttle
and this may be improved by returning the mixture control
temporarily to the "Rich" position.

Gliding

12. With flaps and undercarriage down a good average
gliding speed is 80 m.p.h. A.S.I. reading with the engine
running slightly faster than idling speed. For gliding turns
with engine idling, 90 A.S.I. reading provides a safe margin.

Approach

13. The normal method of approaching to land is by means
of a straight glide, (at the speeds mentioned above) with the
use of some engine until the aerodrome boundary is passed. Note
the following:-

(i) Prior to the approach, reduce speed to about 150 m.p.h.,
A.S.I. reading, and lock the cockpit hood in the open
position; select wheels "Down" and press the operating
lever (or operate the hand pump); keep the lever
depressed until the green lamps light, indicating that
the wheels are locked down and safe for landing. If
the hand pump is used (see para.14), pumping must be
continued until increased resistance is felt and the
green lamps light. When the engine pump has been used,
it may always be confirmed that the wheels are down
and locked by operating the hand pump until increased
resistance is felt.

(ii) After lowering the undercarriage, select flaps "Down",
at a speed not exceeding 120 A.S.I. reading, and press
the oil valve operating lever, or operate the handpump,
until the flap indicator shows flaps fully down. As
soon as the flaps are depressed there is an appreciable
nose down change in trim which can be relieved by
adjusting the elevator trimming tabs.

(iii) In the event of an unsuccessful landing the aeroplane
should be taken-off again without raising the flaps.
It can be climbed with undercarriage and flaps down.

(iv) Before landing check the air pressure in the brake
system to ensure availability of the brakes; the
pressure should be not less than 120 lb./sq.in. for
efficient braking.

(v) If for any reason a landing is being made with the
flaps up increase the approach speed by 10 m.p.h.,
A.S.I. reading.

Undercarriage EMERGENCY operation

14. If difficulty is experienced in selecting wheels
"Down", or the wheels fail to drop (indicated additionally by
the failure of the red lights to extinguish), select wheels "Up"
again and press the operating lever for 15 seconds or operate
R.T.P./126
FS/5

the handpump, after which select wheels "Down" immediately.
If this action fails to lower the undercarriage, reduce speed
to 90 m.p.h., A.S.I. reading and press with both feet on the
undercarriage emergency release knobs and at the same time
select wheels "Down".

Landing

15. Landing is normal. The brakes are powerful and on
smooth ground may be applied without fear of the aeroplane
turning on to its nose, even with the C.G. in the forward
position.

Shutting down

16. The engine should be allowed to idle for a short
period before switching off, the fuel being turned off first
and the switches out only when irregular firing becomes
noticeable. Switch off the undercarriage indicator. Set flaps
up and make certain that the safety catch of the hydraulic
selector is covering the wheels "Up" position.

Diving

17. The maximum diving speed is 380 m.p.h., A.S.I.
reading. At less than one-third throttle opening, r.p.m. must
not exceed 3,000; at more than one-third throttle opening the
engine speed may exceed 3,000 r.p.m. for periods of not more
than 20 seconds with a momentary maximum speed of 3,600 r.p.m.
The boost pressure is automatically limited to + 6¼ lb./sq.in.
It is not unusual for the engine to run erratically during a
steep dive. When diving the trimming tabs should be set as for
level flight; they must not be used to assist recovery from a
dive. The radiator flap should be set in the closed or normal
position and the cockpit hood may be open or closed.

Forced landing due to engine failure

18. Unless a field of ample size is available the
undercarriage should be left up. If there is sufficient time
the selector should be set to flaps "Down" and the handpump used
to depress the flaps fully.

Side-slipping

19. Side-slipping at a steep angle results in the nose
dropping, but gentle side-slips can be used if necessary.

Flying in poor visibility

20. When necessary to fly at low altitude, it is advisable
to open the cockpit hood and lower the flaps fully. In this
condition a speed of 80 - 90 m.p.h., A.S.I. reading may be
maintained with engine r.p.m. of 1,700 - 1,800 without vibration
and with good control. In addition, some pilots prefer to lower
the undercarriage. In hot weather it may be necessary to lower
fully the radiator flap owing to the reduction of air flow
through the radiator occasioned by the depressed wing flap.

Stalling and spinning

21. **Stalling.** - With the flaps and undercarriage up the aeroplane stalls at a speed of 72 m.p.h., A.S.I. reading. With flaps and undercarriage down the stalling speed is 55 m.p.h., A.S.I. reading.

22. **Spinning.** - Spinning of Hurricanes is prohibited (A.M.O.A.15/1938). The following extract from an Experimental Establishment report is included in order that a recovery may be made from an inadvertent spin.

"The aeroplane is easy to spin, more noticeably so at the extended aft centre of gravity. The first three turns are irregular, but subsequent turns are smooth in general. At the extended aft centre of gravity turns to the right tend to be less smooth, having a slightly variable rate of rotation. The first turn of the spin is quick with the nose well down, but after two more turns the aeroplane assumes a more normal attitude.

Measurements of heights and times show no definite variation, with change in position, of the centre of gravity or with changes in the direction of the spin.

The following table gives the average time and height loss recorded during the spins:-

Height at entry into spin:- 18,000 ft. (I.C.A.N.) Air Temp.18°C.
Height loss for 3 turn spin — 1,200 feet.
Time taken for 3 turn spin — 11 seconds.
Height loss for 8 turn spin — 3,200 feet.
Time taken for 8 turn spin — 23 seconds.

The recovery appears to be unrelated to the number of turns made, i.e. 3 or 8, the rotation being stopped within one or two turns subsequent to the correct sequence of control movements for recovery, the subsequent height loss being about 1,000 feet. A further 1,000 feet is lost in returning to level flight. The average total height lost from initiation of the spin to attainment of level flight is about 3,800 feet for a three turn spin and about 5,800 feet for an eight turn spin.

Recovery in all the above spins was made by applying full opposite rudder and then slowly easing the control column forward towards the central (neutral) position. The height loss in recovery is very sensitive to movement of the control column Forward movement of the control column beyond a position just a of central, or a coarse movement forward of the control column, increases the height lost and it must be emphasised, therefore, that the control column be eased forward slowly to a position just aft of central <u>after</u> full opposite rudder has been applied. In general it has been found preferable to apply full opposite rudder, and then make a slight pause before easing the control column forward.

It appears that the aeroplane emerges from a spin in a stalled state which persists for a considerable portion of the resultant dive if backwards pressure is exerted on the control column. If however the control column is pushed forward in recovery so that no effort is made to flatten out from the dive until a reasonable airspeed is reached, the stalled condition is

avoided but the height lost is prohibitive. It will be seen,
therefore, that if recovery is made according to Flying Training
Manual Part I., the loss of height during the recovery is normal
considering the wing loading. On the other hand there is fear
of flicking into a spin in the other direction because the aeroplane emerges from the spin in a stalled state. Coarse backward
movement of the elevator, therefore, at even a later stage of
the curved path in the dive recovery may result in further de-
terioration of the lateral control by virtue of the increased
loading or acceleration. Quick application of the rudder in the
dive recovery phase is required to keep the aeroplane straight,
and correct the tendency to 'flick'.

The instructions laid down in the Flying Training Manual
Part I., Chapter III, paragraph 134, are applicable to the
Hurricane, but should be amplified in the light of the foregoing
remarks.

Fuel capacity and consumptions

23. **Effective fuel capacity.-**

Two main tanks - 33 gallons each = 66 gallons
One reserve tank   = 28   "
     Total effective capacity   94 gallons

Fuel consumptions.- The following table will be found
useful in determining endurances:-

Maximum fuel consumptions
(at altitudes stated)

Condition of flight	r.p.m.	Gallons per hour	Total capacity endurance	Endurance per 5 gallons
Climbing	2,600	81 (at 12,000 ft.)	1.16 hrs.	3.7 mins.
All-out level	3,000	89 (at 17,000 ft.)	1.05 "	3.4 "
Max. cruising (automatic rich)	2,600	64 (at 8,000 ft.)	1.47 "	4.7 "
Max. cruising (automatic weak)	2,600	47 (at 12,000ft.)	2.0 "	6.4 "
Most economical cruising	1,900	20 (at 17,000 ft.)	4.7 "	15 "

Oil capacity

24.   The oil tank has a total capacity of 10½ gallons and an effective capacity of 7½ gallons.

Notes concerning the Merlin II engine

25.   The following should be carefully noted.
Note:-   The automatic mixture control lever has two positions only i.e. "Rich" and "Weak"; there are no intermediate positions. The adjustment of the mixture strength to meet the varying conditions of altitude is effected by the automatic unit on the engine.   The mixture control lever is returned to the "Rich" position by the closing movement of the throttle control lever.

(i) <u>Limiting operational conditions.</u>-

Take-off (up to 1,000 ft. or for 3 mins.)	Maximum r.p.m. Minimum r.p.m. at maximum boost (+6¼ lb./sq.in.)	2,850* 2,080
Climb	Maximum r.p.m. at maximum boost (+6¼ lb./sq.in.)	2,600*
Maximum cruising (mixture control "Rich")	Maximum r.p.m. at maximum boost (+4¼ lb./sq.in.)	2,600
Economical cruising (mixture control "Weak")	Maximum r.p.m. at maximum boost (+2¼ lb./sq.in.)	2,600
All-out level (5 mins. limit)	Maximum r.p.m. at maximum boost (+6¼ lb./sq.in.)	3,000
Maximum dive (See para.17)	Momentary maximum r.p.m. at maximum boost (+6¼ lb./sq.in.)	3,600

*These r.p.m. will not be obtained with a fixed-pitch airscrew.

(ii) <u>Oil pressures.</u>-

Normal	60 lb./sq.in.
Emergency minimum (5 mins. limit)	45 lb./sq.in.

R.T.P./126
F8/7

(iii) <u>Oil inlet temperatures.</u>-

Minimum for opening up	15°C
Maximum for continuous cruising	90°C
Maximum for climbing	90°C
Emergency maximum	95°C
(5 mins. limit)	

(iv) <u>Coolant temperature.</u>-

The engine which employs ethylene glycol as the cooling medium, should not be opened up to full power until the radiator temperature exceeds 70°C. The maximum permissible temperature in flight is 120°C and the recommended cruising temperature should not exceed 95°C.

Correction of A.S.I. reading for Position Error

26.   Note the following.-

At	80	m.p.h.	A.S.I.	reading	add	6.0	m.p.h.
"	100	"	"	"	"	3.2	"
"	120	"	"	"	"	0.5	"
"	140	"	"	"	subtract	1.7	"
"	160	"	"	"	"	4.0	"
"	180	"	"	"	"	6.0	"
"	200	"	"	"	"	7.5	"
"	220	"	"	"	"	8.7	"
"	240	"	"	"	"	9.5	"
"	260	"	"	"	"	9.7	"

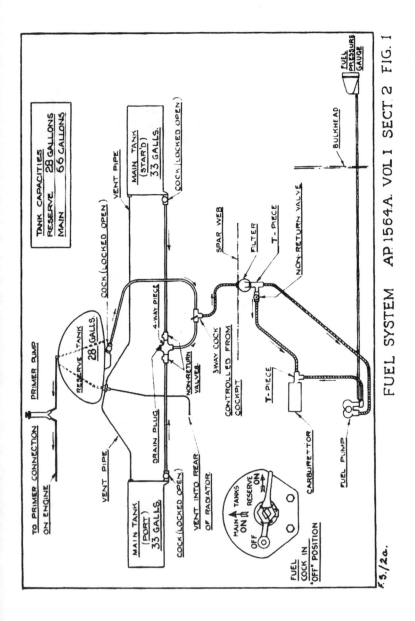

FUEL SYSTEM   AP 1564A. VOL I SECT 2   FIG. 1

F.S./2a.

84

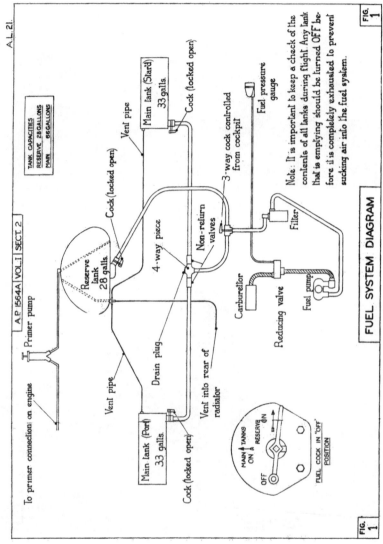

A.P. 1564A | VOL.I | SECT. 2

TANK CAPACITIES
RESERVE 28 GALLONS
MAIN 66 GALLONS

To primer connection on engine

Primer pump

Vent pipe

Reserve tank 28 galls.

Cock (locked open)

Main tank (Stard) 33 galls.

Cock (locked open)

4-way piece

Non-return valves

3-way cock controlled from cockpit

Fuel pressure gauge

Note: It is important to keep a check of the contents of all tanks during flight. Any tank that is emptying should be turned OFF before it is completely exhausted to prevent sucking air into the fuel system.

Filter

Carburettor

Reducing valve

Fuel pump

Drain plug

Vent pipe

Vent into rear of radiator

Main tank (Port) 33 galls.

Cock (locked open)

MAIN TANKS ON

RESERVE ON

OFF

FUEL COCK IN "OFF" POSITION

FUEL SYSTEM DIAGRAM

FIG. 1

FIG. 1

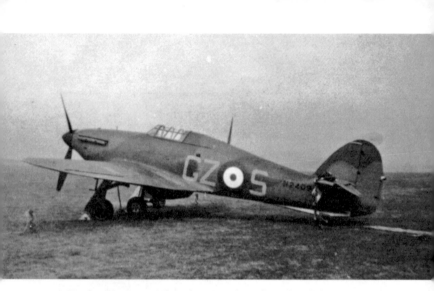

1. A Hawker Hurricane Mk I of 32 Squadron, flown by Flight Lieutenant Peter Brothers, during the 'Phoney War'. This machine has the three-bladed De Havilland two-pitch duralumin propeller.

2. Sergeant Laurence 'Rubber' Thorogood of 87 Squadron with his Hurricane at Exeter during the Battle of Britain. Disney characters were painted on all 87's Hurricanes.

3. Sergeant Thorogood with his 87 Squadron Hawker Hurricane Mk I at Bibury during the Battle of Britain – showing the Rotol airscrew to good effect.

4. Sergeant Thorogood preparing to fly from Bibury during the Battle of Britain – this picture well illustrates the well-worn appearance of an operational Hurricane.

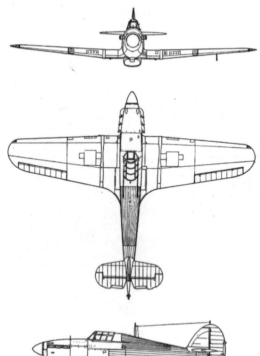

Above: 5. An arrowhead formation of early Hawker Hurricane Mk Is shortly after the type entered service in 1938.

Right: 6. The Hawker Hurricane as drawn for the benefit of wartime plane spotters.

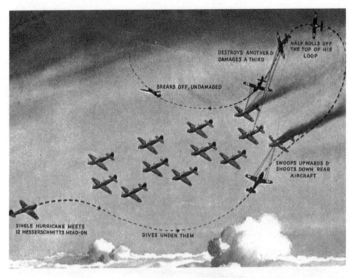

7. A Hawker Hurricane wreaking havoc on a formation of Me 109s: wishful thinking from a British wartime propaganda publication.

8. Hawker Hurricanes in 'vic' formation during the Battle of Britain. Useless in combat against the enemy's loose, line abreast formation of two fighting pairs known as the Schwarm, many young RAF pilots paid the price for this lack of preparedness when war came.

9. Squadron Leader Ian 'Widge' Gleed DFC of 87 Squadron with his personal Hurricane painted with Disney's cat 'Figaro'.

10. Squadron Leader Ian 'Widge' Gleed DFC airborne in his personal Hurricane, leading 87 Squadron on a West Country patrol during the Battle of Britain.

Left: 11. Squadron Leader Ian 'Widge' Gleed of 87 Squadron photographed from an unusual angle in a Hawker Hurricane Mk II on the Scilly Isles in 1941. Note the unusually faired rear-view mirror. Sadly Gleed, an 'ace', was killed in action whilst a Spitfire wing leader over Tunisia.

Below: 12. During the Second World War, only one RAF fighter pilot won the Victoria Cross: Hurricane pilot Flight Lieutenant James Brindley Nicholson of 249 Squadron. Nicholson's signal act of valour took place over Southampton on 16 August 1940. The VC is pictured here signing as part of a quartet with other wounded aircrew recuperating at The Palace Hotel, Torquay. Sadly Nicholson failed to return from a bombing sortie in the Far East and remains missing.

Top: 13. A 32 Squadron Hawker Hurricane Mk I damaged in a taxiing incident just before the Battle of Britain.

Middle: 14. An 87 Squadron Hawker Hurricane Mk I being maintained at Exeter during the Battle of Britain.

Bottom: 15. The Hawker Hurricane Mk IIC of Squadron Leader Ian 'Widge' Gleed DFC in 1942. Armed with 20 mm cannon, these aircraft were used as night intruders.

Top: 16. A Hawker Hurricane night-fighter of 87 Squadron being maintained in 1942.

Middle: 17. Night-fighter: Squadron Leader Peter Townsend DFC, 85 Squadron's Commanding Officer, taxis out during the 1941 Blitz on London.

Bottom: 18. After the battle: a Hurricane survivor, recently used in the 1969 film *Battle of Britain*, seen at an airshow in England that year.

3

MAINTAINING THE HAWKER HURRICANE

Military aircraft represent the forefront of aviation technology – then and now. Although fighters like the Hawker Hurricane appear somewhat antiquated when compared to the computerised fast jets – and even pilotless drones – of today, it is important to remember that in their day these too were advanced aeroplanes. Every aircraft, of course, comprises various systems, each the responsibility of a particular technician – and the Hawker Hurricane was no exception. To service and maintain the Hurricane was a big responsibility. That this was often undertaken under fire or in hostile and remote desert or jungle environments is testimony to the dedication and commitment of the groundcrews concerned – unsung heroes all. The following pages are extracted from the Hurricane Mk I Manual, published by the Air Ministry in March 1939, and include dedicated sections for the aircraft's rigger, fitter, wireless operator/mechanic, and armourer. Like Pilot's Notes, this is an absolutely essential document to understanding the safe operation of a Second World War Hawker Hurricane fighter.

SECTION 3

MAINTENANCE
AND HANDLING OPERATIONS

SECTION 3

LIST OF CONTENTS

R.T.P./126
FS/2

FITTER

INSTRUMENT MAKER

WIRELESS OPERATOR MECHANIC

ARMOURER

R.T.P./126
F8/3

LIST OF ILLUSTRATIONS

SECTION 3

MAINTENANCE
AND HANDLING OPERATIONS

Notes

1. The information given in this Section does not cover all the operations that may be involved during maintenance of the aeroplane; it is intended only to implement the Maintenance Schedule, Vol.II, Pt.2 of this publication.

2. For the maintenance of the following, reference should be made to the relevant Air Publications listed below:-

Engine	A.P.1590B.
Air compressor	A.P.1519.
Instruments	A.P.1275.
Browning guns	A.P.1641C.
Firing control mechanism	A.P.1641E.
Brake system	A.P.1464B.

3. Of the following paragraphs dealing with the removal and assembling of components, the majority refer to the removal of components and, providing additional or contrary instructions for assembling are not given, the procedure for assembling may be assumed to be the same as that for removal but in the reverse order.

RIGGER

GENERAL

Ground equipment

4. The following equipment is required for the efficient handling and maintenance of the aeroplane (ref. A.P.1564A/M.2):-

Universal jacking trestle, No.4, fitted with a 6 in. x 3 in. ash cross beam and suitable blocks at each end, for front end of fuselage.

Universal jacking trestle, type B, fitted with suitable blocks at each end of its beam, for rear end of fuselage.

Handling bar, for rear end of fuselage.

2-ton screw jacks, type B, for bottom of each undercarriage leg.

Side-tracking skates, for undercarriage wheels.

Universal jacking trestles, No.5, for main plane.

Lifting brackets, inner, for outer planes.

Lifting brackets, outer, for outer planes.

Lifting handles, inner, for outer planes.

Lifting handles, outer, for outer planes.

Extractor, for main plane joint pins.

Incidence board, inner, rib B.

Incidence board, outer, rib U.

Dihedral board, front spar.

R.T.P./126
FS/4

Key, for turnbutton fasteners and tank filler caps.
Protecting sleeves, rubber, for struts through main
   fuel tanks.
Studs, for marking main fuel tank covers.
Grease gun, Tecalemit.
Grease gun, Enot.
Air pump, for tyres.
Air pump, for charging pneumatic system.
Air and oil pump, Vickers, for compression legs.
Brake gear valve tools, Dunlop.
Air compressor tools, B.T.H.

Jacking and lifting points

5.   At the front end, the fuselage may be lifted on the
jacking pads incorporated in the engine mounting whilst the
centre section may be jacked beneath the front and rear spar
pin joints.   The rear end of the fuselage may be trestled
beneath the handling bar after it has been fitted through the
tube incorporated in the fuselage joints (lower) just forward
of the tail wheel;   the bar is introduced from either the port
or starboard side through corresponding holes in the fairing.
An emergency jacking point is also provided at the lower end of
each undercarriage compression leg.

6.   Should the aeroplane, with engine installed, be
raised into the flying position on the undercarriage wheels or
on the emergency jacking points at the lower end of each
compression leg, it is essential that the rear end of the
fuselage is anchored to a ground ring or weight of approximately
2 cwt. as a precaution against the fuselage over-balancing on to
its nose.   A rope may conveniently be attached around the bottom
of the tail wheel leg but, when carrying out rigging operations,
care must be taken that the tying down does not put any strain
upon the fuselage.

7.   For handling the outer planes, the lifting brackets
should be screwed into the sockets provided in the undersurface
of the plane at the root end and at the tip, the lifting handles
then being bolted into their brackets; the handles are of such
a length that they project beyond the leading and trailing edges
of the outer plane.

Rigging

8.   General.- The main plane, the tail plane and the fin
are fixed and therefore rigging of the aeroplane is limited to a
general check of the angularity of the main plane and the tail
plane relative to the fuselage, of the verticality of the fin
and the checking of the ranges of movement of the control
surfaces.   On similar port and starboard diagonal dimensions,
a tolerance of 2 in. is allowed, the measurements being taken
from the tips of the planes to suitable points at the nose and
tail of the aeroplane.   The ranges of movement of the control
surfaces are given in the Leading Particulars; the tolerances
given are not hard and fast but when they are exceeded, the
structure as a whole should be examined to determine the cause
of the distortion.   The rigging of the outer planes may be
checked by placing the incidence and dihedral boards in the
positions shown in fig.7, having first placed the aeroplane in
the rigging position as described in para.9.

9. **Rigging position.-** The fuselage should be
supported on adjustable trestles beneath the jacking points
on the engine mounting and rear fuselage (see para.5) until
the undercarriage and tail wheels are clear of the ground;
the trestles should then be adjusted until the fuselage is
level both longitudinally and transversely.   Longitudinal
level is checked by placing a straightedge and level across
the levelling clips on port side struts GH and EF (see fig.7),
transverse level being similarly obtained from the levelling
clips on side struts GH, port and starboard.

10. **Checking ailerons, elevator and rudder.-** With the
aeroplane in the rigging position (see para.9), set the rudder
bar at right-angles to the fuselage centre line (see para.16),
the upper end of the control column in line with the lower
portion and the control column as a whole 7° 30' aft of the
vertical.   Check that the trailing edges of the main plane
and ailerons are in alignment, that the rudder is in line with
the centre line of the fuselage (not the fin centre line) and
that the elevator is in line with the tail plane.

11. **Checking the rear fuselage.-** The rear fuselage may
be checked for overall alignment and freedom from twist as
follows, referring to Sect.6, Chap.1, Fig.2 for the designa-
tion of the fuselage joints:-

   (i)   Place the fuselage in the rigging position as
         described in para.9.

   (ii) Drop plumblines from the centre of joint U and the
         midpoint of cross strut HH to align on a cord
         representing the plan centre line of the fuselage,
         the cord being stretched tightly between two weights
         (or over two supports) a few inches above and
         parallel with the ground.

   (iii) Drop further plumblines from the midpoints of cross
         struts PP, OO and JJ and, if the fuselage is true
         about the plan centre line, these plumblines will
         align on the ground cord.

   (iv) Check the rear fuselage for freedom from twist by
         means of a spirit level laid across the plug ends
         at joints R.

   (v)   Make any necessary adjustments for truing-up the
         rear fuselage by tensioning the bracing wires in
         the top and bottom panels, care being taken to
         ensure that the tension of the wires in adjacent
         panels is approximately equal.

12. **Ailerons.-** Secure the trailing edges of the
ailerons in line with the trailing edges of the main plane
(no droop is intended) and the spade grip in line with the
control column; for this latter operation, the lugged bracket
of the flying controls locking gear may generally be employed
but care should be taken that the gear does maintain the
spade grip in its neutral position.   Connect the cables to
the tie-rods, setting the cables symmetrically about the pulleys
in the outer planes and the cable drum in the fuselage; tighten
the cable turnbuckles to suit.

P.S./5

13.   During flight trials of a new aeroplane it is
sometimes found that when the hand is removed from the control
column one aileron tends to rise and the other to drop,
showing that the ailerons are not in exact balance. This
tendency is corrected by the attachment of a suitable length
of $^3/16$ in. manilla cord to the upper side of the trailing
edge of the up-going aileron. Normally, correct trim is
obtained by this method during the manufacturer's flight
trials for each new aeroplane, and unless the ailerons are
subsequently damaged they should remain in correct trim whilst
in service.

14.   Upon fitting a new aileron, it will be necessary
to remove any cord already fitted to the other aileron before
checking the trim by flying the aeroplane "hands off". If the
trial flight reveals the ailerons to be out of balance, the
length of cord to be applied to the up-going aileron will have
to be determined by trial. When the correct length has been
found by further trial flights, the cord should be attached to
the upper side of, and mid-way along, the trailing edge of the
up-going aileron; the length of cord attached should not
exceed 24 in. The cord should be secured by means of a
serrated-edge fabric strip, $2\frac{1}{4}$ in. wide, doped to the undersurface, around the edge, and on to the upper surface.

15.   Elevator.- Place the aeroplane in the rigging
position (see para.9) and secure the elevator in its neutral
position, i.e. in line with the tail plane; adjust the lengths
of the elevator cables by means of the turnbuckles at their
front ends until the control column is set 7° 30' aft of the
vertical.

16.   Rudder.- Place the rudder in line with the fuselage
centre line (not the fin centre line) and secure the rudder bar
at right-angles to the fuselage centre line; for this latter
purpose, the struts of the flying controls locking gear may
conveniently be employed, checking that the struts do retain
the rudder bar in the correct position. Adjust the cables to
their correct tension by means of the turnbuckles beneath
fuselage cross strut JJ (see Sect.6, Chap.1, Fig.2).

17.   Rudder balance flap.- The balance flap cables should
be fitted in similarly-positioned holes in each arm on either
side of the flap, the cable length being adjusted so that the
flap is in line with the trailing edge of the rudder when the
rudder is in line with the fuselage centre line. When the
cables terminate at the inner holes, the flap remains approximately
parallel with the centre line of the aeroplane through all
angular movements of the rudder; to reduce the degree of
balance, move the cables outboard.

18.   Tail trimming flaps.- When the cockpit indicator
on the handwheel bracket is at zero the trailing edges of the
tail trimming flaps should be in line with the trailing edge
of the elevator. The chain around the sprocket of the cockpit
handwheel should be symmetrically disposed about the sprocket,
the ends of the chain being approximately 11 in. from the
centre of the sprocket. The chains around each worm gear within
each half-elevator, should be disposed about the sprockets so
that their ends are approximately $9\frac{1}{2}$ in. from the centre of
their respective corner sprockets. In front of the elevator
spar, the lengths of cable running forward from the ends of the
bowden casings to the nipples connecting with the fuselage control

cables should be approximately 9 in.; also the connector in the
balance cable should be positioned not more than ½ in. on either
side of the centre line of the aeroplane.

19.   The control should be operated to move the flaps to
their extreme position, up and down, noting that the cable connectors do not foul the fairleads; should the connectors foul
the fairleads the position of the chain on the handwheel
sprocket should be slightly altered. It should also be noted
that, from the fairlead clipped to fuselage cross strut NN, the top control cable passes to starboard and the bottom cable to port.

FUSELAGE

Airscrew

20.   Removal.- Remove the locknut, securing nut and
washer at the nose of the spinner; withdraw the spinner. Remove
the fixing stud and base plate by removing the six nuts, washers
and split-pins securing the base plate to the front flange of
the airscrew hub. Unlock the tabwashers and remove the twelve
nuts securing the front flange of the airscrew hub; remove the
front flange and airscrew.

UNDERCARRIAGE

Compression leg

21.   Warning.- It is extremely important to note that
the air pressure must be released before attempting any dis-
mantling operations; failure to observe these precautions may
result in a serious accident .

22.   General.- Each oleo-pneumatic compression leg contains
3.28 pints of type A anti-freezing oil (Stores Ref.34A/43 and 46)
with air at the following pressures to suit various loadings of
the aeroplane; the table is not to be taken as authorizing weights
in excess of those laid down in the Weight Sheet Summary.
     Weight of aeroplane (lb.) 5,850   6,000,   6,100   6,200
     Pressure (lb.per sq.in.)   362   370   377   385
When checking the air pressure and/or the oil level, the aeroplane
should be supported with the appropriate leg clear of the ground.

23.   The compression legs are supplied as spares with the
correct quantity of oil, but with air at atmospheric pressure;
they should be stored in this condition with the air cylinder
uppermost. It is advisable however to check the oil level (see
para.26) before charging with air to the pressure stated in
para.22; it is also advisable-to check the oil level of a
compression leg which has been installed on a aeroplane and
from which oil has escaped through the air valve due to the
valve having been opened to permit easy closure of the leg when
testing undercarriage movements and clearances.

24.   Once the compression legs are charged with oil and
air as required, it is advisable not to interfere with them
unless there is evidence of air or oil leakage. The following
notes will assist in the diagnosis of faults:-

F.S./6

(i) With the oil level correct, the <u>air pressure is too low</u> if less than 3½ in. of the sliding portion of the piston tube is exposed.

(ii) With the oil level correct, the <u>air pressure is too high</u> if more than 4½ in. of the sliding portion of the piston tube is exposed.

(iii) With the air pressure correct, the <u>oil level is too low</u> if the piston travel is excessive and the aeroplane rolls laterally on a turn.

(iv) With the air pressure correct, the <u>oil level is too high</u> if the leg is harsh in action.

(v) Excessive quantities of oil on the piston and attachment fittings usually denote that the <u>gland packings are worn</u> and need replacement. A leakage from this source can be temporarily remedied by tightening the gland nut but new rings should be fitted (<u>see</u> para.32) as soon as is convenient.

25. <u>Checking air pressure</u>.- Trestle the aeroplane (<u>see</u> para.5) until the undercarriage wheels are clear of the ground and connect the pipeline from the Vickers pump to the air valve; charge the line to the pressure required in the compression leg. Open the air valve two turns and read the pressure on the gauge incorporated in the pump. If a cylinder is used for charging purposes, an air pressure gauge should be incorporated in the pipeline from the cylinder to the air valve.

26. <u>Checking oil level</u>.- If the aeroplane has just landed or taxied, the oil will be in an aerated condition and it is therefore advisable to wait for approximately 15 minutes before checking the oil level. Trestle the aeroplane until the undercarriage wheels are clear of the ground; unscrew the air valve slightly and wait until the air pressure inside the compression leg is equal to that of the atmosphere. Recharge the compression leg with air until the internal pressure is approximately 50 lb. per sq.in.; allow the oil to settle for a few minutes and then open the oil level plug three or four turns. If the air escaping through the oil level valve is free of oil, the oil level is too low but if large quantities of oil are ejected with the air, the oil level is too high; if the escaping air only carries a small amount of oil mist, the level may be taken as correct.

27. <u>Lowering oil level</u>.- Trestle the aeroplane until the undercarriage wheels are clear of the ground. Unscrew the oil valve slightly and allow air to pass through the leg from the pump or cylinder until oil no longer escapes with the air; if the air is passed through the leg too rapidly, it may lower the oil level more than required. Shut off the air supply and wait two or three minutes for the oil to settle to a common level both inside and outside the piston tube; repeat the process until the escaping air only carries a small amount of oil mist.

28. <u>Raising oil level</u>.- After trestling the aeroplane until the undercarriage wheels are clear of the ground, pump in an excess of oil and lower the oil level as described in para.27.

29. Lubrication.- When lubricating the gland at the
lower end of the cylinder tube, it is important that the gland
should only receive sufficient oil for its proper lubrication;
if large quantities of oil are forced into the gland, some may
find its way into the cylinder tube and increase the oil content
of the leg.

30. Checking gland packings.- It may be found that a leg
which has been standing in one position for a long period is
somewhat sluggish in action due to the oil attacking the
composition of the packing rings and causing temporary adhesion
to the piston. This should rectify itself after a short period
of taxying, but if it persists the gland should be removed and
cleaned.

31. Removing piston tube and gland packing.- Unscrew the
oil level valve and release the air from the cylinder, at the
same time pumping in oil through the air valve; when oil only is
expelled, screw down the oil valve and remove the gland capping
ring, the scraper ring and the gland nut. Remove the six bolts
situated around the cylinder tube midway between the gland and
the lugged collar for the radius rod and side stay; this will
permit the splined ring within the cylinder to be withdrawn when
the piston tube is removed. Continue pumping oil into the
cylinder until the gland tubular capping ring and the packing
are forced out from the cylinder tube. Unscrew and remove the
packing supporting ring; withdraw the piston tube and with it
the internal splined ring.

32. Fitting new gland packing rings.- The new rings
should be soaked in type A anti-freezing oil for at least twelve
hours before they are required for fitting. With the oil and
air valves closed, invert the cylinder tube and, after ensuring
that the oil has been well drained from the cylinder tube, pour
in 3.28 pints of type A anti-freezing oil; insert the piston tube
but do not displace the oil. Having removed the stub axle from
the piston tube, slip the packing supporting ring over the piston
tube and screw it into the cylinder tube. Slip the new packing
ring over the piston tube (with its feather edge inwards) and
follow it with the tubular capping ring; tap the packing into
place, using a wooden drift upon the outer end of the tubular
capping ring. Screw the gland nut down on to the ring and
slightly increase the pressure to ensure that the packing is
in its correct position; release the gland nut about one turn to
permit the packing to expand and work automatically. Fit the
scraper ring and gland capping ring over the piston tube; tighten
the gland capping ring and lock it with wire. When replacing
the six securing screws for the internal splined ring, it is
essential that the copper washers are annealed immediately before
use.

Wheels

33. Removal.- Note the position of the stirrup in order
that it may be refitted exactly in its original position; in most
cases there is only one possible position of the stirrup that
will allow the bolt to register with both the slotted nut of the
axle and the shank of the stirrup. Jack the aeroplane until the

R.T.P./126
FS/7

undercarriage wheels are clear of the ground, remove the split-pin through the stirrup locking nut and remove the stirrup. Remove the nut and bolt securing the wheel retaining nut; unscrew the wheel retaining nut and withdraw the wheel from the axle. After refitting the wheel and stirrup, the position of the stirrup should be checked by retracting the undercarriage.

34. <u>Repacking bearings with lubricant</u>.- The lubricant should be smeared over the central portion of the wheel axle before the wheel is refitted; care must be taken not to apply more lubricant than is necessary, as any excess will be thrown outwards on to the brakes by the rotation of the wheels.

Micro-switches

35. <u>Testing</u>.- The plungers of the micro-switches, which are in circuit with the warning devices, should operate under a load of 1 lb. ± 4 oz.

Single undercarriage units

36. <u>Retraction</u>.- By disconnecting the latch operating cable of one unit, it is possible to retract the other unit separately, but this practice is not desirable as damage to the gear may result if the latch should slip. When it is required to retract a single undercarriage unit, the other unit should be held down by external means, e.g., a weight or a picket.

TAIL WHEEL UNIT

Compression leg

37. <u>General</u>.- All parts of the compression leg are self-adjusting for wear except the friction band, which may need adjustment (see para.38) to prevent undue oscillation of the wheel when taxying. The free play, up and down, in the compression leg should not exceed ⅛ in. If excessive movement is present, remove the bolt securing the top attachment fitting; remove the fitting and the spigot cap. Place the requisite number of steel washers on top of the main spring and reassemble the leg. When checking the wear between the inner and outer tubes, it should not be possible to insert a 0.030 in. feeler for any appreciable distance.

38. <u>Adjusting friction band</u>.- The damping of the castoring action provided by the friction band may be varied by altering the tightness of the band by means of the clip bolt. If the distance tube is removed, care should be taken that it is replaced, as undue tightness of the band will interfere with the correct functioning of the self-centring device.

HYDRAULIC SYSTEM

General

39. Absolute cleanliness is essential for the satisfactory operation of the hydraulic system; a diagram of the system is given in fig.13. It is essential that the fluid is maintained

at the correct level in the handpump, otherwise air is likely
to be pumped into the system; the handpump reservoir should be
full when the aeroplane is in flying position. When replenishing, the filter must remain in the filler neck and only clean
fluid should be used; care should be taken that the fluid is
not spilled as it may remove the protective coating from parts
with which it comes in contact. When it is necessary to drain
any part of the system and retain the fluid for further use, the
receptacle used must be scrupulously clean as ordinary oil or
grease may injure the gland and jointing compositions employed
in the system. When pipelines are disconnected, the ends of the
pipes must be protected against the entry of dirt and drain
plugs or other components must be thoroughly examined before
reassembly to ensure freedom from foreign matter.

Filling

40. Trestle the aeroplane in the flying position with the
undercarriage wheels just clear of the ground and proceed as
follows:-

(i) With the handle of the selector gear set at neutral,
pour type A anti-freezing oil (Stores Ref.34A/43 and 46)
into the handpump reservoir and operate the handpump
until the level ceases to fall; refill the reservoir and
again operate the handpump.

(ii) Continue to operate the handpump and fill the reservoir
alternately until the fluid level is no longer lowered
by the operation of the handpump.

(iii) Disconnect the return pipe at the engine-driven pump,
allow it to fill, reconnect the pipe to the pump and
refill the reservoir.

(iv) By a similar procedure, fill the larger pipe connecting
the control valve to the filter, using the handpump
if necessary.

(v) Set the handle of the selector gear to WHEELS UP and,
at the piston rod end of one of the undercarriage jacks,
unscrew the pipe union a few turns to cause a vent.

(vi) Operate the handpump until fluid runs freely from the
vent, retighten the pipe union and refill the reservoir.

(vii) At the other undercarriage jack, repeat the process set
out in (v) and (vi) above and again fill the reservoir.

(viii) Operate the handpump to bring the undercarriage into the
retracted position and, if necessary, refill the
reservoir.

(ix) Set the handle of the selector gear to WHEELS DOWN and,
at the anchored end of one of the undercarriage jacks,
unscrew the pipe union a few turns to cause a vent.

(x) Operate the handpump until fluid runs freely from the
vent, retighten the pipe union and refill the reservoir.

FS/8

(xi) At the other undercarriage jack, repeat the process
set out in (ix) and (x) above and again fill the
reservoir.

(xii) Operate the handpump to bring the undercarriage into
the alighting position and, if necessary, refill the
reservoir.

The jacks and pipelines of the undercarriage system should now
be full of fluid.

41. Fill the flap system in a similar manner to that
described for the undercarriage in para. 40.

42. After filling the flap system, any air remaining in
the hydraulic system should then be expelled as follows:-

(i) Lower the aeroplane on to its wheels and start the
engine.

(ii) With the handle of the selector gear set at neutral
and with the control lever depressed, allow fluid to
flow from the engine-driven pump through the control
valve and control box to the reservoir; the engine
should be run sufficiently fast to enable the engine-
driven pump to expel any air that remains in the system.

(iii) With the engine still running, release the control
lever and allow fluid to circulate in the engine-driven
pump by-pass system for a minute or two.

Handpump

43. The filter in the filler neck requires cleaning after
each filling of the hydraulic system. Should leakage occur at
the point of emergence of the shaft carrying the handle, remove
the wire which locks the gland nut, tighten the nut and relock
with wire; care must be taken not to over-tighten the nut which
might cause binding of the shaft. The test pressure for the handpump is 800 lb. per sq.in.

Filter

44. Cleaning.- Unscrew the cap at the bottom of the
filter, remove the filter element and wash it in petrol; the
element should be dried by means of an air-blast before replacement.
When replacing, care should be taken that the washer above the
element is assembled with its lipped rim downwards and that no
foreign matter remains inside.

Control valve

45. If there is any sign of leakage at the connections,
new copper-asbestos washers should be fitted; if the inlet
connection is removed, no particular care is required in its
replacement but if either the outlet connection to the filter and
reservoir, or the outlet connection to the control box is removed,
care must be taken to ensure that the springs and centralizing
caps are correctly fitted on reassembly. No adjustment may be
made to the screw which controls the spring-loading of the relief

valve. The blow-off pressure is 800 lb. per sq.in. and the
test pressure 1,200 lb. per sq.in.

Control box

46.   Normally, no attempt should be made to alter the
setting of the relief valves which control the release pressures
but, in a case of emergency only, adjustment may be made by
loosening the locknut and screwing or unscrewing the adjusting
pin.   Should there be any evidence of leakage, the tightness of
the connections should be tested but, if this appears to be
correct, new copper-asbestos washers should be fitted.   The test
pressure for the return connection is 250 lb. per sq.in. and
that for the other connections is 1,750 lb. per sq.in.; the blow-
off pressure for WHEELS UP is 1,400 ± 50 lb. per sq.in. and for
WHEELS DOWN is 850 ± 50 lb. per sq.in.; the blow-off pressure
for FLAPS UP is 850 ± 30 lb. per sq.in. and for FLAPS DOWN is
370 ± 15 lb. per sq.in.

Jacks

47.   The test pressure is 1,200 lb. per sq.in. except for
the ⅜ in. B.S.P. union on the flap jack where it is 700 lb. per
sq.in.

48.   <u>Adjusting for length</u>.- Length adjustment of the jacks
may be effected by altering the position of the eye which is
screwed into the outer end of the piston rod.   Release the
locknut and its securing tabwasher; remove the eye.   Fit a new
tabwasher, screw the eye into the desired position, tighten the
locknut and lock it with its tabwasher.

49.   <u>Checking positions of undercarriage jacks</u>.-   The
length and the position of each jack relative to the undercarriage
may be checked by removing the bolt connecting the jack to the
triangulated lever.   When fully extended, the length of the piston
rod must be such that, with the undercarriage locked down, the
eye of the jack can be placed outboard of the fork on the
triangulated lever and not more than $3/32$ in. from it.

PNEUMATIC SYSTEM

Charging

50.   With the aeroplane on the ground, if the pressure in
the system is less than 150 lb. per sq.in. (as shown on the
"supply" scale of the pressure gauge in the cockpit) it should
be increased to not more than 300 lb. per sq.in. by means of a
handpump or compressed air cylinder.   Access to the charging
connection, mounted on the port side of the fireproof bulkhead,
is obtained by removing the port intermediate side panel of the
engine cowling.

Oil trap

51.   <u>Draining</u>.- Slacken off the locknut and unscrew the
drain plug in the bottom of the trap; after two or three turns,
A.T.P./126
FS/9

the oil should flow through the small hole in the side of the drain connection and may be caught in a suitable receptacle. If necessary, the drain plug may be removed completely.

52. Cleaning.- Detach the inlet and outlet pipes by unscrewing each union nut and, with a C-spanner, unscrew the top half of the trap. Slacken the bolt closing the supporting bracket and withdraw the trap downwards; lift out the cap embodying the top pipe connection. Clean the trap with a dry rag, taking care that the drain and the pipe in the cap are free from foreign matter.

Oil reservoir

53. Replenishing.- Slacken off the locknut and unscrew the plug in the overflow connection. Remove the filler cap and insert a filter funnel in the filler neck; pour in treated castor oil to Specification D.T.D.72 (Stores Ref.34A/5 and 45) until the oil commences to flow through the small hole in the underside of the overflow connection. Tighten the overflow plug and the locknut; replace the filler cap.

54. Draining.- Slacken off the locknut and unscrew the plug in the overflow connection two or three turns, detach the air pipe from the bottom connection and allow the oil to drain away through a funnel and tube into a suitable receptacle.

Air cylinder

55. Draining.- Detach the air pipe at each end of the cylinder by unscrewing the union nuts; release the cylinder by removing the bolts from the securing straps. Swing the straps clear and withdraw the cylinder downwards and to starboard; unscrew the union from one end of the cylinder and drain any condensed moisture.

Air filter

56. Draining.- Slacken off the locknut and unscrew the drain plug in the bottom of the filter; after two or three turns the oil should flow through the small hole in the side of the drain connection and may be caught in a suitable receptacle. If necessary, the drain plug may be removed completely.

57. Cleaning.- Detach the inlet and outlet pipes by unscrewing each union nut and, with a C-spanner, unscrew the top half of the filter. Slacken the bolt closing the supporting bracket and withdraw the filter downwards; lift out the cap embodying the top pipe connection and remove the felt filter element. Wash the felt element in petrol and dry it by means of an air-blast. Clean the internal surfaces of the filter with a dry rag, taking care that the drain connection and the pipe in the cap are free from foreign matter; replace the filter element. Assemble the remainder of the filter and replace it in its mounting bracket.

Pressure reduction valve

58. Adjusting.- To adjust the delivery pressure, remove the split-pin securing the screwed plug within the end of the

valve casing and screw the plug in to decrease the pressure
or out to increase the pressure; replace the split pin.

FITTER

FUSELAGE

Hand-starting gear

59. Removal of handles from stowage.- The starting
handles are stowed in the wheel recess beneath the centre
section, one on each side wall. To remove a handle, unscrew
the wing nut on the securing bracket and swing the bolt
downwards; then lift the clip, disengage the starting handle
and withdraw it forwards.

60. Adjustment of chain from handle shaft sprocket.-
Slacken the nuts attaching the bearing brackets of the handle
shaft to engine mounting struts XZ, port and starboard (see
Sect.6, Chap.1, Fig.2), and slide the bearing brackets forward
to tighten the chain or rearward to loosen it.

61. Adjustment of chain driving magneto sprocket.-
Remove packing washers from under the magneto feet to tighten
the chain or add washers to loosen it.

62. Adjustment of chain driving engine sprocket.-
Slacken the nuts attaching the bearing bracket to engine
mounting strut XY, starboard (see Sect.6, Chap.1, Fig.2)
and slide the bearing with its double sprocket forward to
tighten the chain or rearward to loosen it; this adjustment
will necessitate adjustment of the other two chains as described
in paras.60 and 61. When tightening the bearing brackets on
the struts after adjustment of the chains, care should be taken
that the sprockets are parallel with one another in order to
avoid twist in the chains.

Airscrew

63. Removal.- Reference should be made to para.20
for the removal of this component.

Engine controls

64. Adjusting for length.- The lengths of both the
throttle and mixture controls may be altered by screwing the
fork-ends along the sliding rods at each end of each control in
the desired direction; the fork-ends are locked with nuts.

65. Adjusting control stops.- The stops are situated
at the forward ends of the throttle and mixture lever slots
in the quadrant plate. Slacken off the two screws in each
stop and slide the stop forward or rearward as required to
increase or decrease respectively the maximum degree of
throttle opening or weakness of mixture.

F.S./10

66. Removal of inner linkage.- At the engine end, uncouple the control at the ball joint and unscrew the sliding rod. Disconnect the throttle control at the cockpit end by removing the split-pin, nut, washer and roller from the bolt securing the fork-end to the throttle lever; disconnect the mixture control at its rear end by removing the split-pin and tabwasher from the headed pin coupling the fork-end to the mixture lever. After removing the bolt from the throttle lever and the headed pin from the mixture lever, withdraw each inner linkage with its olives and tubelets from the respective casing tube by pulling on the rear sliding rod.

67. Inspection of inner cable.- The cable may be inspected by removing the locking barrel from the screwed terminal rod, sliding the inspection tubelet back and then, in turn, moving each olive and tubelet along the cable until it has been examined throughout its length.

68. Adjustment of inner linkage.- A linkage is satisfactorily adjusted when there is no end play between the olives and the tubelets; increasing the tension beyond this point makes the control heavy in operation. The adjustment is made by screwing up the locking barrel to the appropriate point on the screwed terminal rod and then screwing the sliding rod along the terminal rod until it is hard against the locking barrel.

69. Assembling of inner linkage.- Insert the linkage into the casing tube. If the fork-end has been removed from the rear end of the linkage, care must be taken that the fixed end is at the front and the adjustable end at the rear; the fixed end of each sliding rod and casing tube is marked with an F, whilst the adjustable ends are marked with an A. Screw the non-adjustable sliding rod on to the front terminal rod, open the inspection hole by moving the spring clip and check that the sliding rod has been screwed right home. Close the inspection hole and connect the control at each end to the adjacent parts of the control system.

Radiator fairing

70. Removal.- Disconnect the two bracing struts at the rear end of the radiator fairing and the control rods to the radiator flap at the port and starboard sides of the flap. Remove the cover plates in the rear wall of the wheel housing; reach through the holes thus disclosed and disconnect the link on the centre stiffener of the radiator fairing from the fork bolt on the lower boom of the centre section rear spar. Support the fairing, remove all the attachment bolts and screws around its upper flange and lower the fairing away from the fuselage.

71. Assembly.- The assembly procedure is the reverse of that for removal with the addition of the following adjustments. The length of the rear bracing struts may be adjusted by slackening the locknuts and screwing the fork-ends in or out as required, the length of the flap control rods being adjusted in a similar manner.

FUEL SYSTEM

Refuelling

72. The points of access to the fuel filler necks are shown in fig.1. Insert the bonding plug on the filling hose in

the bonding socket adjacent to the filler cap and remove the
cap; after filling, disconnect the bonding plug and socket,
screw on the cap and replace the access door.

Filter

73.   Cleaning.- Turn the fuel distributing cook to the
OFF position. Hold up the locking spring and unscrew the wing
nut securing the stirrup; swing the stirrup clear of the bottom
casing and withdraw the latter together with the strainer unit
and spring. Wash the strainer unit in petrol and reassemble
the filter; do not use rag for cleaning the strainer unit.

Reserve tank

74.   Draining.- Remove the split-pin which locks the
sleeve of the drain valve situated at the bottom of the sump.
Fit a suitable piece of hose to the nozzle of the drain valve,
unscrew the sleeve a few turns and drain the fuel through the
hose into a convenient receptacle. When the fuel has ceased to
flow, retighten the sleeve and lock it with a split-pin.

75.   Removal of sump.- Set the control handle of the fuel
distributing cook to the OFF position. Cut the wire locking the
isolating cock of the reserve tank sump in the ON position, turn
the cook to the OFF position and disconnect the fuel pipe from
the cook, moving the freed end out of the way. Place a funnel,
to which is attached a length of hose, under the cook, turn the
cock to the ON position and drain the fuel into a suitable
receptacle. Remove the twelve small bolts securing the sump to
the tank shell and thus remove the sump.

Main tanks

76.   Draining.- Set the handle of the fuel distributing
cook to the OFF position. Remove the door situated at the
inboard edge of the tank bottom covering and then the wire
locking the isolating cook in the tank sump in the ON position;
turn the cook to the OFF position. Uncouple the fuel delivery
cook at the tank and loosen the coupling at the other end of
the pipe; this coupling will be found on the rear wall of the
wheel housing on the centre line of the aeroplane. Fit a
suitable length of hose to the isolating cook, open the cook
and drain the fuel into a suitable receptacle.

77.   Removal of handhole covers.- After draining the
fuel tank as described in para.76, the handhole covers may
easily be removed from the outboard sides and bottom surfaces
of the tank by unscrewing the twelve securing bolts.

OIL SYSTEM

Draining

78.   The oil system should be drained when the oil is hot
to ensure adequate draining and in order that the viscosity
valve shall not close the oil cooler circuit; the system is

R.T.F./126
F8/11

drained by separately draining the oil tank and the oil
cooler as described in paras.80 and 83 respectively.

Filter

79. **Cleaning**.- Remove the locking wire and release
the adjusting screw at the top of the filter. Unscrew the top
cap and remove the inner sealing cap, the spring and the gauze
filter. Clean the filter in petrol and dry by means of an air-
blast; do not use rag for cleaning the gauze. When reassembling,
the filter should be filled with oil before replacing the top
cap and great care must be taken that an airtight joint is
obtained.

Oil tank

80. **Draining**.- Remove the under-fairing strip at the
bottom rear edge of the oil tank and then the wire locking the
drain plug situated at the bottom rear corner of the tank about
midway along its length. Unscrew the valve of the drain plug
a few turns and drain the oil through a funnel into a suitable
receptacle.

81. **Removal**.- Remove the front and intermediate side
cowling panels, the leading edge fillet on the port side and
the gap fairing between the centre section and port outer
plane. Remove the upper cover over the port main fuel tank and
the port side fairing strip under the centre section front spar.
After draining the oil tank as described in para.80, disconnect
the vent pipe at its connection in the top of the rear wall of
the tank by removing the jubilee clips and sliding the rubber
hose along the vent pipe. Disconnect the inlet and outlet
pipes in the inboard end wall of the tank and the bonding wire
from the socket fitting at the filler cap seating by removing
the attaching screw. Support the tank and remove the four bolts
attaching the tank feet to the brackets on the centre section
front spar; remove the tank, replacing the bolts and rubber pads
to prevent their loss.

82. **Assembly**.- The assembly procedure is the reverse of
that for removal but in addition the following points should be
noted. The rubber pads should be arranged so that one is placed
between the tank foot and the bracket, and the other between the
tank foot and the washer under the bolt head; it is important
that the tank feet attachment bolts are locked with wire.

Oil cooler

83. **Draining**.- Remove the door in the bottom surface of
the radiator fairing and then the wire locking the drain plugs
situated in the bottom surface of the radiator; the front plug
is the oil cooler drain plug. Remove the drain plug and drain
the oil cooler with the aid of a funnel and a hose leading to a
suitable receptacle; when the oil has ceased to flow, replace
the drain plug and wire it to the coolant radiator drain plug.
If the oil does not flow freely, uncouple either the oil inlet
or outlet connection at the top of the cooler; access to these
connections may be obtained through the door in the top of the
radiator fairing above the flap.

84.   Removal.- Remove the radiator fairing as described in para.70 and, if necessary, drain the oil cooler as described in para.83. Disconnect the two pipes between the oil cooler and the viscosity valve. Remove the bolts attaching the oil cooler to the radiator shell; six bolts are situated at the top of the cooler whilst two smaller bolts are situated at each end. Lift the oil cooler vertically until the drain plug extension in its lower surface clears the hole in the connecting portion between the two halves of the coolant radiator; remove the cooler.

Viscosity valve

85.   Cleaning filter.- Unscrew the large screwed plug at that end of the valve which is adjacent to the pipe leading to the oil cooler; the nut which locks the centre screwed plug to this large screwed plug must not be unscrewed or removed under any circumstances as it is sweated in position after the valve has been calibrated. Remove the large screwed plug taking great care not to damage the bellows during removal; without removing the filter from the valve head, clean the gauze in petrol and dry it by means of an air-blast. The screwed plug, at that end of the valve which is adjacent to the pipe leading to the oil tank, may be removed for inspection of the valve at that end if necessary.

COOLING SYSTEM

Draining

86.   Remove the door in the under-surface of the radiator fairing and then the wire locking the drain plugs situated in the bottom surface of the radiator; the rear plug is the coolant radiator drain plug. Remove the drain plug and drain the coolant radiator with the aid of a funnel and a hose leading to a suitable receptacle; when the coolant has ceased to flow, replace the drain plug and wire it to the oil cooler drain plug.

Filling

87.   With the tail wheel of the aeroplane on the ground, remove or open the following vents:-

  (i) Radiator drain plug.
  (ii) Plug on top of the return pipe from the radiator
         to the engine, about 12 in. aft of the centre
         section front spar.
  (iii) Four vent plugs in the engine outlet pipes, two
         front and two rear.
  (iv) Drain cock on base of engine-driven pump.
  (v) Drain tap on each side of carburettor.

88.   Remove the filler cap from the header tank and pour in slowly, through a fine-mesh strainer, sufficient coolant to obtain a flow from the radiator drain hole; screw in the drain plug and lock it with wire to the oil cooler drain plug.

R.T.P./126
FS/12

89. Continue to pour in coolant as above and, as the coolant content of the system is increased, the coolant will flow in turn from each of the above-mentioned vents, each vent being closed and looked as soon as coolant flows from it; coolant flowing from the vents should be caught in suitable receptacles so that the total quantity remaining in the system may be checked. When the coolant is level with the rim of the filler neck of the header tank, replace the filler cap and run the engine as for warming-up; this will disperse any trapped air. Stop the engine and check the level of the coolant; top up if the level has dropped. Run the engine again until the coolant temperature reaches 60°C, when the engine should be stopped and the header tank topped up if necessary; the system should require 15 gallons of coolant.

Header tank

90. Removal.- Drain the cooling system as described in para.86. Slacken the clip attaching the vent pipe hose connection to the top of the tank and ease off the vent pipe; disconnect the bonding strips at each pipe connection to the header tank. Slacken the clips attaching the three hose connections, one under the tank and two in the front face; loosen the hose on the tank branches. From the connection in the front face of the tank, remove the thermometer bottle and stow it in a position where it is unlikely to be damaged, taking care to avoid sharp bends in the capillary tubing. Disconnect the bonding wire at the rear web of the port rear foot and remove the bolts attaching the four tank feet to their mounting brackets; remove the tank, easing off the loosened hose connections.

91. Assembly.- The installation procedure is the reverse of that for removal described in para.90, but in addition the following points should be noted. When mounting the tank, place a rubber packing over each bolt hole in the mounting brackets, thread the washer and another rubber packing on to each bolt and insert the bolts from below; there should thus be a rubber packing between the tank foot and the bracket, and between the bracket and the washer under the bolt head.

Radiator

92. Removal.- Drain the oil cooler as described in para.83 and remove it as described in para.84; drain the cooling system as described in para.86. Slacken the clips securing the two hose connections at the top of the radiator and loosen the hose on the radiator branches; disconnect the bonding wire at the front starboard edge of the radiator. Support the radiator, remove the four attachment bolts and thus remove the radiator downwards.

INSTRUMENT MAKER

Pressure head

93. Setting.- The setting of the pressure head is given in the Leading Particulars.

WIRELESS OPERATOR MECHANIC

Undercarriage indicator

94. Testing circuits.- Switch on the indicator circuit at the cut-out switch when the green lamps should light for both the port and starboard undercarriage units. Operate the change-over switch and note that the green lamps light in the alternative circuit for each undercarriage unit.

Undercarriage warning buzzer

95. Testing.- With the engine throttle lever in the "closed" position, raise by hand the latch locking one of the undercarriage side stays until the lever operating the micro-switch is just engaged; the warning buzzer should then sound. Repeat the operation raising the other latch. Then move the engine throttle lever forward to slightly more than one-third of its travel and raise each latch as before; this time the buzzer should not sound. Throughout these operations it should be noted that when a latch is lifted the corresponding green lamp on the indicator should not be alight.

96. Cleaning contacts.- Unscrew the five screws round the outside of the instrument and gently pull the buzzer from its case. Disconnect the wires from the terminals outside the case and remove the gauze cover by taking out the two counter-sunk screws on the top. Unscrew the six countersunk screws from the back of the unit and remove the diaphragm assembly. Clean the contacts by passing a slip of fine emery cloth between them or, if very dirty, remove the adjusting screws and clean both contacts with a magneto file.

97. Adjusting contacts.- Apply the working voltage to the lead-out wires and adjust the contact screw to produce the correct note; relock the contact adjusting screw with the locknut provided. Replace the gauze cover and re-check the buzzer for the correct note before replacing the unit in its case.

Fuel tank gauges

98. Removal.- Disconnect the electrical leads at the gauge and remove the twelve bolts round the securing flange. The gauge may then be lifted from the tank, great care being taken not to bend the float arm.

Bonding

99. Inspection.- To facilitate examination of the bonding system, a diagram of the bonding points is given in fig.12.

R.T.P./126
FS/13

Guns

100. <u>Alignment</u>.- Remove the split-pin and release the
slotted nut at the bottom of the front mounting bracket; at the
rear mounting bracket, release the two locknuts adjacent to the
knurled knob at the side of the bracket. To adjust the elevation
of a gun, rotate the knurled knob at the bottom of the rear
mounting fork until the gun has the required elevation; to adjust
the gun laterally, rotate the knurled knob at the side of the
mounting bracket. It will usually be possible to rotate the
knurled knobs with the fingers, but should they prove too stiff,
a $5/32$ in. diameter tommy-bar may be inserted in holes provided
round their rims. After adjustment, the setting should be
locked by tightening the locknuts at the side of the rear mounting
bracket; the inner nut should first be tightened with a $\frac{3}{8}$ in.
spanner, but not excessively, and then locked with the outer nut.
Finally, the slotted nut at the bottom of the front mounting
bracket must be tightened and the split-pin replaced.

Parachute flares

101. <u>Loading</u>.- Before the flare can be placed in the
launching tube, the suspension lug and safety pin must be removed
from the central part of the flare casing; the lug is $11\frac{1}{2}$ in.
from the bottom of the case and the safety pin is adjacent to
the lug. Push forward the projecting pin at the side of the door
in the front under-fairing of the rear fuselage, when the door
should fall open. With the large end uppermost, pass the flare
into the chute with the looped end of the static cord lying on top
of the flare; close and secure the door. Remove an appropriate
access door in the side of the fuselage and draw the looped end
of the static cord through the top ring of the chute; attach it
to the forked bolt on joint G by the toggle pin provided. Stow
any surplus cord in the canvas pocket on the flare and replace
the access door.

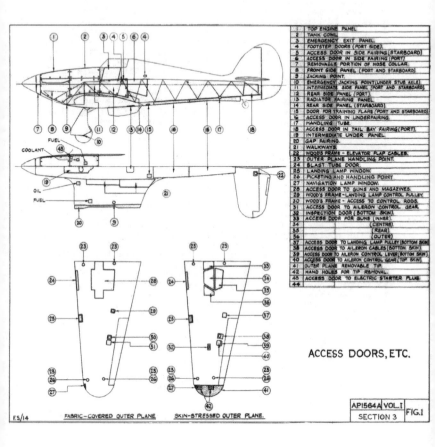

1	TOP ENGINE PANEL.
2	TANK COWL.
3	EMERGENCY EXIT PANEL.
4	FOOTSTEP DOORS (PORT SIDE).
5	ACCESS DOOR IN SIDE FAIRING (STARBOARD)
6	ACCESS DOOR IN SIDE FAIRING (PORT)
7	REMOVABLE PORTION OF NOSE COLLAR.
8	FRONT SIDE PANEL (PORT AND STARBOARD).
9	JACKING POINT.
10	EMERGENCY JACKING POINT (UNDER STUB AXLE).
11	INTERMEDIATE SIDE PANEL (PORT AND STARBOARD).
12	REAR SIDE PANEL (PORT).
13	RADIATOR FAIRING PANEL.
14	REAR SIDE PANEL (STARBOARD).
15	DOOR FOR TRAINING FLARE (PORT AND STARBOARD).
16	ACCESS DOOR IN UNDERFAIRING.
17	HANDLING TUBE.
18	ACCESS DOOR IN TAIL BAY FAIRING (PORT).
19	INTERMEDIATE UNDER PANEL.
20	GAP FAIRING.
21	WALKWAYS.
22	WOOD'S FRAME - ELEVATOR FLAP CABLES.
23	OUTER PLANE HANDLING POINT.
24	BLAST TUBE DOOR.
25	LANDING LAMP WINDOW.
26	PICKETING AND HANDLING POINT.
27	NAVIGATION LAMP WINDOW.
28	ACCESS DOOR TO GUNS AND MAGAZINES.
29	WOOD'S FRAME - LANDING LAMP CONTROL PULLEY.
30	WOOD'S FRAME - ACCESS TO CONTROL RODS.
31	ACCESS DOOR TO AILERON CONTROL GEAR.
32	INSPECTION DOOR (BOTTOM SKIN).
33	ACCESS DOOR FOR GUNS (INNER).
34	(CENTRE)
35	(REAR).
36	(OUTER).
37	ACCESS DOOR TO LANDING LAMP PULLEY (BOTTOM SKIN)
38	ACCESS DOOR TO AILERON CABLES (BOTTOM SKIN)
39	ACCESS DOOR TO AILERON CONTROL LEVER (BOTTOM SKIN)
40	ACCESS DOOR TO AILERON CONTROL GEAR (TOP SKIN)
41	OUTER PLANE REMOVABLE TIP.
42	HAND HOLES FOR TIP REMOVAL.
43	ACCESS DOOR TO ELECTRIC STARTER PLUG.
44	

FUEL

COOLANT

OIL

FUEL

ACCESS DOORS, ETC.

FABRIC-COVERED OUTER PLANE.   SKIN-STRESSED OUTER PLANE.

F.S./14

API564A	VOL.I	FIG.1
SECTION 3		

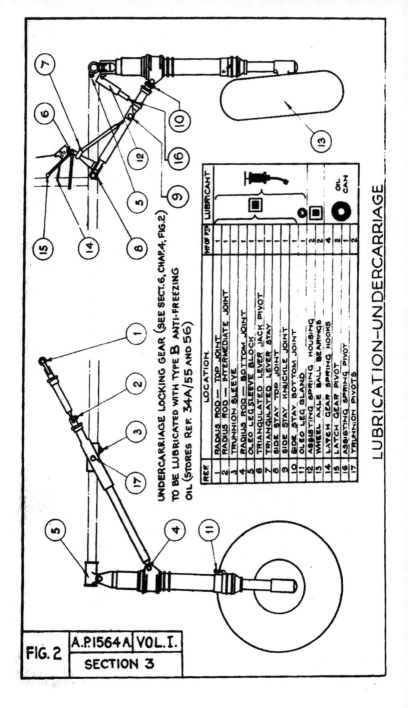

UNDERCARRIAGE LOCKING GEAR (SEE SECT. 6, CHAP. 4, FIG. 2)
TO BE LUBRICATED WITH TYPE B ANTI-FREEZING
OIL (STORES REF. 34A/55 AND 56)

REF.	LOCATION.	Nº OF PTS	LUBRICANT
1	RADIUS ROD — TOP JOINT	1	
2	RADIUS ROD — INTERMEDIATE JOINT	1	
3	TRUNNION SLEEVE	1	
4	RADIUS ROD — BOTTOM JOINT	1	
5	OLEO LEG SLEEVE BLOCK	1	
6	TRIANGULATED LEVER JACK PIVOT	1	
7	TRIANGULATED LEVER STAY	1	
8	SIDE STAY TOP JOINT	1	
9	SIDE STAY KNUCKLE JOINT	1	
10	SIDE STAY BOTTOM JOINT	1	
11	OLEO LEG GLAND	1	
12	ASSISTING SPRING HOUSING	2	
13	WHEEL AXLE BALL BEARINGS	2	
14	LATCH GEAR SPRING HOOKS	4	
15	LATCH GEAR PIVOT	2	
16	ASSISTING SPRING PIVOT	1	
17	TRUNNION PIVOTS	2	

LUBRICATION—UNDERCARRIAGE

FIG. 2	A.P.1564A VOL.I.
	SECTION 3

121

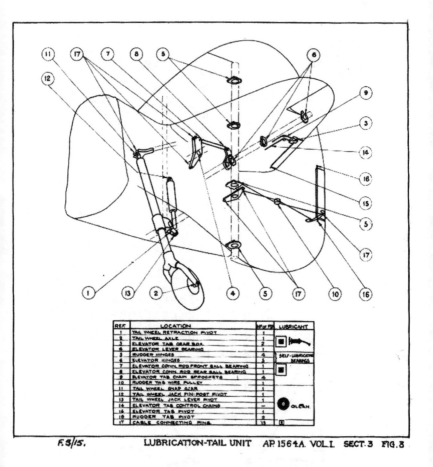

REF	LOCATION	N°of PTS	LUBRICANT
1	TAIL WHEEL RETRACTION PIVOT	1	
2	TAIL WHEEL AXLE	1	
3	ELEVATOR TAB GEAR BOX	2	
4	ELEVATOR LEVER BEARING	1	
5	RUDDER HINGES	4	SELF-LUBRICATING BEARINGS
6	ELEVATOR HINGES	5	
7	ELEVATOR CONN. ROD FRONT BALL BEARING	1	
8	ELEVATOR CONN. ROD REAR BALL BEARING	1	
9	ELEVATOR TAB CHAIN SPROCKETS	1	
10	RUDDER TAB WIRE PULLEY	4	
11	TAIL WHEEL SNAP GEAR	1	
12	TAIL WHEEL JACK PIN-POST PIVOT	1	
13	TAIL WHEEL JACK LEVER PIVOT	1	OIL CAN
14	ELEVATOR TAB CONTROL CHAINS	—	
15	ELEVATOR TAB PIVOT	1	
16	RUDDER TAB PIVOT	2	
17	CABLE CONNECTING PINS	13	

REF.	LOCATION	Nº OF PTS	LUBRICANT
1	CONTROL COLUMN JOINT	1	
2	UNIVERSAL JOINT	1	
3	CRANK BEARINGS	2	
4	CONNECTING ROD REAR END.	1	
5	ELEVATOR LEVER BEARING	1	
6	RUDDER BAR PEDESTAL.	1	
7	BRAKE LEVER & PARKING CATCH PIVOTS	2	OILCAN
8	CONNECTING ROD FRONT END.	1	
9	RUDDER BAR ADJUSTING GEAR.	SLIDE & SCREW	
10	RELAY VALVE CONTROL CONNᵍ ROD ENDS	2	OILCAN
11	CHAINS AND SPROCKETS	—	
12	CONTROL CABLE CONNECTING PINS	4	
13	CONTROL COLUMN BALL BEARINGS	2	
14	TORQUE TUBE BALL BEARING	1	

LUBRICATION   A.P. 1564A. VOL.I. SECT.3 FIG.4.

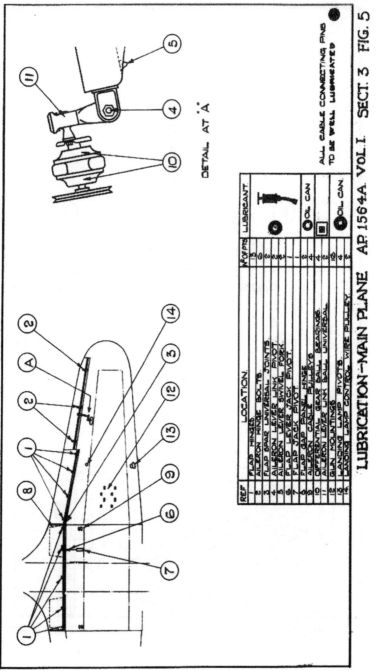

DETAIL AT 'A'

REF	LOCATION.	NºOFPTS	LUBRICANT
1	FLAP HINGES	13	
2	AILERON HINGE BOLTS.	2	
3	FLAP SPAR UNIVERSAL JOINTS	2	
4	AILERON LEVER LINK PIVOT	2	
5	AILERON LEVER SWIVEL FORK	2	
6	FLAP LEVER JACK PIVOT	1	
7	FLAP JACK PIVOT		
8	FLAP GAP PANEL HINGE	2	OIL CAN
9	AILERON CABLE PULLEYS	4	OIL CAN
10	DIFFERENTIAL GEAR BALL BEARINGS	4	
11	AILERON LEVER LINK BALL UNIVERSAL	2	
12	GUN MOUNTINGS	12	OIL CAN
13	LANDING LAMP PIVOTS	4	
14	LANDING LAMP CONTROL WIRE PULLEY	2	

ALL CABLE CONNECTING PINS
TO BE WELL LUBRICATED

LUBRICATION—MAIN PLANE   AP. 1564A. VOL.I.   SECT. 3   FIG. 5

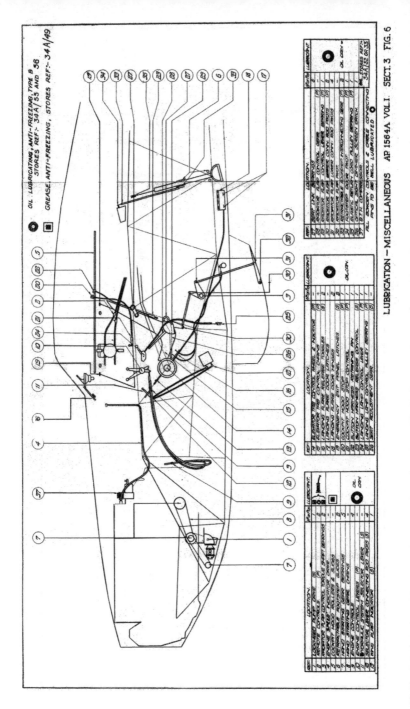

LUBRICATION — MISCELLANEOUS   AP 1564A VOL.I.   SECT.3   FIG. 6

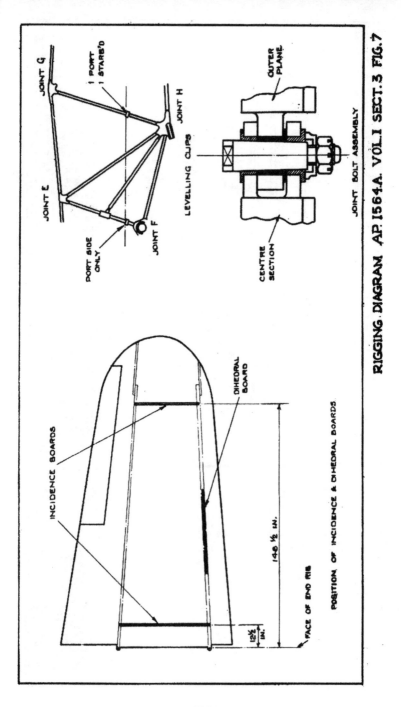

RIGGING DIAGRAM AP.1564A. VOL.I SECT.3 FIG.7

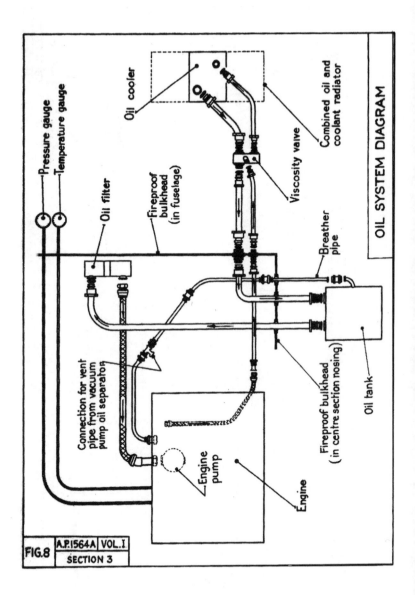

Pressure gauge

Temperature gauge

Oil filter

Fireproof bulkhead (in fuselage)

Oil cooler

Combined oil and coolant radiator

Viscosity valve

Breather pipe

Connection for vent pipe from vacuum pump oil separator

Engine pump

Engine

Fireproof bulkhead (in centre section nosing)

Oil tank

OIL SYSTEM DIAGRAM

FIG.8   A.P.1564A   VOL.I
SECTION 3

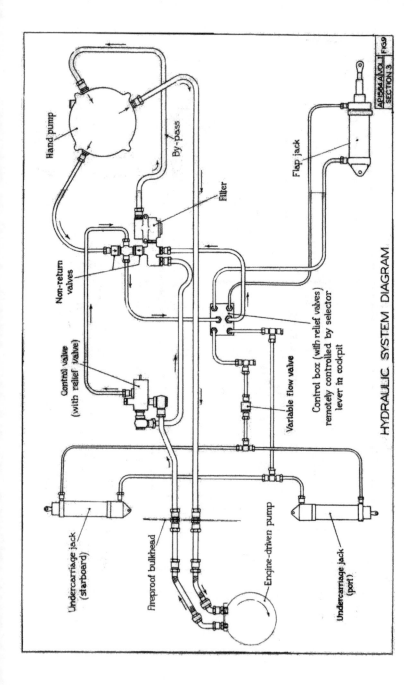

HYDRAULIC SYSTEM DIAGRAM

Hand pump

By-pass

Filter

Flap jack

Non-return valves

Control valve (with relief valve)

Control box (with relief valves) remotely controlled by selector lever in cockpit

Variable flow valve

Undercarriage jack (starboard)

Fireproof bulkhead

Engine-driven pump

Undercarriage jack (port)

AP1564A VOL 1 SECTION 3 FIG.9

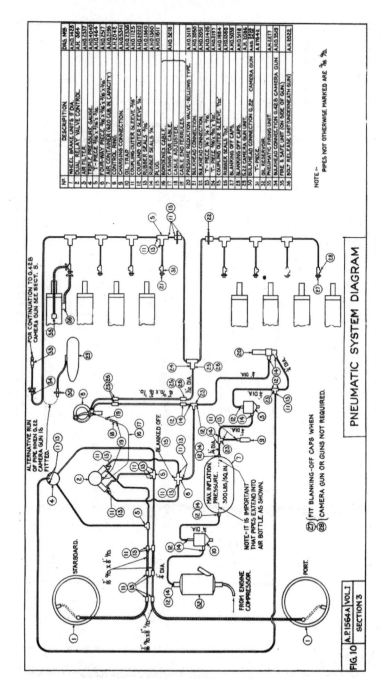

Nº	DESCRIPTION	DRG Nº8
1	WHEEL BRAKE UNITS 8" DIA	AH0.1428
2	DUAL RELAY VALVE CONTROL	A.H. 364
3	AIR FILTER	AH0.2337
4	TRIPLE PRESSURE GAUGE	AH0.4040
5	T - PIECE 3/16 x 3/16 x 3/16	AH0.464
6	FOUR-WAY PIECE 3/16 x 3/16 x 3/16 x 3/16	AH0.2196
7	AIR CONTAINER (820 CUB IN CAPACITY)	AH0.2517
8	CONTROL RING	A.H.2042
9	CHARGING CONNECTION	A.H0.5341
10	OIL TRAP	AH0.2336
11	COUPLING OUTER SLEEVE 3/16	AH0.1125
12	COUPLING OUTER SLEEVE 1/4	AH0.2220
13	RUBBER SEALS 3/16	AH0.1360
14	RUBBER SEALS 1/4	AH0.1560
15	PLUG	AH0.611
16	BOWDEN CABLE	
17	CASING FOR CABLE	
18	CABLE ADJUSTER	AH0.5218
19	CABLE END FERRULES	
20	PRESSURE REDUCTION VALVE - BELLOWS TYPE.	AH0.5119
21	BULKHEAD CONNECTION	AH0.2050
23	BULKHEAD CONNECTION	AH0.2051
24	T - PIECE 1/4 x 1/4 x 3/16	AH0.1426
25	T - PIECE 3/16 x 3/16 x 7/32	AH0.2191
26	COUPLING OUTER SLEEVE. 7/32	AH0.1984
27	RUBBER SEALS 7/32	AH0.1360
28	BLANKING OFF CAPS.	AH0.5039
29	BLANKING OFF CAPS.	AH0.5118
30	G.22 CAMERA GUN UNIT	A.H. 2086
31	BULKHEAD CONNECTION G.22	A.H. 2293
32	T - PIECE,	A.1764-2
33	OIL RESERVOIR	
34	PNEUMATIC FIRING UNIT.	A.H.2177
35	BULKHEAD CONNECTION G.42.B CAMERA GUN	AH0.3549
35	FIRE & SAFE UNIT (ON SIDE OF GUN)	
36	BOLT RELEASE UNIT (UNDERNEATH GUN)	AH.6022

NOTE :-

PIPES NOT OTHERWISE MARKED ARE 3/16 o/D.

PNEUMATIC SYSTEM DIAGRAM

FIG. 10	A.P.1564A	VOL.I
	SECTION 3	

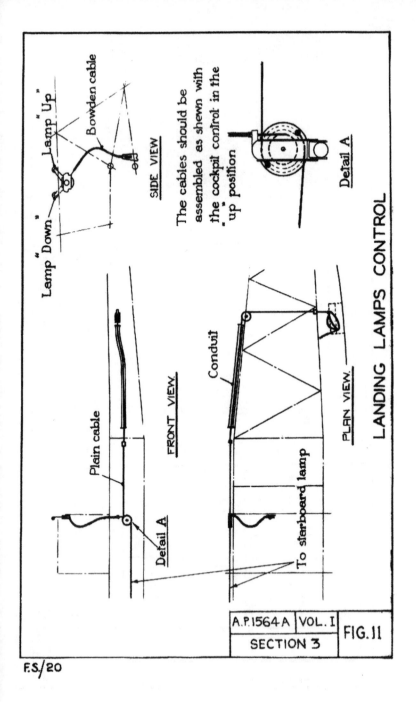

Lamp "Up"

Lamp "Down"

Bowden cable

SIDE VIEW

The cables should be assembled as shewn with the cockpit control in the "up" position

Detail A

Plain cable

FRONT VIEW.

Detail A

Conduit

PLAN VIEW.

To starboard lamp

LANDING LAMPS CONTROL

| A.P.1564 A | VOL. I | FIG. 11 |
| SECTION 3 | | |

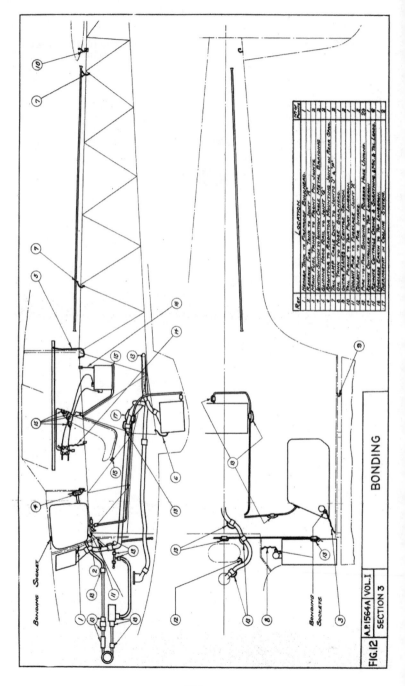

Ref	Location	No. off
1	Header Tank to Firewood Bulkhead.	1
2	Mounting Fuel Tank to Joint. Pin Joints.	2
3	Ignition Switch to Ignition Cable. Metal Breathing.	2
4	Silicon Head Rail. vs Joint.	2
5	Generator to Radiator Mounting Joints or Rear 5mm.	2
6	Tail Lamp Cable Duct to Joints ⅛ & ⅛".	1
7	Oil Tank to Main Bulkhead.	2
8	Outer Flying to Centre Section.	2
9	Tail Plane to Rib Post Longeron.	1
10	Coolant Pipe to Fireplace Joint ⅛.	1
11	Coolant Pipe to Rib Intake.	1
12	Coolant Pipe to Air Intake.	1
13	Bonding Sockets Plain Washer Mare Varnish.	28
14	Remote Controller to Rib Longeron.	1
15	Remote Controller Engine & Smartning Attac. & Tel Lever.	6
16	Instrument Unit on Engine Station.	2

BONDING

FIG.12	A.P.1564A	VOL.I
	SECTION 3	

Bonding Socket

Bonding Sockets

Bonding Sockets

SECTION 4

REMOVAL AND ASSEMBLY
OPERATIONS

P.S./1

LIST OF CONTENTS

F.S./2

TAIL UNIT

ALIGHTING GEAR

FLYING CONTROLS

FUEL SYSTEM

OIL SYSTEM

COOLING SYSTEM

HYDRAULIC SYSTEM

PNEUMATIC SYSTEM

F.S./3

SECTION 4

REMOVAL AND ASSEMBLY
OPERATIONS

General

1. Of the following paragraphs dealing with the removal and assembly of components, the majority refer to the removal of components and, providing additional or contrary instructions for assembly are not given, the procedure for assembly may be assumed to be the same as that for removal but in the reverse order.

Division for transport

2. For transport purposes, Hurricane I aeroplanes are packed in cases measuring internally 29 ft. 6 in. long x 9 ft. 6 in. wide x 8 ft. 3 in. high, each case containing one complete aeroplane with engine installed; the aeroplane is divided into the following units before being packed:-

   (a) Airscrew
   (b) Port outer plane
   (c) Starboard outer plane
   (d) Rudder
   (e) Fin
   (f) Tail plane and elevator
   (g) Engine, fuselage and centre section

Instructions for assembling the aeroplane from these units will be found in the following paragraphs.

FUSELAGE

Engine

3. Removal. - (i) By raising the tail, set the aeroplane approximately in flying position and place chocks under the wheels to prevent fore-and-aft movement.

   (ii) Turn the fuel distributing cock to the OFF position.

   (iii) Drain the oil tank (see Sect.3, para.80).

   (iv) Drain the cooling system (see Sect.3, para.86).

   (v) Remove the airscrew (see Sect.3, para.20) and hub.

P.S./4

(vi) Remove the following cowling:-

    (a) Engine and rear top-panels
    (b) Engine and intermediate side-panels
    (c) Front and intermediate under-panels
    (d) Leading-edge fillet

(vii) Remove the stays supporting the arch cowl rail over the engine and then the arch cowl rail itself.

(viii) Remove the bolts attaching the vertical cowl rail to the horizontal top cowl rail and then remove the horizontal top cowl rail.

(ix) Remove the bolts attaching the lower cowl rail at each end and those attaching the nose collar diaphragm to the spigots on the engine mounting.

(x) Remove the nose collar and the lower cowl rail.

(xi) Remove the starter chains and the starter sprockets from the countershaft above the electric starter.

(xii) Remove the air intake at the flange at the rear of the engine.

(xiii) Disconnect the bonding wire to the coolant pipe.

(xiv) Remove the exhaust manifolds and the cooling pipes from the electrical generator.

(xv) Remove the pipe from the air compressor to the oil reservoir of the pneumatic system.

(xvi) Remove the drain pipes from the fuel pump and the supercharger.

(xvii) Remove the drain plug on the engine-driven pump of the hydraulic system and drain the fluid into a suitable receptacle.

(xviii) Remove the oil vent pipe between the engine connection and the T-piece.

(xix) Remove the large flexible inlet pipe between the engine oil pump and the oil filter and then the smaller flexible oil outlet pipe from the engine.

(xx) Remove the coolant pipe between the engine pump and the joint just forward of the centre section front spar.

(xxi) Disconnect the flexible inlet pipe and the pressure gauge banjo fitting at the engine fuel pump; tie the banjo fitting with cord to the nearest structural member, taking care to avoid sharp bends in the capillary tube.

(xxii) Disconnect the flexible pipe from the non-return valve at the carburettor T-piece.

(xxiii) Remove the priming pipe and the boost gauge pipe at their engine ends.

(xxiv) Disconnect the oil thermometer bottle and the oil pressure gauge banjo at the oil relief valve on the starboard side of the engine and tie them to the adjacent structure, care being taken to avoid sharp bends in the capillary tubes.

(xxv) Remove the flexible pipes at the engine-driven pump of the hydraulic system.

(xxvi) Disconnect the two leads at the accumulator in the fuselage and stow them at once on the dummy terminal block below the accumulator; access is through the door in the starboard side fairing. Note. - It is important that this disconnection is made before any other electrical leads are disconnected.

(xxvii) Disconnect the two leads from the electric starter motor; push down the rubber sleeves to uncover the connections.

(xxviii) Remove the ignition leads from the magnetos and the leads from the front end of the generator; stow the latter on the dummy terminal block on the engine mounting.

(xxix) Disconnect the throttle and mixture control rods at the levers on the engine; move the throttle control in the cockpit to the "closed" position.

(xxx) At the rear of the engine, remove the engine-speed indicator drive and the bowden cable from the boost cut-out lever; tie the latter to the adjacent structure.

(xxxi) Attach the engine hoisting sling to the engine (as detailed in A.P.1590B, Vol.I) and to the hoist hook, adjusting the hoist so that it just takes the strain; remove the engine holding-down bolts.

(xxxii) Hoist and swing the engine forward to clear, making sure that no fittings, cables, pipes, etc. are left in such a position that they impede the removal of the engine; lower the engine into a suitable cradle.

4. Installation. - The installation of the engine is the same as the removal procedure described in the previous paragraph, but in the reverse order; reference should also be made to the installation notes in A.P.1590B, Vol.I. The engine holding-down bolts should be assembled in the following manner:-

(i) Place a piece of packing (supplied with the engine) between each engine bearer and each engine foot; the rubber packings should be placed beneath the rear feet and the Ferobestos packings beneath the front feet.

F.S./5

(ii) At each of the front feet, first insert the rear bolt, with a washer in place under its head; screw it downwards into the engine bearers and pass the locking strip over the bolt head. Then fit a washer over each front bolt and pass each bolt upwards through the engine bearer, the packing, the engine foot, another washer, the rear bolt locking strip and finally through a third washer; screw a slotted nut on to each bolt and lock it with a split-pin.

(iii) At the rear feet, the two bolts for the port foot are 6¼ in. long under the head and those for the starboard foot are 5¼ in. long. Each of the four bolts should be fitted with a washer and passed up through the engine bearer, the lower packing, the engine foot, the upper packing, the capping strip and finally through a second washer; a slotted nut should then be screwed over each bolt and locked with a split-pin.

Engine and mounting

5. Removal. - (i) By raising the tail, set the aeroplane approximately in flying position and place chocks under the wheels to prevent fore-and-aft movement.

(ii) Turn the fuel distributing cock to the OFF position.

(iii) Drain the oil tank (see Sect.3, para.80).

(iv) Drain the cooling system (see Sect.3, para.86).

(v) Remove the airscrew (see Sect.3, para.20) and hub.

(vi) Remove the following cowling:-

(a) Engine and rear top-panels
(b) Engine and intermediate side-panels
(c) Intermediate under-panel
(d) Leading-edge fillet

(vii) Remove the stays supporting the arch cowl rail over the engine and the two fore-and-aft rails which support the intermediate under-panel.

(viii) Remove the exhaust manifolds and then the oil tank as described in Sect.3, para.81.

(ix) Remove the flexible pipes which run from the fuel filter to the engine pump and the carburettor.

(x) Remove the oil vent pipe between the engine connection and the T-piece.

(xi) Remove the large flexible inlet pipe between the engine oil pump and the oil filter and then the smaller flexible oil outlet pipe from the engine.

(xii) Remove the coolant pipe between the engine pump and the joint just forward of the centre section front spar.

(xiii) Remove the pipes of the hydraulic system which run between the engine-driven pump and the fireproof bulkhead.

(xiv) Remove the pipe from the air compressor to the oil reservoir of the pneumatic system.

(xv) Remove the boost gauge pipe between the engine and the fuel trap.

(xvi) From the engine mounting, remove the clips attaching the capillary tubes for the fuel pressure gauge, the oil temperature and the oil pressure gauges.

(xvii) From the engine mounting, remove the clips attaching the ignition leads and those attaching the electrical generator leads.

(xviii) Remove the cover plates on the fireproof bulkhead at fuselage joints A.

(xix) At their joints on the fireproof bulkhead, disconnect the horizontal top cowl rail and the fillet rail.

(xx) Disconnect the priming pipe at the engine connection and the pressure gauge banjo fitting at the engine fuel pump; tie the banjo fitting with cord to the nearest structural member, taking care to avoid sharp bends in the capillary tube.

(xxi) Disconnect the oil thermometer bottle and the oil pressure gauge banjo at the oil relief valve on the starboard side of the engine and tie them to the adjacent structure, care being taken to avoid sharp bends in the capillary tubes.

(xxii) Disconnect the two leads at the accumulator in the fuselage and stow them at once on the dummy terminal block below the accumulator; access is through the door in the starboard side fairing. Note. - It is important that this disconnection is made before any other electrical leads are disconnected.

(xxiii) At the starboard bottom rear strut of the engine mounting, disconnect the leads from the electric starter to the terminal block and the adjacent socket, also the lead from the push switch to the magnetic relay; tie these leads to the adjacent structure.

(xxiv) Remove the ignition leads from the magnetos and the leads from the front end of the electrical generator; tie the ignition leads to the engine mounting and the generator leads to the fireproof bulkhead.

(xxv) Disconnect the throttle and mixture control rods at the levers on the engine; move the throttle control in the cockpit to the "closed" position.

(xxvi) At the rear of the engine, remove the engine-speed indicator drive and the bowden cable from the boost cut-out lever; tie the latter to the adjacent structure.

F.S./6

(xxvii) Attach the engine hoisting sling to the engine (as detailed in A.P.1590B, Vol.I) and to the hoist hook, adjusting the hoist so that it just takes the strain; remove the engine mounting attachment bolts at joints A, port and starboard.

(xxviii) At the lower boom of the front centre section spar, remove the bolts attaching the lower rear struts of the engine mounting and the pins attaching the engine mounting bracing wires to the shackles; tie the bracing wires to the lower rear struts of the engine mounting.

(xxix) Swing the engine and mounting forward and hoist it away from the centre section, making sure that no fittings, cables, pipes etc. are left in such a position that they impede removal of the engine and mounting; lower the engine and mounting into a suitable cradle.

6. **Installation**. - The installation of the engine mounting complete with engine is the same as removal procedure described in the previous paragraph, but in the reverse order and with the following additions:-

(i) Set the fuselage in the rigging position (see Sect.3, para.9), using the jacking points at the lower ends of the compression legs.

(ii) Drop plumblines from the centre of the airscrew boss, the centre of joint U and the mid-point of the centre section front spar.

(iii) Adjust the bracing wires in engine mounting bay ZB until these three plumblines are in fore-and-aft alignment; the wires are provided with turnbuckles so that the wires themselves need not be turned.

Cockpit seat

7. **Removal**. - (i) At the lower end of the rear strap of the pilot's harness, remove the pin attaching the shackle to the bracket at the rear of the seat; the strap atop will come away and, to avoid loss, should be replaced on the shackle by means of the pin.

(ii) Remove the nuts attaching the harness strap links to the spigots on the sides of the seat and pull the rear harness strap up through the hole in the back of the seat; stow the harness out of the way.

(iii) Remove the split-pins locking the quadrant bolts to the bosses on the seat and remove the bolts, quadrants and distance tubes. **Note**. - The seat should not be supporting any load when the quadrant bolts are removed.

(iv) Remove the split-pins locking the spigots to the bosses on the seat and remove the bosses; the latter may be unscrewed by means of the flats provided on the outer flanges for a $9/16$ in. spanner.

(v) Support the seat and remove the bolts attaching it at the upper brackets; lift the seat out of the cockpit.

Radiator flap

8. **Removal**. - (i) Disconnect the radiator flap control rods at the flap and operate the control lever in the cockpit until the indicator is in the CLOSED position; this latter operation will lift the control rods out of the way.

(ii) Cut the locking wires and remove the two bolts attaching each of the hinge pins at the forward end; withdraw the flap downwards and rearwards.

9. **Assembly**. - The installation procedure is the reverse of that for removal, but in addition the following points should be observed:-

(i) The hinge pin attachment bolts should be locked with 18 s.w.g. iron wire.

(ii) After assembly, set the control lever in the cockpit to the CLOSED position when the gap between the flap trailing edge and the fuselage underfairing should be 3½ in.; if this dimension is not obtained, the length of the flap control rods must be adjusted.

(iii) The length of the flap control rods may be adjusted by slackening the locknuts at their upper ends, disconnecting the fork-ends and screw them in or out as required. Access may be obtained through a door in the underfairing between the two control rods.

Radiator Fairing

10. **Removal**. - See Sect.3, para.70.

11. **Assembly**. - See Sect.3, para.71.

MAIN PLANE

Gap fairing

12. **Removal**. - (i) With the flaps down (or removed), remove the locknut and fixing bolt attaching the upper main panel of the fairing to the upper rear panel; this bolt is situated on the inner side of the upper fairing above the universal joint between the flap spars.

(ii) Release the fixing of the lower main and rear panels in a similar manner.

(iii) Remove the three screws at the leading edge and thus remove the upper and lower main panels.

(iv) Remove the washer-head bolts attaching the upper and lower rear panels and thus remove these panels.

F.S./7

13. **Assembly.** - (i) Assemble the upper and lower main panels by means of three screws at the leading edge and secure the lower rear panel in position by means of the washer-head bolts.

(ii) Place the main fairing in position and bolt it to the lower rear panel with the fixing bolt, leaving approximately ¾ in. gap between the brackets.

(iii) Secure the upper rear panel in position by means of the washer-head bolts and bolt it to the main fairing with the fixing bolt.

(iv) Tighten the upper fixing bolt, and adjust the lower fixing bolt to suit, until the fairing is in contact with the skin of the outer plane and centre section at all points; lock the fixing bolts by means of the locknuts.

Flaps

14. **Removal.** - (i) Lower the flaps and disconnect the flap jack at its attachment to the flap lever.

(ii) Uncouple the universal joints and disconnect the flap indicator control cable at its attachment to the eyebolt on the centre section flap spar.

(iii) Remove the radiator fairing (see Sect.3, para.70).

(iv) Remove the bolts attaching the centre bearing of the flap spar to the bracket mounted on the fuselage plan bracing struts.

(v) Remove the bolts attaching the remaining flap spar bearings to the centre section and outer plane ribs; remove the flaps.

15. **Assembly.** - The assembly procedure is the reverse of that for removal, but in addition the following points should be noted. To ensure accurate alignment with the flap spar, the bearings should be adjusted during assembly by means of the shims provided. The shims should be introduced between the bearings and the ribs of the centre section, any shims not so required being used as packing beneath the head of the corresponding bolt of the bearing. When inserting the bolt, care should be taken not to use undue force lest the fibre locking device in the nut be dislodged; it is advisable to see that the end of the bolt has a small amount of taper at the tip.

CENTRE SECTION

Removal

16. (i) First remove the engine mounting complete with engine as described in para.5 and then remove the following cowling:-

  (a) Rear side panels
  (b) Front and rear walkways
  (c) Trailing-edge fillet
  (d) Covering under trailing edge
  (e) Cover strip at rear of wheel housing

(ii) Remove the fireproof bulkhead inboard of the oil tank, by removing the fibre blocks, the plates and fibre bushes at the oil vent pipe and the bolts holding the two portions together.

(iii) Fit a hoisting bar through the fuselage in the angle formed by struts AB and AD; attach the fuselage slinging gear and hook it to the hoist.

(iv) Fit the handling bar through the tube between fuselage joints Q and jack up the rear fuselage with an adjustable trestle.

(v) Close the isolating cock at the reserve fuel tank in the fuselage and drain the main fuel tanks in the centre section (see Sect.3, para.76).

(vi) Drain the oil cooler (see Sect.3, para.83) and the oil tank (see Sect.3, para.80).

(vii) Drain the hydraulic system by opening the drain cock at the engine-driven pump, removing the filler cap in the handpump casing as a vent and operating the handpump.

(viii) Remove the outer planes (see para.21).

(ix) Remove the bolts attaching the rear walkway support to the innermost trailing edge rib of the centre section; the support should be left attached to the cross tube.

(x) Remove the brackets on the centre section inner girder which support the fillet rail.

(xi) Remove the main fuel tanks from the centre section (see para.37) and the flying controls from the cockpit (see paras.32, 34, 35 and 36).

(xii) Remove the pipes between the main fuel tanks and the T-piece on the rear wall of the wheel housing.

(xiii) Remove the fuel pipe between the T-piece on the rear wall of the wheel housing and the 3-way cock on the port longeron at joint B.

(xiv) Remove the fuel pipe from the 3-way cock to the fuel filter connection at the front spar and then the vent pipes from the main fuel tanks.

(xv) Remove the underfairing and radiator fairing (see Sect.3, para.70).

F.S./8

(xvi) Remove the two oil pipes between the oil cooler
and the viscosity valve.

(xvii) Remove the coolant pipes between the radiator and
the joint just forward of the centre section rear spar;
disconnect the remaining coolant pipe at the radiator.

(xviii) Remove the radiator (see Sect.3, para.92) and the
oil cooler (see Sect.3, para.84).

(xix) From the port longeron just aft of joint F, remove
the clip attaching the pipes from the flap jack.

(xx) Remove the pipes from each end of the air cylinder;
the port pipe may be disconnected at the union adjacent to
the cylinder and starboard pipe at the union to the rear of
the mid-point of fuselage starboard strut AB.

(xxi) At joint F1, remove the bolt through the tubular
rivet attaching the bracket which supports the T-piece in the
gun-firing pipes of the pneumatic system.

(xxii) Remove the clips attaching the brake-operating
pipes of the pneumatic system to the lower longeron just aft
of joints B, port and starboard.

(xxiii) At the latches locking the undercarriage in the
DOWN position, disconnect the leads from the micro-switches
and remove the pin attaching the two springs to the pivot arm;
remove the bolts attaching the pivot tube and push out the
tube, leaving the bowden cables attached to the latch.

(xxiv) From the pulleys on the centre section, free the
cables operating the undercarriage latch gear.

(xxv) Remove all clips attaching the cable ducts to the
centre section structure.

(xxvi) At the electric fuel contents gauge on each main
fuel tank, lift the wire clip and remove the socket which
houses the leads from the indicator in the cockpit.

(xxvii) At the outer ribs, remove the fibre fairleads for
the landing lamp control cables; withdraw the cables inboard,
coil them and stow them out of the way.

(xxviii) Remove the bolts attaching the fireproof bulkhead
to the front spar.

(xxix) Support joint F1 by means of a cable or c
attached to any convenient point on the fuselage structure
and remove the bolts attaching the joint to the rear spar.

(xxx) Disconnect the pipes (from the undercarriage jacks)
at the T-pieces situated on the starboard side just above and
to the rear of the centre section front spar.

(xxxi) At the control box of the hydraulic system, remove
the pipes to the flap jack.

(xxxii) Disconnect the air-speed indicator tubes at the unions just outboard of joint F, port.

(xxxiii) Disconnect the cables from the terminal blocks on the top boom of the centre section outer girder and draw them back through the duct on the front face of the rear spar; remove the duct, coil the cables and stow them out of the way.

(xxxiv) Disconnect the control cable of the flap indicator at its attachment to the eyebolt on the centre section flap spar.

(xxxv) Remove the bolts attaching the rear heelboard support to the lower longeron; remove the rear heelboard support.

(xxxvi) Remove the undercarriage (see para.29).

(xxxvii) Support the centre section by means of adjustable trestles placed as close under the outer girders as practicable and slacken off the wires in bays BD and DF.

(xxxviii) Disconnect the struts in the inner bay of the centre section at joints B and F; swing the freed ends clear.

(xxxix) Remove the strut between the rear spar lower boom and joint H.

(xl) Remove the bolts securing the top booms of the spars to the fuselage at joints B and F.

(xli) Lower the trestles on which the centre section is now resting and hoist the fuselage until it clears, making sure that no fittings, cables, pipes etc. are left in such a position that they impede the removal of the centre section.

(xlii) Remove the centre section.

17. Assembly. - The installation procedure is the reverse of that given for removal but with the following additions:-

(i) Drop plumblines as when checking the rear fuselage (see Sect.3, para.11).

(ii) Drop plumblines from the mid-points of the front and rear spars.

(iii) Adjust the wires in bays BD and DF until the lines dropped from the spars are in fore-and-aft alignment with the other plumblines.

(iv) Adjust all control cables to the proper tautness; fit new split-pins and locking wires as required.

F.S./9

Front spar

18. **Removal**. – (i) Remove the engine mounting complete with engine (see para.5).

(ii) Sling the aeroplane from joints A (see para.16, sub-para.(iii)), or alternatively, place a trestle under a wooden beam supporting the fuselage across joints D.

(iii) Remove the outer planes (see para.21).

(iv) Remove the rear side panels and the front walkways; this cowling is additional to that removed under (i) above.

(v) Remove the leading edge fairing (see para.19) and the oil tank (see Sect.3, para.81).

(vi) Remove the oil filter from the front face of the front spar opposite joint B, starboard.

(vii) Remove the main fuel tanks from the centre section.

(viii) Remove the starboard top fairing angle.

(ix) Remove the fuel filter from the front face of the front centre section spar.

(x) Disconnect each end of the coolant pipe elbow which passes through the front centre section spar and remove the bolts attaching the flange on the elbow to the spar.

(xi) Remove the undercarriage (see para.29).

(xii) From the undersurface of each spar, remove the two screws securing each end of the lower boom of each outer girder; at the web bracing joints with the lower boom, remove the three bolts at the front joint and, at the rear joint, the three bolts and eyebolt.

(xiii) Remove the undercarriage latch gear from the channel section at the front end of each inner girder and disconnect the electrical leads from the micro-switches on the latch gear.

(xiv) Remove the pulleys (which carry the latch gear operating cables) from the brackets mounted on the spar stiffeners above the latches; stow the latch gears, cables and pulleys out of the way.

(xv) Remove the air cylinder (see Sect.3, para.55).

(xvi) Remove the web plate of the channel fitting attaching the inner girder to the front spar.

(xvii) Disconnect the port side fairing angle from the brackets on the front spar top boom.

(xviii) Slide the lower boom of the outer girder forwards out of the rear spar; should the boom be tightly held in place, it will be necessary to remove the outer trailing edge rib and tap the boom rearwards until it clears, using a mallet and a block of wood.

(xix) Dismantle the joint of the outer girder with the
top boom of the front spar.

(xx) Dismantle the joint of the inner girder with the
large channel fitting on the front spar.

(xxi) Support the front spar and remove the three bolts
attaching the top boom at joints B, port and starboard.

(xxii) Lower the front spar to clear the spool fittings
at joints B and remove forwards.

Leading edge fairing

19. Removal. - (i) Remove the cover over the starboard
main fuel tank.

(ii) Remove the screws attaching the top edge of the
fairing and the screw at the inboard lower corner.

(iii) Remove the four nuts, on the rear faces of the
spar booms, which attach the two intermediate formers to the
spar.

(iv) From each end former, remove the two bolts which
attach these formers to the spar shear plates; remove the
fairing in a forward direction.

Fuel tank covers

20. Assembly of new covers. - New covers are only
drilled with a certain number of location holes and therefore
the remaining holes must be drilled on assembly; there are
eight attachment points on the upper cover and seven on the
lower. The method of determining the positions of the holes
for the attachment screws is as follows:-

(i) Into the plug and cap fittings on the face of the
tank, screw the special marking studs (ref. Sect.3, para.4).

(ii) Apply the cover to the centre section and secure
the edges to the fairing strips by a sufficient number of
screws to hold it in place. Note. - On the starboard side
only, the holes along the front edge of the top cover must be
drilled on assembly; the positions of these holes may be
determined by scribing from below, or by an adaption of the
method outlined in this paragraph.

(iii) With a mallet, strike the covering at points above
the special studs so that the points of the latter will mark
the inner surface of the cover.

(iv) Remove the cover and, at the point marked by the
studs, drill 3/8 in. diameter holes.

F.S./10

(v) Replace and secure the cover with 2 B.A. screws to the fairing formers, and with 2 B.A. countersunk screws and drawsunk washers to the tank plug-and-cap fittings.

OUTER PLANES

Removal

21. (i) Trestle the aeroplane until it is approximately in its flying position.

(ii) Remove the gap fairing between the centre section and the outer plane (see para.12) and, if the flaps have not been removed, uncouple the outer plane flap spar from the centre section flap spar.

(iii) Disconnect the two aileron cables and the landing lamp control cable at the gap between the outer plane and the centre section, immediately aft of the rear spar.

(iv) Disconnect the navigation and landing lamp leads at the terminal block on the centre section end rib; access may be obtained through a door in the upper surface of the centre section.

(v) When removing the port outer plane, disconnect the tubes to the pressure head and, if the outer planes are of the skin-stressed type, disconnect the pressure head heater lead at the terminal block on the centre section end rib.

(vi) Disconnect the pipe for the pneumatic gun-firing gear at the joint on the trailing edge portion of the inner end rib.

(vii) Disconnect the gun heating pipes and the electrical bonding wires at their joints just aft of the rear spars.

(viii) Screw the lifting brackets into the sockets provided in the undersurface of each outer plane (see Sect.3, fig.1) and bolt the lifting handles in place; place trestles under both outer planes to take the load off the pin-joints and to maintain the stability of the aeroplane when one outer plane has been removed.

(ix) Remove the nuts and washers from the main plane joint pins and extract the joint pins with the special extractor supplied.

(x) Ease the plane away by means of the lifting handles and, after removing the trestles out of the way, lower the plane on to a suitably padded support.

Assembly

22. (i) Trestle the aeroplane until it is in the rigging position (see Sect.3, para.9).

(ii) Support the outer plane on adjustable trestles so that the plug-ends at the root end of the outer plane are adjacent to and just below the fork-ends of the centre section.

(iii) Using the lifting brackets and lifting handles, offer the outer plane up to the centre section and insert three of the taper joint pins as far as they will go into the fork joints.

(iv) Drive in the fourth joint pin as far as it will go to align the holes in the plug-end and fork-end.

(v) Withdraw this latter joint pin and, with a special B.& S.No.9 taper reamer, open up the holes until the reamer is home up to the collar.

(vi) Insert and tap home the taper joint pin and assemble the special washer, nut, and split-pin (see Sect.3, fig.7).

(vii) Repeat the process at the other three joints in succession, taking front and rear joints alternately.

(viii) With the aid of the dihedral and incidence boards, check the rigging of the main plane in accordance with the rigging diagram (see Sect.3, fig.7).

(ix) Couple up the outer plane services uncoupled when the outer plane was removed (see para.21); remove the lifting handles and brackets.

(x) Replace the gap fairing between the centre section and the outer main plane (see para.13).

Aileron

23. Removal. - (i) At the aileron lever, uncouple the connecting rod between the aileron control gear and the aileron.

(ii) Remove the nuts from the aileron hinge bolts that pass through the aileron spar.

(iii) Remove the aileron, leaving the bolts attached to the outer plane.

TAIL UNIT

Removal

24. (i) Remove the metal fairing between the tail plane, fin and fuselage.

(ii) Disconnect the rudder control cables at the rudder lever.

(iii) Remove the elevator connecting rod and disconnect the control cables at each end of the elevator lever in the tail plane; access to the lower end of the lever is obtained by removing the port side panel in the tail bay fairing.

F.S./11

(iv) Remove the pulleys for the elevator control cables from the bracket on the rear face of the tail plane front spar and pull the elevator cables through the spar from the front; replace the pulleys.

(v) Open the Woods frames in the upper surface of the tail plane at the rear inner corner and disconnect the cables to the tail trimming flaps.

(vi) Remove the fairleads for the trimming flap cables situated in the web of the tail plane front spar and pull the cable through from the front; replace the fairleads but do not lock the nuts.

(vii) Disconnect the electrical lead to the tail navigation lamp at the terminal block on fuselage strut TU, port.

(viii) Remove the rudder, fin, elevator and tail plane (in that order) as described in paras.25, 26, 27 and 28 below.

Rudder

25. **Removal**. - After performing the necessary operations as described in para.24 above, proceed as follows:-

(i) Disconnect the wireless aerial at the rear insulator.

(ii) Disconnect the balance flap cables at the housing for the hinge bearing on the rudder post.

(iii) Detach each hinge by removing the two bolts holding it to the hinge bracket on the rear finpost.

(iv) Remove the rudder, taking care not to wrench the lead for the tail navigation lamp during withdrawal.

Fin

26. **Removal**. - After performing the necessary operations as described in paras. 24 and 25 above, proceed as follows:-

(i) Remove the four bolts attaching the lower end of the front finpost at fuselage joint S1, and also the packing washers.

(ii) Detach the front finpost from fuselage cross strut RR by withdrawing the two bolts sufficiently to clear the packing block on the strut and to permit the removal of the shims (if any); the bolts should be left in the finpost to keep the distance tubes in place.

(iii) Detach the rear finpost from the rear end of the top longerons by withdrawing the four attachment bolts and removing the shims (if any); as in sub-para.(ii) above, the bolts should only be withdrawn sufficiently to clear the fittings on the fuselage.

(iv) Remove the four bolts attaching the bottom end of
the rear finpost; lift the fin upwards and remove it clear
of the fuselage.

(v) Push home the two bolts left in the front finpost
(see sub-para.(ii)) and the four bolts in the rear finpost
(see sub-para.(iii)) and replace the nuts.

Elevator

27. Removal. - After performing the necessary
operations as described in paras.24, 25 and 26 above, proceed
as follows:-

(i) Remove the control cable fairleads for the tail
trimming flap from the front face of the tail plane rear
spar; access is obtained through the Woods frames in the
upper surface of the tail plane at the rear inner corner.

(ii) Detach each hinge by removing the two bolts holding
it to the hinge bracket on the tail plane rear spar.

(iii) Remove the elevator in a rearward direction, taking
care that the connectors on the trimming flap cables do not
foul the tail plane rear spar.

(iv) If necessary, remove the bolt connecting the two
half-elevators; each half-elevator may be removed separately
if required.

Tail plane

28. Removal. - After performing the necessary
operations as described in paras.24, 25, 26 and 27 above,
remove the four bolts attaching the tail plane to the fuselage
at joints R and T, port and starboard, and lift the tail plane
clear.

ALIGHTING GEAR

Undercarriage

29. Removal. - (i) With the undercarriage in the
DOWN position, jack up the aeroplane until the wheels are just
clear of the ground.

(ii) Disconnect the hydraulic jack by removing the bolt
attaching it to the triangulated lever on the sidestay;
replace the bolt, nut and washer in the lever and tie the free
end of the jack to the channel fitting on the centre section
spar.

(iii) Disconnect the assisting spring gear at its
attachment to the shackle on the sidestay; care should be
taken to hold the lower portion of the gear and allow it to
ease off to its full extension gradually.

F.S./12

(iv) Disconnect the sidestay at the compression leg by removing either one of the two bolts.

(v) Remove the compression leg fairing by withdrawing the bolts attaching the fairing clips and removing the clips.

(vi) Disconnect the radius rod at the compression leg by removing the bolt; swing the free end upwards and tie it to any convenient part of the centre section structure.

(vii) Release the pressure in the pneumatic system by depressing the valve at the charging connection and, at the upper end of the compression leg, uncouple the lower end of the flexible tube from the pipeline running down to the brake unit; remove the clip attaching the end of the flexible tube to the air valve on the compression leg.

(viii) Remove the split-pin locking the special ball nut for the assisting spring on the compression leg pivot bolt.

(ix) Whilst supporting the compression leg and assisting spring gear, unscrew and withdraw the pivot bolt; remove the compression leg and the assisting spring gear.

(x) At the joint of the sidestay with the inner girder, remove the split-pin and the slotted nut at the rear end of the pivot bolt and withdraw the bolt; the head of the bolt is on the front face of the front spar lower boom.

(xi) Whilst supporting the sidestay, wedge the end of a piece of wood into the bore of the pivot distance piece and withdraw the distance piece rearwards; remove the sidestay. Note. - If required, the sidestay may be disconnected at the elbow joint.

Assembly

30. When assembling the undercarriage care must be taken to ensure full freedom of movement without undue slackness in the joints.

(i) Assemble the two portions of the sidestay if they have been disconnected at the elbow joint. Test for freedom of movement by holding the lower portion upwards and allowing the upper portion to fall; the upper portion should just be capable of swinging downwards under its own weight.

(ii) Assemble the upper end of the sidestay assembly on the fitting at the inner girder joint with the front spar; note that the thin washer should be placed under the bolt head on the front face of the spar boom.

(iii) Test the sidestay assembly for freedom of movement; when raised and allowed to fall, it should fall freely under its own weight but there should not be any sideplay.

(iv) Offer up the compression leg (axle inboard) to the forked sleeve at the front end of the lower boom of the centre section outer girder and insert the pivot bolt from the outboard side.

(v) Remove the locking plate on the inboard side of the forked upper end of the compression leg and place the large washer over the end of the pivot bolt.

(vi) Screw the special ball nut for the assisting spring gear on to the end of the pivot bolt; tighten the nut and lock it in place with a split-pin. (It is unnecessary to separate the assisting spring gear from the ball nut).

(vii) Replace the locking plate, turning the pivot bolt by its head (if necessary) to ensure that the ball nut fits inside the locking plate with the ball uppermost.

(viii) Swing the compression leg fore-and-aft and sideways to test for freedom of movement; should there be too much play in the universal sleeve on the outer girder boom, the sleeve must be replaced.

(ix) Attach the radius rod to the compression leg; the bolt head should be on the inboard side.

(x) Raise the locking latch assembly and tie it back clear of the sidestay triangulated lever to avoid damage.

(xi) Attach the sidestay to the compression leg.

(xii) Attach the lower end of the assisting spring gear to the shackle on the sidestay.

(xiii) At the upper attachment of the assisting spring gear, set the ball on the ball nut aft to the limit allowed by the locking plate, i.e. 3^0 approximately; this may be done by turning the pivot bolt.

(xiv) With the undercarriage retracted, check to ensure a small clearance between the upper end of the assisting spring gear and the spar plate; lock the locking plate attachment bolt.

(xv) Attach the hydraulic jack to the fork at the top of the sidestay triangulated lever, making sure that the flat faces of the fork face inboard.

(xvi) Lower the locking latch assembly into position. There should be a clearance of 0.03 in. between the end of the latch gear tube and the face of the fork; in plan view, the centre line of the latch gear tube should line up with the centre of the front cheek of the fork.

(xvii) Attach the fairing to the compression leg.

(xviii) Test the undercarriage for freedom of movement. Raise the undercarriage by selecting WHEELS UP and operating the handpump; set the selector lever to WHEELS DOWN and the undercarriage should fall under its own weight (see also Sect.3, para.36).

F.S./13

Tail wheel unit

31. **Removal.** - (i) Trestle the aeroplane until the tail wheel is clear of the ground.

(ii) Remove access panel in the port side of the tail bay fairing and disconnect the tail wheel compression leg at its upper fixing by removing the securing bolt.

(iii) At the lower fixing, remove the wire locking the four bolts for the securing cap; remove the four bolts and withdraw the tail wheel unit downwards.

(iv) **Unless the tail wheel unit is to be replaced immediately**, it will be advisable to remove the V-strut assembly that provides the upper fixing point for the compression leg; this is effected by removing a bolt at fuselage joints R, port and starboard.

FLYING CONTROLS

Control column assembly

32. **Removal.** - (i) Remove the intermediate and rear side cowling panels.

(ii) Remove the cockpit seat (**see** para.7).

(iii) From the heelboards, remove the screws attaching the pipe connections of the pneumatic system; the nuts are fixed in the brackets so detached.

(iv) Remove the heelboards; whilst the attachment screws are being removed, the 4 B.A. nuts may be held against rotation by inserting a box spanner through the holes in the underside of the heelboard support tubes.

(v) **Disconnect the elevator control tube at both ends** and remove it.

(vi) Disconnect the brake control bowden cable at the lever on the control column; hold the lever forward and, with a suitable instrument inserted in the slot at its base, lift the cable nipple clear and slide the cable out through the slot.

(vii) Remove the clips attaching the bowden cable and the rubber tubes of the pneumatic system to the control column; coil the cable and stow where convenient.

(viii) Disconnect the rubber tubes at their upper ends and tie them out of the way to the mounting tube of the control column assembly.

(ix) Disconnect the aileron torque tube at the universal joint at the bottom of the control column.

(x) **From the control column mounting tubes, remove the** bolts attaching the crank bearing brackets.

(xi) Remove the control column assembly with the bearing brackets. As soon as the bearing brackets are clear, slip them off the cranks and replace them on the mounting tubes; replace the attachment bolts, screwing on the nuts finger tight only. Care should be taken to prevent the distance tubes within the mounting tubes from falling out of position.

33. **Installation.** - The installation procedure is the reverse of that for removal but the following point should be observed. When re-assembling the cranks in the bearings, a laminated brass shim ($1^1/8$ in. o/d x $^{13}/16$ in. i/d x $^1/64$ in. thick) should be fitted between the inner faces of the bearings and the shoulders of the cranks to take up possible end play.

Cockpit aileron controls

34. **Removal.** - After carrying out the operations described in para.32, sub-paras. (i) to (iv) inclusive, proceed as follows:-

(i) At the rear end of the aileron torque tube, disconnect the aileron cables at the turnbuckles immediately outboard of the cable drum.

(ii) Remove the three bolts attaching the housing for the torque tube bearing to the support bracket on the centre section rear spar.

(iii) Remove the torque tube, complete with cable drum; replace the bolts removed under (ii) above to retain the cable guard.

Cockpit elevator controls

35. **Removal.** - After carrying out the operations described in para.32, sub-paras. (i) to (iv) inclusive, proceed as follows:-

(i) At the ends of the elevator lever countershaft, remove the caps of the rudder cable fairleads; remove the cables and replace the caps.

(ii) Disconnect the elevator cables at each end of the elevator lever and stow the freed ends out of the way.

(iii) At the rear end of the flying controls mounting tubes, remove the bolts attaching the supporting plug-ends for the elevator lever countershaft.

(iv) Remove the complete countershaft assembly by withdrawing it rearwards.

Rudder bar assembly

36. **Removal.** - After carrying out the operations described in para.32, sub-paras. (i) to (iv) inclusive, proceed as follows:-

F.S./14

(i) At the rudder lever, disconnect the rudder cables and uncouple the connecting rod to the brake relay valve of the pneumatic system; the shackle should remain with the connecting rod.

(ii) Remove the bolts attaching the front heelboard support tubes to the bottom longeron; remove the support tubes.

(iii) Remove the bolts attaching the rudder pedestal support tubes to the pedestal and to the brackets on the flying controls mounting tubes.

(iv) Remove the pedestal support tubes, taking care to avoid damage should it be found necessary to drive them with a hammer.

(v) Turn the rudder bar fore-and-aft as far as possible and lift out the complete assembly.

FUEL SYSTEM

Main fuel tank

37. Removal. - (i) Remove the upper and lower tank covers and drain the tank (see Sect.3, para.76).

(ii) At the electric fuel gauge, lift the wire clip and withdraw the socket which houses the leads from the indicator in the cockpit.

(iii) Disconnect the fuel pipe from the cock situated in the inboard lower edge of the tank.

(iv) Disconnect the vent pipe at the connection in the front upper edge of the tank, holding the pipe connection at the tank against rotation by a $\frac{1}{4}$ in. spanner fitted over the flats provided.

(v) Disconnect the bonding wire from the socket fitting at the filler cap seating by removing the attaching screw.

(vi) Remove the bolts by which the two struts that pass through the tank are attached to the joints on the centre section structure.

(vii) Remove the locking wire, bolt, washer and rubber pad from each of the four tank feet.

(viii) Lift the tank out vertically, taking care to see that the struts through the tank do not foul the centre section structure or damage the tank.

(ix) Remove the struts and, to avoid loss, replace the rubber pad, washer and bolt.

38. Installation. - The installation procedure is the reverse of that for removal but the following points should be noted. The rubber pads should be arranged so that one is under

each tank foot, and one between the tank foot and the washer
under the bolthead; the bolts should be locked with wire.

Reserve fuel tank

39. Removal. - (i) Remove the rear top and intermediate
side cowling panels.

(ii) Remove the bolts attaching the rearmost portions
of the horizontal top cowl rails; remove these cowl rails.

(iii) Set the handle of the fuel distributing cock in
the cockpit to the OFF position.

(iv) Cut the wire locking the isolating cock at the
reserve tank sump in the ON position and turn the cock to the
OFF position.

(v) Disconnect the fuel pipe at this cock and move
the freed end out of the way.

(vi) Place a funnel (to which is attached a length of
hose) under the cock; turn the cock to the ON position and
drain the fuel into a suitable receptacle.

(vii) On the port side, disconnect the vent pipe in the
undersurface of the tank, holding the pipe connection at the
tank against rotation by a $\frac{1}{2}$ in. spanner fitted over the flats
provided.

(viii) Disconnect the priming pipe at the top of the
rear face of the tank by removing the nut and sliding off
the banjo.

(ix) At the electric fuel gauge, lift the wire clip
and withdraw the socket which houses the leads from the
indicator in the cockpit.

(x) Disconnect the bonding wire from the outer web
of the port front foot.

(xi) At each of the four tank feet, remove the slotted
nuts and bolts holding the four clamps closed; swing the
clamps clear and lift the tank out vertically.

OIL SYSTEM

Oil tank

40. Removal. - See Sect.3, para.81.

41. Assembly. - See Sect.3, para.82.

Oil cooler

42. Removal. - See Sect.3, para.84.

F.S./15

Oil filter

43. **Removal**. - (i) Drain the oil tank (see Sect.3, para.80).

(ii) At the bottom of the filter, uncouple the flexible pipe to the engine.

(iii) At the top of the filter, uncouple the pipe to the tank; disconnect the other end of the pipe at the tank and move the filter end of the pipe clear of the filter.

(iv) Support the filter and remove the bolts attaching the bracket cap; remove the filter.

Viscosity valve

44. **Removal**. - (i) Place a suitable receptacle beneath the viscosity valve to catch the oil liberated when the pipes are disconnected.

(ii) Disconnect and remove the two pipes between the oil cooler and the viscosity valve.

(iii) At the viscosity valve, disconnect the two pipes from the fireproof bulkhead.

(iv) Remove the two bolts attaching the viscosity valve to the bracket on fuselage strut FH1.

45. **Installation**. - The installation procedure is the reverse of that for removal. To ensure the correct attitude of the valve on the strut, the bolts attaching the valve to the mounting should not be tightened until all four pipes are connected to the valve.

COOLING SYSTEM

Radiator

46. **Removal**. - **See** Sect.3, para.92.

Header tank

47. **Removal**. - **See** Sect.3, para.90.

48. **Assembly**. - **See** Sect.3, para.91.

HYDRAULIC SYSTEM

General

49. Absolute cleanliness is essential for the satisfactory operation of the system and, therefore, when pipelines are disconnected, the ends of the pipes must be protected against the entry of dirt. When it is desired to retain the fluid for further use, the receptacle into which it is drained must be scrupulously clean; mineral oil or grease may injure the gland and jointing compositions employed in the

system. Care should be taken that the fluid is not spilled as it may remove the protective coating from parts with which it comes in contact.

Control valve

50. Removal. - (i) Disconnect the pipes at the two banjo fittings and the smaller pipe entering the valve from above.

(ii) Remove the two bolts attaching the valve to the bracket on fuselage strut CD.

(iii) Remove the two bolts attaching the operating lever bracket to the valve; the valve may then be removed downwards.

Filter

51. Removal. - (i) Disconnect the outlet pipe from the top of the handpump at the non-return valve above the cruciform 4-way piece; disconnect the two pipes below this non-return valve at the front and rear sides of the cruciform 4-way piece.

(ii) Disconnect the two pipes coupled to the underside of the special 4-way piece attached to the side of the filter.

(iii) Unscrew and remove, from the special 4-way piece as one unit, the two non-return valves and cruciform 4-way piece; unscrew and remove the special 4-way piece from the filter.

(iv) Disconnect the outlet pipe at the filter and remove the two bolts attaching the filter to the bracket on the fuselage strut EH.

Handpump

52. Removal. - (i) Disconnect the outlet and inlet pipes in the upper part of the casing and then the outlet pipe at the bottom of the casing; a hose and funnel should be held in readiness to convey the fluid into a suitable receptacle.

(ii) Slacken off the bolt clamping the handle to the pump-operating shaft and remove the handle.

(iii) Support the pump casing and remove the bolts attaching it to the brackets on fuselage struts EF, EH and FCH; remove the pump casing.

Control box

53. Removal. - (i) Uncouple the two connecting rods from the selector gear.

F.S./16

(ii) Disconnect the six pipes entering the rear face of the control box; a hose and funnel should be held in readiness to convey any fluid into a suitable receptacle.

(iii) Remove the four bolts attaching the control box to its bracket when the control box may be removed downwards.

Selector gear

54. Removal. - (i) Disconnect the connecting rods to the control box and the cables operating the catch and latch gears; remove the instruction plate by removing three screws.

(ii) Remove the two bolts attaching the selector gear mounting bracket to fuselage strut CF.

(iii) Remove the three bolts attaching the selector gear spindle to the mounting bracket; the outer portion of the bracket will then drop away and the selector gear may be removed.

Jacks

55. Removal. - (i) Disconnect the two pipes at the jack and drain off the fluid into a suitable receptacle.

(ii) Disconnect the jack at each end.

PNEUMATIC SYSTEM

Oil reservoir

56. Removal. - (i) Detach the upper air pipe and drain the reservoir (see Sect.3, para.54).

(ii) On the rear face of the fireproof bulkhead, remove the four nuts and washers attaching the U-bolts and then withdraw the U-bolts from the front face of the fireproof bulkhead.

(iii) Remove the reservoir and the block on which it is mounted.

57. Installation. - The installation procedure is the reverse of that given for removal but instead of draining the reservoir it should be filled as described in Sect.3, para.53.

Oil trap

58. Removal. - (i) Drain the oil trap as described in Sect.3, para.51 and detach the two air pipes.

(ii) With a C-spanner, unscrew and remove the top half of the trap.

(iii) Slacken off the bolt closing the supporting bracket and withdraw the trap downwards.

Air cylinder

59. Removal. - See Sect.3, para.55.

Air filter

      60. <u>Removal</u>. - <u>See</u> Sect.3, para.57.

Brake relay valve

      61. <u>Removal</u>. - (i) Detach the four air pipes and uncouple the connecting rod to the rudder bar at the relay valve lever.

      (ii) Remove the moulded cover by pulling it off against its retaining spring clips.

      (iii) Remove the small spring clip from the cylindrical fitting connecting the bowden inner cable to the operating chain.

      (iv) Raise the cable connector by depressing the brake lever on the spade grip of the control column, hold the connector in the raised position, release the brake lever and slide the cable and ball end out of the connector; replace the spring clip on the connector.

      (v) Slacken the locknut and remove the bush which provides the adjustment for length of the bowden cable and is screwed into the frame of the relay valve; withdraw the bowden cable.

      (vi) Remove the four bolts attaching the relay valve to the bracket when the valve may be removed.

      62. <u>Installation</u>. - The installation procedure is the reverse of that given for removal but care should be taken that the cylinders project forward and to port and that the starboard cylinder is approximately 10° to port of a fore-and-aft line; the attachment bolts will then secure the valve in its correct position.

F.S./17

SECTION 5

ELECTRICAL INSTALLATION

F.S. /1

SECTION 5

LIST OF CONTENTS

LIST OF ILLUSTRATIONS

F.S./2

SECTION 5

ELECTRICAL INSTALLATION

INTRODUCTION

1.   The diagrams issued with this Section are provided to assist in following the various electrical services. The circuits have been numbered in accordance with the fuse position.   For example, the first fuse in the 8-way box is in the reflector gun sight circuit, this circuit has therefore been numbered 1.   The various terminal blocks have also been numbered with the prefix T.B., and where the same terminal block occurs on one or more diagrams, it bears the same number.

2.   Alternative circuits are shown in figs.4,5 and 12.   The dotted circuits illustrate the manner in which some existing aeroplanes may be wired, while the full-line circuits illustrate how future aeroplanes will be wired.   In fig.5 two types of undercarriage indicator are shown.   To change over from one to the other, all that is necessary is to connect the cable from the numbered terminal of the old type indicator to the corresponding lettered terminal of the new type of indicator.

3.   Referring to fig.4, the dotted circuit refers to aeroplanes wired for G.42 cine camera gun, while the full-line circuit illustrates aeroplanes wired for G.42B cine camera gun. An examination of fig.4 will show the manner in which the two circuits differ.   If a septocel 7 cable is used,in which one of the cores is brown, this core must be connected to the terminal to which the slate-cored cable is shown connected.

4.   Two dimmer switches type D are shown on fig.12. The old type D is now obsolete and will be replaced in future by the new type D.   It should be noted that both old and new type D dimmer switches bear the same Stores Ref. number.   The manner in which the new type of dimmer switch may be adapted to the existing wiring is shown in the illustration.

5.   The location diagram, fig.1, shows the physical position of all the terminal blocks, and some of the remaining electrical equipment.   The schematic diagram shows at a glance the source of supply for the various services.   For example, it will be seen that the landing lamps are connected directly across the accumulator, whereas the navigation lamps are connected across the generator positive and negative.   The generator controls circuit, fig.3, illustrates how the main terminal blocks are connected back to the generator or the accumulator as the case may be.   The remaining circuits are self explanatory.

F.S./3

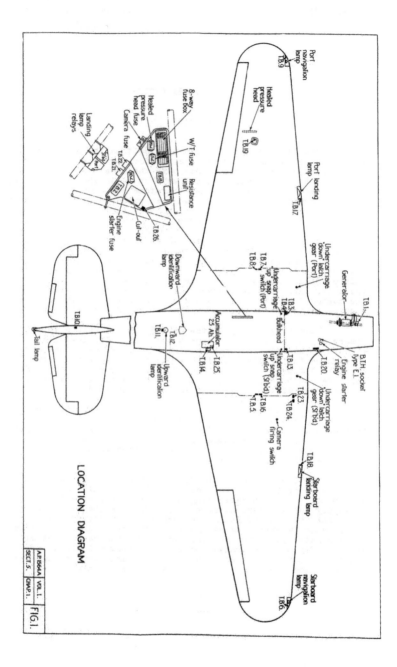

LOCATION : DIAGRAM

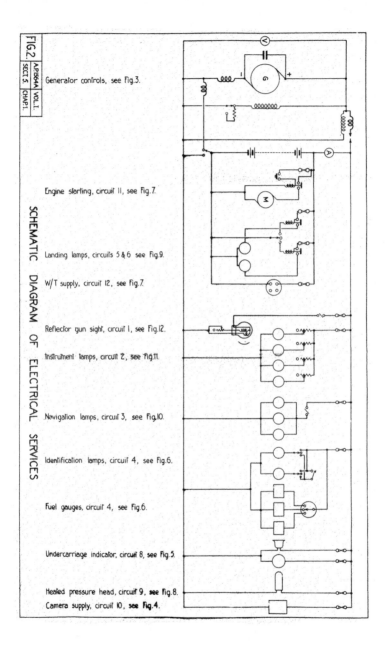

FIG.2. | A.P.1564A | VOL.I.
SECT.5. | CHAP.1.

SCHEMATIC DIAGRAM OF ELECTRICAL SERVICES

Generator controls, see Fig.3.

Engine starting, circuit 11, see Fig.7.

Landing lamps, circuits 5 & 6 see Fig.9.

W/T supply, circuit 12, see Fig.7.

Reflector gun sight, circuit 1, see Fig.12.

Instrument lamps, circuit 2, see Fig.11.

Navigation lamps, circuit 3, see Fig.10.

Identification lamps, circuit 4, see Fig.6.

Fuel gauges, circuit 4, see Fig.6.

Undercarriage indicator, circuit 8, see Fig.5.

Heated pressure head, circuit 9, see Fig.8.
Camera supply, circuit 10, see Fig.4.

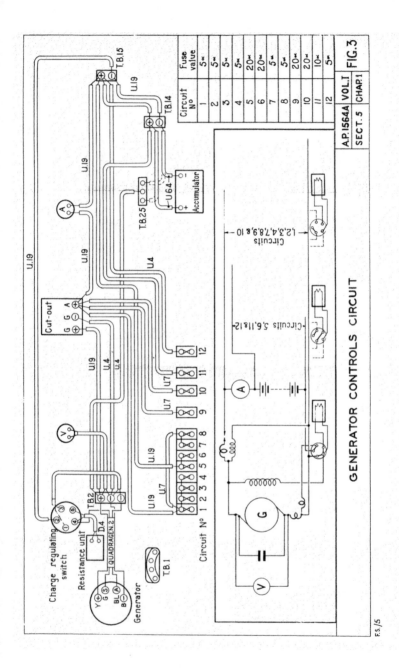

GENERATOR CONTROLS CIRCUIT

Circuit Nº	Fuse value
1	5~
2	5~
3	5~
4	5~
5	20~
6	20~
7	5~
8	5~
9	20~
10	20~
11	10~
12	5~

A.P.1564A	VOL.I	FIG.3
SECT. 5	CHAP.1	

F.S.J/5

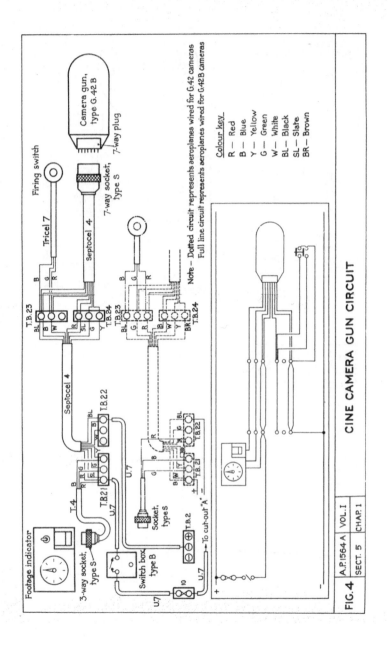

Footage indicator

Firing switch

Tricel 7

Camera gun, type G.42.B

7-way plug

7-way socket, type S

Septocel 4

Note – Dotted circuit represents aeroplanes wired for G.42 cameras
Full line circuit represents aeroplanes wired for G.42B cameras

Colour key

R — Red
B — Blue
Y — Yellow
G — Green
W — White
BL — Black
SL — Slate
BR — Brown

T.B.23
T.B.24
T.B.23
T.B.24

Septocel 4

T.B.22
T.B.22

T.B.21
T.B.21

U.7
U.7

3-way socket, type S

Socket, type S

T.B.2

To cut-out "A"

Switch box type B

FIG. 4   CINE CAMERA GUN CIRCUIT

| A.P.1564 A | VOL. I |
| SECT. 5 | CHAP. 1 |

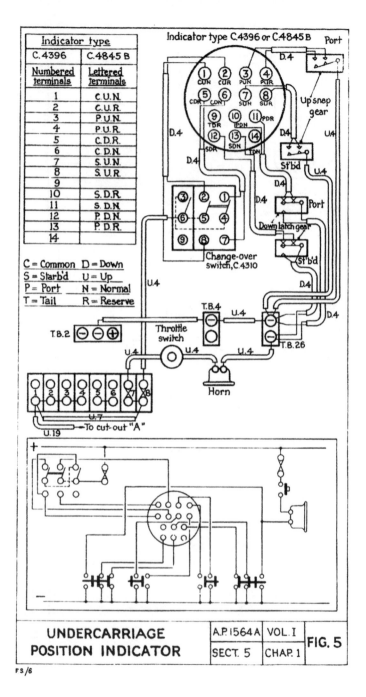

Indicator type	
C.4396	C.4845 B
Numbered terminals	Lettered terminals
1	C.U.N.
2	C.U.R.
3	P.U.N.
4	P.U.R.
5	C.D.R.
6	C.D.N.
7	S.U.N.
8	S.U.R.
9	
10	S.D.R.
11	S.D.N.
12	P.D.N.
13	P.D.R.
14	

C = Common D = Down
S = Starb'd U = Up
P = Port N = Normal
T = Tail R = Reserve

Indicator type C.4396 or C.4845 B

Port

Up snap gear

St'bd

Port

Down latch gear

St'bd

Change-over switch, C.4310

T.B.4

T.B.2

Throttle switch

T.B.26

Horn

To cut-out "A"

UNDERCARRIAGE POSITION INDICATOR

| A.P.1564 A | VOL. I | FIG. 5 |
| SECT. 5 | CHAP. 1 | |

FS/6

170

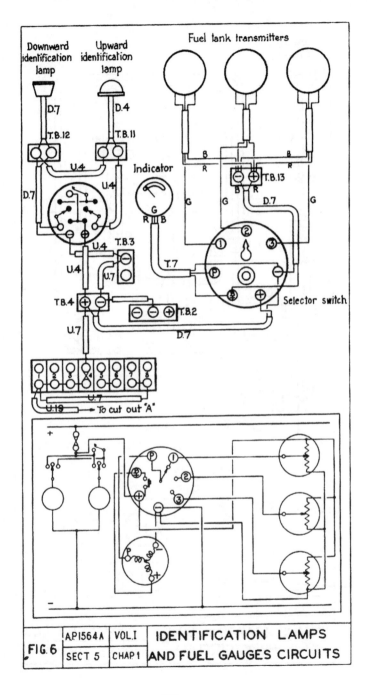

| FIG.6 | API564A | VOL.I | IDENTIFICATION LAMPS |
| | SECT 5 | CHAP 1 | AND FUEL GAUGES CIRCUITS |

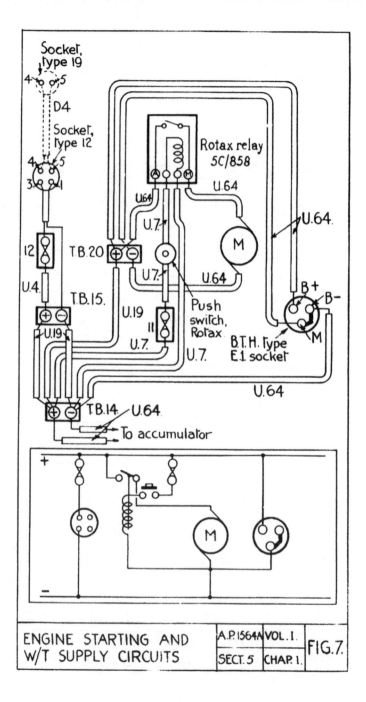

ENGINE STARTING AND W/T SUPPLY CIRCUITS

A.P.1564A VOL.1. SECT.5 CHAP.1. FIG.7.

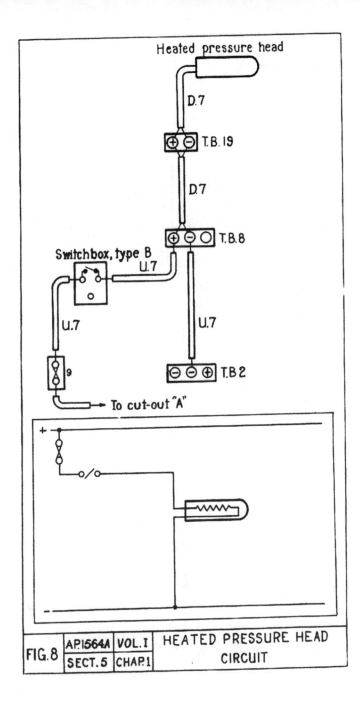

Heated pressure head

D.7

T.B.19

D.7

T.B.8

Switchbox, type B

U.7

U.7

U.7

9

T.B 2

To cut-out "A"

| FIG.8 | AP.1564A | VOL. I | HEATED PRESSURE HEAD |
| | SECT. 5 | CHAP.1 | CIRCUIT |

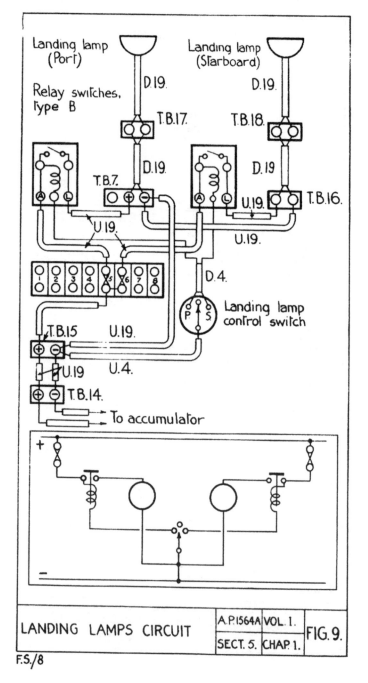

LANDING LAMPS CIRCUIT	A.P.1564A	VOL. 1.	FIG. 9.
	SECT. 5.	CHAP. 1.	

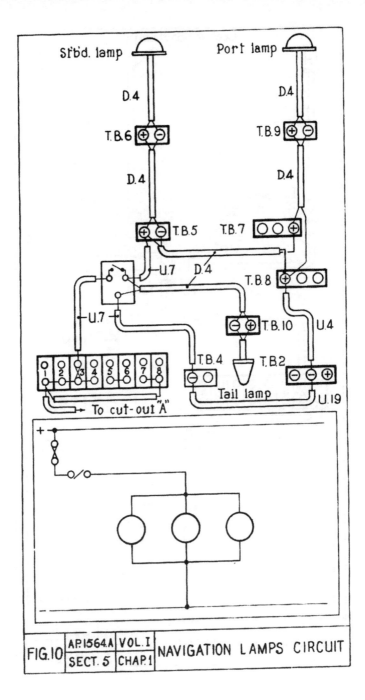

FIG.10	A.P.1564A	VOL.I	NAVIGATION LAMPS CIRCUIT
	SECT. 5	CHAP.1	

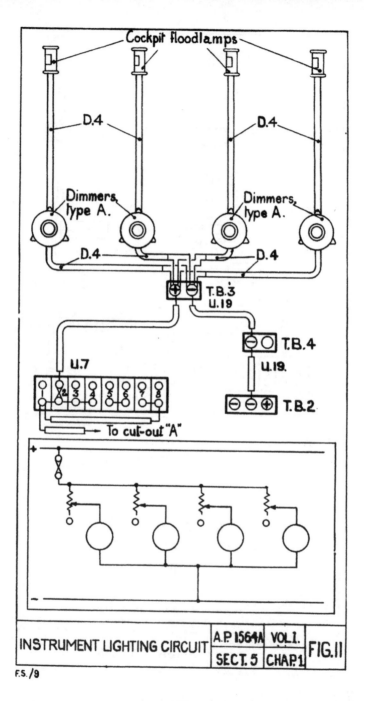

Cockpit floodlamps

D.4   D.4

Dimmers, type A.   Dimmers, type A.

D.4   D.4

T.B.3
U.19

T.B.4

U.19.

T.B.2

U.7

To cut-out "A"

+

−

INSTRUMENT LIGHTING CIRCUIT	A.P. 1564A	VOL.1.	FIG.11
	SECT. 5	CHAP.1	

F.S./9

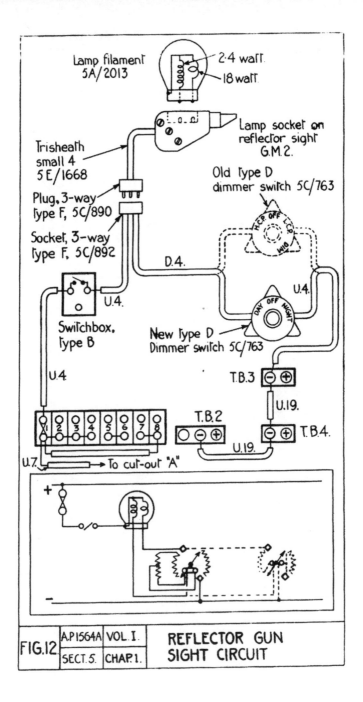

Lamp filament
5A/2013

2·4 watt.
18 watt.

Lamp socket on
reflector sight
G.M.2.

Trisheath
small 4
5 E/1668

Old type D
dimmer switch 5C/763

H.C.P. OFF L.C.P.

Plug, 3-way
type F, 5C/890

Socket, 3-way
type F, 5C/892

D.4.

U.4.

Switchbox,
type B

U.4.

DAY OFF NIGHT

New type D
Dimmer switch 5C/763

U.4

T.B.3

U.19.

T.B.2

T.B.4.

U.19.

U.7.→ To cut-out "A"

+

−

FIG.12	A.P.1564A	VOL.I.	REFLECTOR GUN SIGHT CIRCUIT
	SECT.5.	CHAP.1.	

December, 1939
Issued with A.L. No.6

AIR PUBLICATION 1564A
Volume I

SECTION 7

ENGINE INSTALLATION

P.S./1

SECTION 7

CONTENTS

LIST OF ILLUSTRATIONS

F.S./2

SECTION 7

ENGINE INSTALLATION

Engine

1. The aeroplane is powered with a Merlin II or III engine; for full particulars of the engine construction and methods of operation reference should be made to A.P.1590B, Vol.I. The engine is supercharged, and cooled by ethylene glycol, its twelve cylinders being ranged in two 6-cylinder mono-blocks set at 60° to one another. Reduction gearing is employed in the drive to the airscrew, which may be either a fixed-pitch wooden airscrew or a variable-pitch metal airscrew, provided with a two-pitch or constant-speed control. The exhaust manifolds in early aeroplanes were of kidney type, but later aeroplanes are fitted with ejector type exhaust manifolds as shown in the photographs in this volume. Boost pressure control is automatic but, in conditions of emergency, the automatic control may be cut-out to obtain maximum permissible boost pressure. The carburation system employs an automatic mixture control and an automatic two-stage enrichment device, the former worked by air intake pressure, and the latter by boost pressure; the enrichment device is provided as a safety measure to ensure that the mixture strength will be suitably enriched at large throttle openings. The ignition timing is interconnected with the manual throttle control lever.

2. An air compressor is driven from the rear end of the starboard camshaft whilst an engine-speed indicator is driven from the rear end of the port camshaft. An electrical generator is mounted on the port side of the crankcase and an electric starting motor is mounted vertically on the right-hand lower side of the wheelcase; a hand turning gear, with an operating handle on each side of the engine, is incorporated with the gear train for the electric starting motor. A dual gear-type fuel pump is driven in tandem from the left-hand side of the wheelcase whilst an oil pump for operating the hydraulic system is mounted at the base of the crankcase. On later aeroplanes the suction for the suction-operated instruments on the instrument-flying panel is obtained from a vacuum pump mounted on the lower face of the reduction gear casing. Gauges are fitted in the cockpit to show engine speed, boost pressure, oil pressure and temperature, coolant temperature and fuel pump pressure.

Fuel system

3. The fuel system (see fig.1 and the relevant illustration in Sect.2) is arranged so that the fuel is normally drawn by the dual engine-driven pumps in approximately equal quantities from

F.S./3

each main fuel tank in the centre section, a reserve tank being fitted in the fuselage immediately in front of the pilot's instrument panel; this latter tank also provides a supply for the engine primer pump. The supply from the main tanks or from the reserve tank is governed by a three-way cock remotely controlled from the cockpit; a fuel filter is fitted between the three-way cock and the engine.

4. **Main tanks.**- Each main fuel tank is of approximately rectangular form (see fig.2) and is constructed from sheet aluminium; four attachment feet are bolted to the tank shell. The top surface is strengthened by small swaged troughs which accommodate the eight specially-housed Simmonds nuts for the attachment of the upper aerofoil surface, seven similar nuts being also incorporated in the tank lower surface for the attachment of the lower aerofoil surface. Within the tank there are two longitudinal baffles and three transverse baffles, two tunnels being fitted between the inboard and outboard sides for the passage of the centre section inter-girder bracing tubes (see Sect.6, Chap.2).

5. The screwed filler cap, situated in the upper front outboard corner of the tank, is fitted with an internally-secured chain and is deeply slotted to facilitate its removal. Access to the filler cap is obtained through a door in the centre section upper tank cover and, to avoid loss, the door is attached internally to the door frame by a length of balloon cord. The outlet connection is situated in a recess in the inboard lower edge of the tank, the vent connection being in the front face near the upper edge of the tank and towards the inboard side. Two handholes are provided for inspection of the interior of the tank, one in the outboard face towards the rear, and one in the underside towards the front. A flush-type electrical fuel contents gauge (see A.P.1275, Vol.I) is situated in a recess in the centre of the upper rear edge of the tank.

6. Each main tank is housed between the centre section inner and outer girders (see Sect.6, Chap.2) and is carried by four brackets, two on each girder upper boom. Each of these brackets has an internally-tapped spigot over which a circular rubber pad is first placed to form the actual seating for the tank foot. The tank is then placed in position over the upper end of the spigot and another similar pad placed on the upper side of the tank foot; the pads are of such a thickness that the spigot does not project through the total thickness. A washer is placed on top of the uppermost pad and a bolt inserted in the spigot; the bolt is then screwed down to compress the pads until stopped by the end of the spigot.

7. **Reserve tank.**- The reserve fuel tank is of approximately semi-circular form (see fig.3) and is constructed from sheet aluminium; the tank is fitted internally with one longitudinal baffle in the centre of which there is a large approximately-rectangular flanged hole. A channel-section bearer, lightened with flanged holes, is fitted at each end across the bottom of the tank; the four tank feet are bolted externally to these cross bearers. The front tank feet are mounted on fuselage cross strut AA and the rear feet

on longerons AC, port and starboard. Each tank foot comprises an
upper and a lower semi-circular portion which are hinged together,
the front feet at their front ends and the rear feet at their outboard
ends. When the tank is in position on the longerons and cross strut,
the ends of the tank feet which are remote from the hinges are bolted
together; rubber blocks are interposed between the feet and the
tubes on which they are mounted in order to damp vibration.

8.   The screwed filler cap, situated in the top of the tank
near the front end and slightly to starboard, is fitted with an
internal retaining chain and has a deep slot to facilitate turning.
Access to the cap is obtained through the upper and rearmost of the
two doors in the top rear panel of the engine cowling; to avoid
loss, the door is attached internally to one of the fastener springs
with a length of balloon cord. The sump, embodying the outlet,
connection and draining connection, is in the underside of the tank
slightly to the front, whilst the vent pipe connection is also in
the underside near the centre of the port side edge. A priming
pipe connection is situated in the rear face of the tank near the
top and a flush-type electrical fuel contents gauge (see A.P.1275,
Vol.I) is situated in a pocket in the upper rear edge of the tank,
slightly to starboard.

9.   Fuel contents gauges.-   The electrical fuel contents gauge
fitted to each fuel tank is of the float and potentiometer type;
a selector switch, in conjunction with a meter, both fitted on the
starboard side of the instrument panel, enables the contents of any
tank to be determined at will. A wiring diagram for the fuel
contents gauges is illustrated in Sect.5.

10.   Pipe-lines.-   A two-way cock is fitted at each tank outlet
connection, the cocks being normally locked in the "open" position
except in such special circumstances as when about to remove a tank.
The two main tanks are interconnected through a T-piece with a non-
return valve on each side, the valves being fitted to prevent any
flow from one tank to the other whatever the attitude of the aeroplane.
From the third arm of the T-piece, a pipe is taken to the three-way
fuel cock which is mounted on the port lower longeron just aft of
joint B. The supply pipe from the reserve tank is lead to the
opposite connection on the cock, the cock being remotely-controlled
by a handle mounted on the port side of the fuselage, in the angle
between struts CF and CF1. From the three-way cock, a flexible
pipe runs to the rear face of the centre section front spar web
where it is coupled to the inlet connection of a filter; the filter
is mounted on the front face of the spar, the connection projecting
through the spar web.

11.   At the top of the filter is the outlet branch which is
connected by a coupler to a T-piece. In early aeroplanes, a non-
return valve is screwed into one branch of the T-piece and, from the
non-return valve, a flexible pipe runs directly to another T-piece
connected by a coupler to the carburettor. In later aeroplanes,

P.S./4

the non-return valve and this latter pipe are not fitted, one branch
of each T-piece being blanked off.   From the other branch of the
T-piece on the filter, a flexible pipe runs to the inlet connection
of the engine fuel pump and, from the outlet connection of the fuel
pump, another flexible pipe runs to the remaining branch of the
T-piece on the carburettor;   in later aeroplanes, this latter pipe-
line includes a pressure-reducing valve from which a balance pipe
is taken to the engine air intake.   In early aeroplanes, the
flexible pipe from the T-piece on the filter to the T-piece on the
carburettor, permits a flow under gravity from the reserve tank to
the carburettor whilst the non-return valve fitted to the filter
outlet prevents the possibility of the pump feeding fuel back into
the reserve tank when the engine is running.   As the capacity of
each fuel pump is in excess of the maximum demands of the engine,
a suitable relief valve is fitted in the dual pump unit.

12.   From a banjo fitting at the priming connection on the
reserve tank, a supply pipe runs to the inlet connection of the
manually-operated primer pump which is mounted on a bracket on
fuselage joint C on the starboard side.   The priming delivery
pipe runs directly from the pump to the engine primer connection,
from which it is distributed by four pipes to the induction manifolds.
The vent pipes of all three fuel tanks meet at a fitting on the
reserve tank vent pipe connection, whence a common vent pipe runs
aft and connects with a pipe projecting from the rear of the radiator.

13.   A fuel pressure gauge, mounted on the starboard side of
the instrument panel in the cockpit, is connected by a capillary
tube, in early aeroplanes to the delivery side of the engine pump
and, in later aeroplanes, to the pressure-reducing valve on the
engine.   From a connection on the engine induction manifold, a
small-diameter tube runs to a fuel trap mounted on the port side
of the front face of the fireproof bulkhead, whence a similar tube
continues to a boost pressure gauge on the starboard side of the
instrument panel in the cockpit.   All joints in the fuel system
are standard unions locked with wire, except in the case of the vent
pipes where all the connections are of rubber hose secured by jubilee
clips bonded with copper strips.

Oil system

14.   The lubrication system of the engine is of the conventional
dry sump type necessitating the use of an external oil tank, the
engine pumps maintaining the oil in constant circulation from the
tank, through the engine and back to the tank;   an oil cooler, a
viscosity valve and an oil filter are also included in the circuit.
The oil tank forms part of the port leading edge of the centre
section (See Sect.6, Chap.2, fig.2) and is attached to the front
spar by means of two pairs of feet situated along the upper and
lower rear edges of the tank;   insulation against vibration is
similar to that used with the main fuel tanks in the centre section.
At the top and bottom, the tank skin projects rearwards beyond the
rear tank wall;   the upper edge meets the forward edge of the outer
cover over the port main fuel tank and is screwed to the cover,

whilst the lower edge engages with a fairing strip beneath the spar.
The flanges of the inner and outer end walls of the tank project
sufficiently beyond the tank skin to provide seatings for the leading
edge fillet and the gap fairing between the centre section and the
port outer plane. The tank when filled contains 7½ gallons of oil,
leaving 3 gallons air space. An oil cooler of increased cooling
area and a differently-graduated viscosity valve are fitted when
the aeroplane is equipped for tropical use.

15. <u>Oil tank</u>.- The tank (<u>see</u> fig.5) is constructed from
duralumin sheet to the profile of the centre section leading edge
at its point of attachment. Two baffles are fitted within the
tank parallel to the centre line of the aeroplane. The outboard
baffle has seven flanged holes approximately evenly spaced; the
inboard baffle has two oval-shaped holes, placed approximately one-
third of the depth of the tank from the top, and is drilled along
the bottom edge with thirteen holes of small diameter. The enclosed
portion between the inboard baffle and the inboard end of the tank
acts when necessary as a partial-circulation chamber for quick
warming of the oil and is of approximately 1¼ gallons capacity.

16. The filler neck, situated centrally in the inboard wall,
is fitted with a screwed cap which is retained against loss by a
short length of chain attached to an internal C-spring; on early
aeroplanes, the filler cap has a deep slot to facilitate its fitting
and removal but, in later aeroplanes, a lugged filler cap is provided.
Access to the filler cap is obtained through a door in the port leading edge fillet between the centre section and the fuselage; the
door is attached with four fasteners and, as a precaution against
its loss, it is secured internally with a length of balloon cord.
The oil inlet and outlet connections are situated in the inboard
wall of the tank, the former at the top; internally, the inlet
connection is extended forward by a short tube with a flared end,
whilst the outlet connection is continued by a plain tube pointing
downwards. The oil inlet connection is incorporated with the
filler neck in an oval-shaped plate which may be removed for cleaning
and inspection of the interior of the tank; for the same purpose,
a circular handhole is provided in the outboard wall. The vent
pipe connection is near the top of the rear wall about half-way
along the length of the tank, and below it, in the bottom rear edge
of the tank, a drainage connection is fitted; the drainage connection
incorporates a screw cock.

17. <u>Oil cooler</u>.- This cooler is of box form, and is housed
between the two halves of the coolant radiator; the top is
constructed of sheet brass whilst the bottom portion, comprising
longitudinal sides and base, is constructed of cupro-nickel.
Baffles (also of cupro-nickel) are so arranged as to divide the
cooler into two longitudinal chambers and to sub-divide each chamber
into three tiered galleries. Ports in the alternate ends of the
horizontal baffles provide means of inter-gallery communication,
inter-chamber communicating ports being provided at the front end
of the longitudinal vertical baffle in the bottom gallery.

F.S./6

18. The oil inlet and outlet branches are mounted at the top of the cooler, the inlet branch communicating with the starboard and the outlet branch communicating with the port longitudinal chamber. In each gallery is housed a bank of honeycomb radiator tubes around which the oil flows, the inlet oil flowing forward along the starboard top gallery, aft along the centre gallery and then forward again along the starboard bottom gallery. At the forward end of the starboard bottom gallery, the oil passes into the port bottom gallery from which, in a reverse sequence of flow direction, it is led to the oil outlet at the rear of the port top gallery. A drain plug, with its mounting communicating with both port and starboard bottom galleries, projects through the inter-communicating channel at the bottom of the coolant radiator (see para.35).

19. **Viscosity valve.-** This valve (see fig.6) comprises a cylindrical casting (M) in which are three chambers (H), (L) and (E), the chamber (E) being provided with inlet and outlet branches, the chamber (L) with an inlet branch, and the chamber (H) with an outlet branch. Between chambers (L) and (E) is a spring-loaded by-pass valve, and between chambers (L) and (H) is a valve of complex design, the operation of which is entirely dependent on the degree of viscosity of the circulating oil.

20. Oil from the engine enters the chamber (H) and according to its degree of viscosity passes through the appropriate valve either into the chamber (E) and thence to the oil tank, or into the chamber (L) and thence to the oil cooler. The oil from the cooler passes directly through the chamber (E) back to the oil tank.

21. A portion of the oil from the engine passes from chamber (H) through a small filter (G) and thence through a small orifice in the plate (J) into the interior of the bellows (C). The oil then passes through a number of small-bore passages (N) into the annular space in the end of the valve, whence it passes through the communicating passage (F) into the chamber (E) (which is approximately at atmospheric pressure) and thence to the oil tank.

22. When the oil is cold and/or viscid, it passes through the orifice in the plate (J) but does not readily pass through the small-bore passages (N), thereby automatically setting up a pressure within the bellows. When this pressure, in conjunction with that exerted by the spring (B), exceeds the pressure exerted by the spring (D), the by-pass valve (A) is lifted from its seating and the oil is by-passed to the tank without passing through the cooler.

23. When the oil has dropped below the required degree of viscosity, the free flow through the small-bore passages prevents the building up of any pressure within the bellows, with the result that the valve (K) is lifted from its seating and the oil flows into chamber (L) and thence to the oil cooler. From the cooler, the oil passes into one side of chamber (E) and out through the other side to the oil tank.

24. Due to the changes of viscosity being necessarily gradual, the action of the valve (K) is gradual. The load of the spring (B) is regulated and set so that the oil from the engine is automatically

by-passed to the tank or directed through the cooler. Should
failure occur of any part of valve (K), oil is automatically directed
through the cooler.

25. Oil filter.- This filter (see fig.7) is mounted on the
front face and to the starboard side of the fireproof bulkhead.
The cylindrical filter body has an upper branch for the inlet and
a lower branch for the outlet connections, a drain plug being
incorporated at its lower end; two locating shoulders are provided
to receive the securing cap. A gauze-covered filter element is
retained within the body by a retaining spring, a sealing cap
and a securing cap fitted with an adjusting screw.

26. Pipe-lines.- The oil system installation is shown in
fig.4 and a diagrammatic arrangement is given in Sect.3. From the
outlet connection on the inboard wall of the tank, a pipe is taken
through a gland in a small bulkhead fitted in the port leading edge
fillet to the upper inlet connection of the oil filter, mounted on
the front face of the fireproof bulkhead on the starboard side;
from the lower connection on the filter a flexible pipe runs to
the inlet connection of the engine oil pump. From the engine
outlet connection, a small flexible pipe connects with a pipe leading
to a double-ended union fitted in the fireproof bulkhead on the
port side just above the centre section spar. From the rear face
of the fireproof bulkhead, a pipe is taken along the port side of
the fuselage to the viscosity valve mounted on fuselage strut FH1;
the pipe is supported on fuselage side struts AD and CF.

27. When the oil is of high viscosity, the viscosity valve
by-passes the oil back to the oil tank thus short-circuiting the
oil cooler; the oil cooler is incorporated in the centre of the
radiator beneath the fuselage and is connected to the viscosity
valve by two short pipes. When the oil has reached a suitable
viscosity, the valve causes the oil to flow through the oil cooler
before returning to the oil tank. From the viscosity valve,
the oil is returned to the oil tank through two lengths of pipe
joined together by a union fitted in the fireproof bulkhead.
From the viscosity valve to the bulkhead, the return pipe is
carried in the same support brackets as the delivery pipe; the
return pipe from the front face of the fireproof bulkhead is
joined, through a gland in the port leading-edge bulkhead, to the
inlet connection of the oil tank.

28. From the vent connection in the upper edge of the oil
tank, a vent pipe is taken through a gland in the port leading-
edge bulkhead and continues along the front side of the centre section
front spar to the crankcase breather on the starboard side of the
engine. The vent pipe is in four sections joined by means of
rubber hose connections secured with jubilee clips; a T-piece is
incorporated between the two sections nearest the engine to provide
a connection for the vacuum pump installation (see Sect.10). The
oil pressure gauge on the starboard side of the instrument panel
is joined by a capillary tube to a banjo fitting on the engine,

F.S./6

whilst a similar tube connects the thermometer bottle on the engine
with the oil temperature gauge, situated on the instrument panel
beneath the oil pressure gauge.

Cooling system

29.   The engine is cooled with ethylene glycol which is passed
around the cooling system (see fig.8) by means of a centrifugal
pump driven from the base of the engine wheelcase.   From the
engine, the coolant is passed through two outlets to the header
tank mounted on the front face of the fireproof bulkhead, and
thence aft to the radiator situated beneath the fuselage, whence
it is passed forward to the single inlet connection on the engine
pump.   The cooling system incorporates a thermostat which by-
passes the radiator when the coolant temperature is low.   The
quantity of cooling air passing through the radiator may be
controlled from the cockpit by a flap fitted to the radiator
fairing.   For tropical use, a radiator with increased cooling
area is fitted.

30.   Header tank.-   This tank, constructed from sheet brass
to the shape shown in fig.9, is carried on two brackets on the
front face of the fireproof bulkhead with a single bolt through each
of the four tank feet.   Rubber packings are interposed between
the tank feet and the brackets, and between the brackets and the
bolt heads to provide insulation against vibration.

31.   Two baffles are fitted across the tank in line with the
centre line of the aeroplane and extend from the bottom of the
tank up to the normal level of the coolant; the baffles are
provided with six flanged holes of varying diameter.   The heated
coolant from the engine is passed into the tank through two inlet
connections riveted through flanged spools into the front face of
the tank; the conical sump is bolted into the bottom surface of
the tank and itself provides the outlet connection.   The pipes
forming the inlet connections are continued internally to the
centre of the tank where they are bent to run upwards towards the
top; near the top they are bent outwards and their upper sides
riveted to the top surface.   A slightly smaller-sectioned pipe
is brazed into each inlet pipe where it is bent upwards, the
smaller pipes projecting downwards into the top of the tank sump.

32.   The tank is normally only filled to half its total
volume, i.e. 4 gallons.   When the coolant is cold it flows
through the smaller-sectioned pipes into the sump and out through
the connection at the bottom, thus mixing with the minimum of cold
coolant and providing rapid warming-up of the engine; under
cruising conditions, the same direction of flow obtains.   Under
high-power running, the rate of flow is increased and a certain
amount of steam is generated; in consequence, the steam (and some
of the coolant) passes up the vertical pipes and is sprayed from
their upper ends into the colder coolant on the outer sides of the
baffles.   Thus the steam is separated from the liquid coolant and
condensed by the colder coolant outside the baffles; the hot

coolant which has passed up the pipes is thereby mixed with the colder coolant and, draining through the holes in the baffles, passes into the sump and out at the outlet connection.

33.   The filler neck, fitted with a screwed filler cap and retaining chain, is situated in the starboard side of the tank; access to the filler cap is obtained through the forward and lower of the two doors in the top rear cowling panel on the starboard side. A vent pipe, connected into the tank through a relief valve situated approximately in the centre of the upper surface of the tank, is taken down the inside of the engine cowling on the starboard side to vent directly to the atmosphere through a rubber connection in the top front corner of the starboard intermediate side panel of the engine cowling.   In the front face of the tank and between the two connections for the return pipes from the engine, a connection for a thermometer bottle is riveted to the tank, a capillary tube being taken from the bottle to the meter on the starboard side of the instrument panel.

34.   Radiator.-   The combined coolant radiator and oil cooler (see fig.8) is suspended beneath the fuselage just aft of the centre section rear spar; at the front it is bolted to brackets on the rear face of the rear spar lower boom and at the rear to brackets on the radiator support tubes which are fitted between fuselage joints H and the lower boom of the centre section rear spar. To protect the radiator from excessive vibration, thick rubber liners are inserted in the attachment bolt housings; the housings are bolted to the attachment brackets which are riveted to the radiator shell at each end of each outboard side. The oil cooler is accommodated between the two halves of the radiator honeycomb, being held in position by two channels on the upper surface which are bolted to small channels on each half of the radiator.

35.   The coolant enters the radiator through a cone-shaped inlet branch fitted to the top surface of the upper half-honeycomb; the inlet branch is fitted internally with two vanes to spread the flow of the coolant.   After passing down through the upper half-honeycomb, the coolant is taken across the bottom of the radiator beneath the oil cooler and continues up through the starboard half-honeycomb to the outlet connection; the outlet connection is of similar construction to the inlet connection, less the flow vanes. A baffle is fitted across each half-honeycomb in line with the centre line of the aeroplane and immediately beneath the centre line of the inlet and outlet branches.   A drain plug is fitted into the undersurface of the radiator beneath the oil cooler, just in front of the drain plug for the oil cooler.

36.   Radiator flap control.-   The radiator is enclosed in a tunnel-type fairing beneath the fuselage, the quantity of air passing through the radiator being controlled by a flap, hinged along its front edge, which forms the rear part of the fairing undersurface.   The flap is operated by two rods (see fig.10),

F.S./7

the upper ends of which are adjustable and attached to levers
mounted on each end of a countershaft.   The countershaft is
supported at each end by a bearing, just inboard of the levers,
secured to the lower longeron FH, port and starboard; at its port
end, the countershaft carries another lever, the upper end of which
is connected by a tube of fixed length to the lower end of the
control hand lever mounted in the cockpit.   The control hand
lever is mounted on the port side of the pilot's seat between
quadrant plates bracketed to fuselage cross strut FC.FC and is
supported by a stay tube from port joint F.   The hand lever may
be set in any one of nine positions by depressing a knob at the
top of the handle, moving the handle to the required position and
releasing the knob; the knob is spring-loaded internally and
operates a catch pin engaging with the notches in the quadrant
plates.

37.   Just inboard of the port bearing, the countershaft carries
a small lever, the upper end of which is connected through a bowden
cable with a flap position indicator mounted on port strut CF1; the
indicator is calibrated to show "degrees of flap movement"

38.   **Pipe-lines.-** The outlet pipe from the header tank sump
(**see** fig.8) runs to starboard and then down almost to the bottom
of the fireproof bulkhead, where it is joined to another length of
pipe which passes rearwards through a gland in the bulkhead; the
pipe continues along the starboard side of the fuselage beneath
the plane-to-fuselage fairing fillet and is clipped to fuselage side
strut CF.   Just aft of joint F, the pipe is joined to a short length
of pipe the aft end of which is coupled to the thermostat bracketed
to fuselage side strut FC.H.   Two pipes run from the thermostat,
one continuing aft and then forwards to the starboard inlet branch
to the radiator and the other passing across the fuselage to the
return pipe from the radiator.   The former pipe is in two parts
coupled together at its aft extremity and is clipped to fuselage
cross strut HH between the coupling and the radiator, whilst the
latter pipe is coupled to a T-joint in the return pipe from the
radiator.

39.   From the port branch connection on the radiator, the return
pipe-line is taken along the centre line of the aeroplane, through
a gland in the web of the centre section rear spar, to a clip on
fuselage cross strut DD and then to port through a gland in the web
of the centre section front spar.   A separate length of pipe is
used between the spars and through the front spar, the joints in
the pipe-line being adjacent to each spar; a vent plug is fitted
between the clip on fuselage cross strut DD and the front joint.
From the joint just in front of the centre section front spar, a
short length of pipe connects directly with the centrifugal pump
on the engine.   After the coolant has been pumped around the
engine, it is returned through two parallel pipes into the front
face of the header tank.   All pipe connections in the cooling
system are made by rubber hose secured with jubilee clips, each
connection being electrically bonded.

Thermostat

40.   The thermostat serves to decrease the time taken in warming-up the engine by returning the coolant through the by-pass directly back to the engine until such time as the coolant has reached a temperature necessitating the use of the radiator; it also prevents cavitation in the engine pump due to increased flow resistance of the radiator when the coolant is cold.

Ignition system

41.   The diagram of the ignition system (see fig.11) shows the connections between the main magnetos, the starting magneto and the control switches; for the operation of the system and the connections between the magnetos and the distributors, reference should be made to A.P.1590B, Vol.I.   The starting magneto is mounted on the starboard engine mounting strut XZ.

Engine controls

42.   Throttle and mixture controls.-   These engine controls (see fig.12) are mounted on the port top longeron CE, close to the pilot's left hand.   The longer (inboard) lever is the throttle control and the shorter the mixture control; the levers are moved forward to "open" the throttle and to weaken the mixture.   The knob on the mixture control lever projects in the way of the throttle control lever to ensure that the mixture control is pulled back to RICH on closing the throttle, thus preventing the mixture from being excessively weakened at small throttle openings.

43.   The two levers are mounted outboard of the longeron on concentric spindles, and are retained in any required position by tightening a series of friction discs mounted on the outer spindle. The spindles project inboard below the longeron, the inner being fitted with a knurled cap whilst the outer carries a small wheel just behind the knurled cap.   By turning the knurled cap, the friction on the mixture control lever may be adjusted, the wheel providing a similar adjustment for the throttle control lever.

44.   Below the spindles, a small box contains a micro-switch unit for the undercarriage warning buzzer, the switch being operated by a cam plate pivoting about a pin at the lower rear corner of the box; this cam plate is actuated by a roller mounted on the bolt attaching the throttle control rod fork-end to the throttle lever.

45.   The two control levers project upward through a plate mounted on the decking shelf; adjustable stops are fitted at the forward ends of the paths of travel of the levers.   Pinned to the lower end of each control lever is a fork-end into which is screwed the end of a flexible push-pull member operating in a conduit; the conduit runs forward and downwards along the port side of the fuselage structure, passes through a gland in the fireproof bulkhead and is

P.S./8

then anchored to a bracket on the front face of the fireproof
bulkhead. A rod, attached to the flexible member, emerges from
the conduit at its anchorage and is connected to its appropriate
lever on the engine by means of a fork-end and pin.

46. **Automatic boost control.**- An automatic boost control is
provided to maintain a constant boost pressure without continual
manipulation of the throttle control. In conditions of emergency,
the boost control cut-out may be used to render the automatic boost
control virtually inoperative, thus enabling the throttle to be
fully opened by the cockpit control lever at any altitude; the
cut-out control is located on the port side of the instrument panel.
A boost gauge, connected with the induction manifold, is mounted on
the starboard side of the instrument panel.

Airscrew controls

47. **Two-pitch control.**- The control lever is fitted on the
port side of the decking just above the throttle and mixture controls,
Teleflex conduit and cable being used between the lever and the relief
valve unit incorporated on the starboard side of the engine crankcase.
From the lever, the conduit runs downwards and forwards through a
gland in the fireproof bulkhead, across to starboard and then forward
to terminate in a swivel end on engine mounting strut AZ.

48. **Constant-speed control.**- The control system is similar
to that used for the two-pitch airscrew (**see** para.47) as far as
the front face of the fireproof bulkhead. From the bulkhead, the
conduit is carried forward along the port side of the engine to the
governor unit on the underside of the engine nosepiece, the connection
being made by means of a 180° - wrap box unit.

Hand starting equipment

49. **Two starting handles** are stowed in the wheel recess beneath
the centre section (**see** Sect.6, Chap.1, fig.13), one on each side
wall. In use, the handles are engaged with the ends of a countershaft carried in brackets on the engine mounting struts XZ. A
sprocket at the starboard end of the countershaft is connected, by
means of a chain, with a sprocket on the inboard end of a small
countershaft mounted on the starboard engine mounting strut XY.
The outboard end of this latter countershaft carries a double
sprocket connected, by means of further chains, to the starter
sprocket on the engine and to the starting magneto.

Electrical starting equipment

50. The wiring diagram for the electrical starting system is
given in Sect.5, fig.7, the power for the system being supplied
by the accumulator in the aeroplane except when an external supply
is available. The external supply plug is connected with a socket
in the aeroplane in which is combined an isolating switch for

automatically cutting out the aeroplane accumulator; the cover
over the sockets must be rotated before the plug can be inserted,
the rotation operating a switch which isolates the negative pole
of the aeroplane accumulator.   The combined socket and isolating
switch is situated on the starboard lower strut of the engine
mounting, and is accessible through a door in the engine cowling
(see fig.13); a hook is provided on the door for the attachment
of the lanyard of the ground cable.   When the power supply has
been connected, the engine may be turned by depressing a pressbutton
switch, situated on the port side of the instrument panel;
this switch operates a relay switch, mounted adjacent to the
external supply socket, which in turn operates an electrical
starting motor mounted on the starboard side of the engine wheel
case.

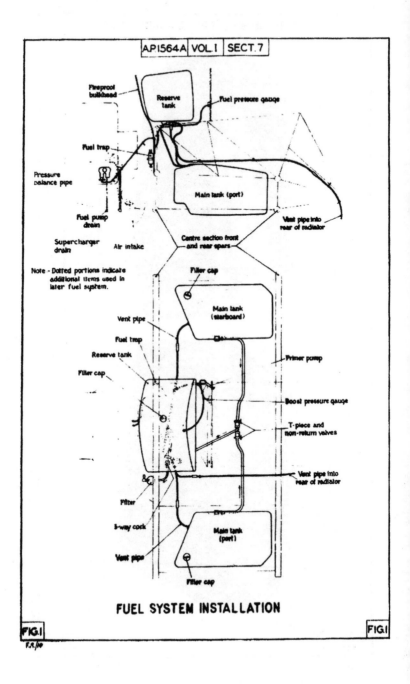

FUEL SYSTEM INSTALLATION

FIG.1
FIG.1

193

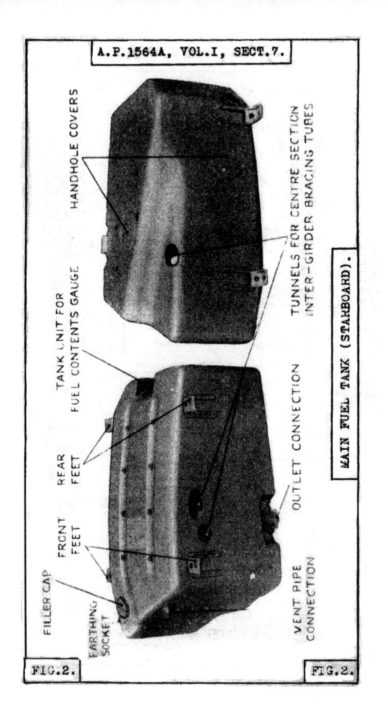

HANDHOLE COVERS

TANK UNIT FOR
FUEL CONTENTS GAUGE

TUNNELS FOR CENTRE SECTION
INTER-GIRDER BRACING TUBES

REAR
FEET

FRONT
FEET

FILLER CAP

EARTHING
SOCKET

OUTLET CONNECTION

VENT PIPE
CONNECTION

MAIN FUEL TANK (STARBOARD).

FIG.2.

FIG.2.

194

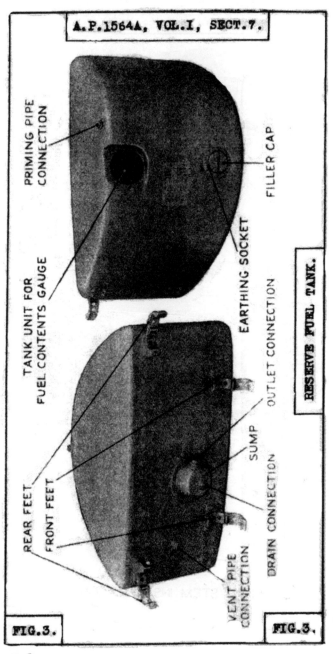

PRIMING PIPE CONNECTION

FILLER CAP

TANK UNIT FOR FUEL CONTENTS GAUGE

EARTHING SOCKET

OUTLET CONNECTION

SUMP

RESERVE FUEL TANK.

REAR FEET

FRONT FEET

DRAIN CONNECTION

VENT PIPE CONNECTION

FIG.3.

FIG.3.

E.S./II.

195

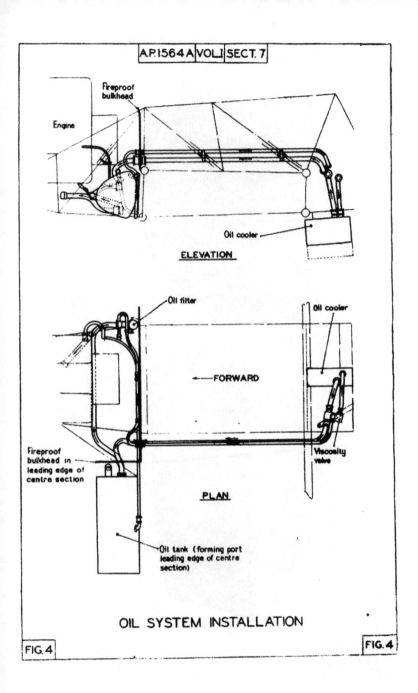

Fireproof bulkhead

Engine

Oil cooler

ELEVATION

Oil filter

Oil cooler

← FORWARD

Fireproof bulkhead in leading edge of centre section

Viscosity valve

PLAN

Oil tank (forming port leading edge of centre section)

OIL SYSTEM INSTALLATION

FIG. 4

FIG. 4

INLET CONNECTION

EARTHING SOCKET

FILLER NECK

OUTLET CONNECTION

VENT PIPE CONNECTION

TANK FEET

DRAIN CONNECTION

OIL TANK.

FIG.5.

FIG.5,

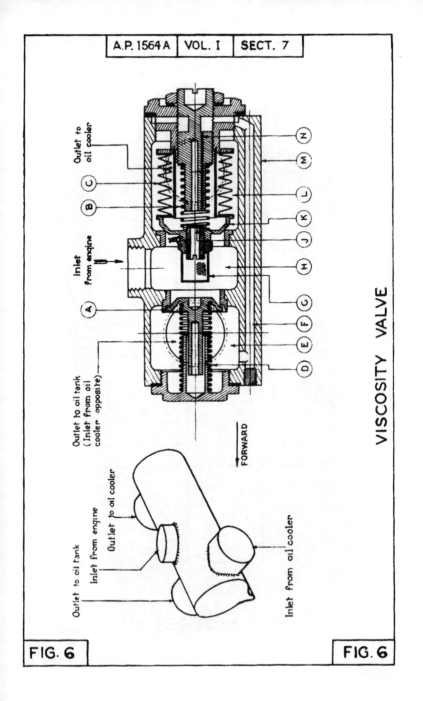

Outlet to oil cooler

Inlet from engine

Outlet to oil tank (Inlet from oil cooler opposite)

FORWARD

VISCOSITY VALVE

Outlet to oil tank

Inlet from engine

Outlet to oil cooler

Inlet from oil cooler

FIG. 6

FIG. 6

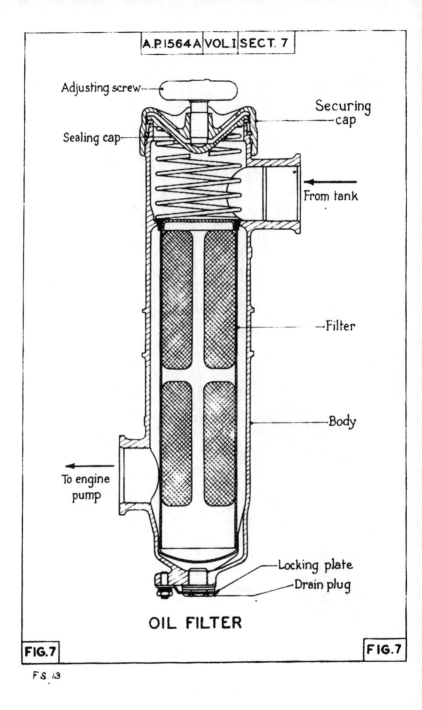

OIL FILTER

FIG.7

FIG.7

F.S. 13

199

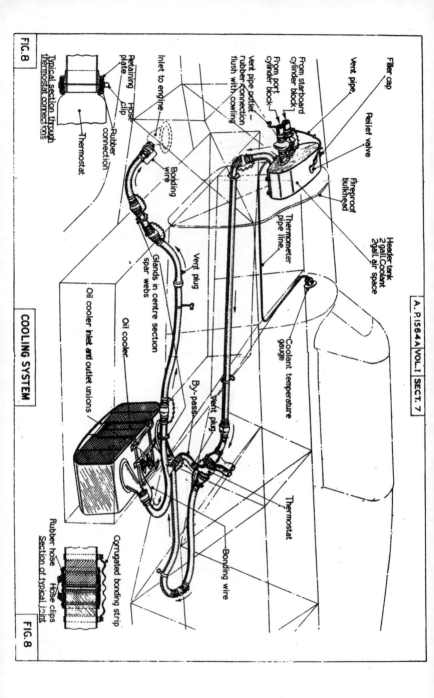

FIG.8

FIG.8

COOLING SYSTEM

Filler cap

Vent pipe

Relief valve

Header tank
2 gall.Coolant
2 gall.air space

From starboard
cylinder block

From port
cylinder block

Fireproof
bulkhead

Vent pipe outlet —
rubber connection —
flush with cowling

Thermometer
pipe line

Inlet to engine

Coolant temperature
gauge

Retaining
plate

Hose
clip

Bonding
wire

Rubber
connection

Thermostat

Vent plug

Glands in centre
section spar webs

Oil cooler

By-pass

Vent plug

Oil cooler inlet and outlet unions

Thermostat

Bonding wire

Typical section through
thermostat connections

Rubber hose
Hose clips
Section of typical joint

Corrugated bonding strip

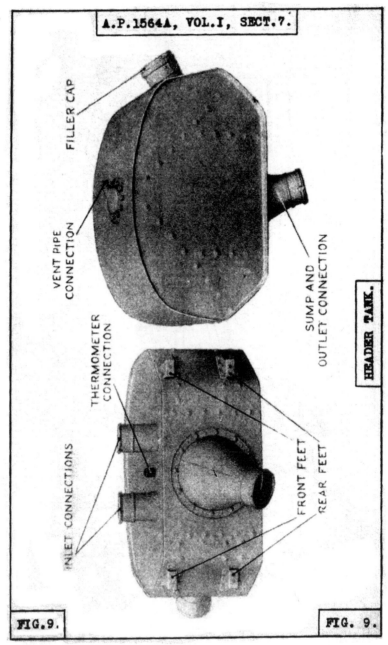

FILLER CAP

VENT PIPE CONNECTION

SUMP AND OUTLET CONNECTION

THERMOMETER CONNECTION

INLET CONNECTIONS

FRONT FEET

REAR FEET

HEADER TANK.

FIG. 9.

FIG. 9.

F.S./14.

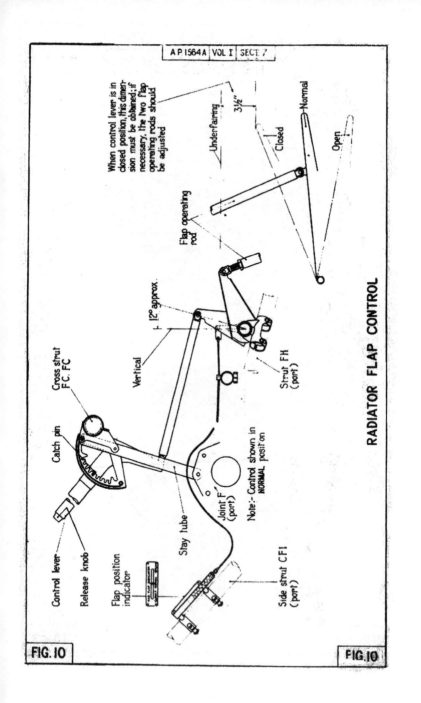

When control lever is in closed position, this dimension must be obtained; if necessary, the two flap operating rods should be adjusted

Underfairing

3½"

Closed

Normal

Open

Flap operating rod

12° approx.

Vertical

Strut FH (port)

Cross strut F.C. FC

Catch pin

Control lever

Release knob

Flap position indicator

Stay tube

Joint F (port)

Note:- Control shown in NORMAL position

Side strut CF1 (port)

RADIATOR FLAP CONTROL

FIG. 10

FIG.10

202

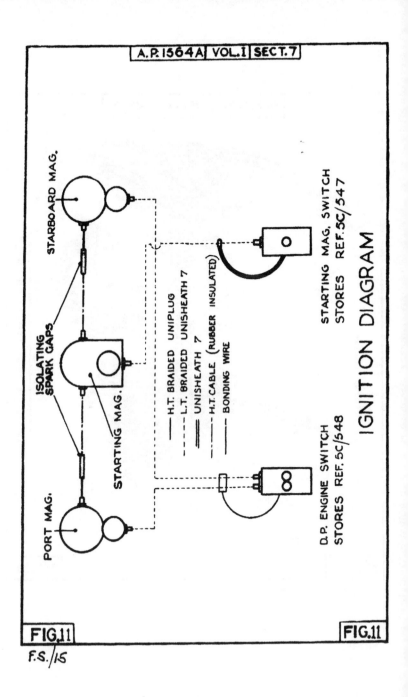

IGNITION DIAGRAM

STARBOARD MAG.

STARTING MAG.

ISOLATING SPARK GAPS

PORT MAG.

STARTING MAG. SWITCH
STORES REF.5C/547

D.P. ENGINE SWITCH
STORES REF.5C/548

—— H.T. BRAIDED UNIPLUG
----- L.T. BRAIDED UNISHEATH 7
▬▬ UNISHEATH 7
—·— H.T. CABLE (RUBBER INSULATED)
——— BONDING WIRE

FIG.11

FIG.11

F.S./15

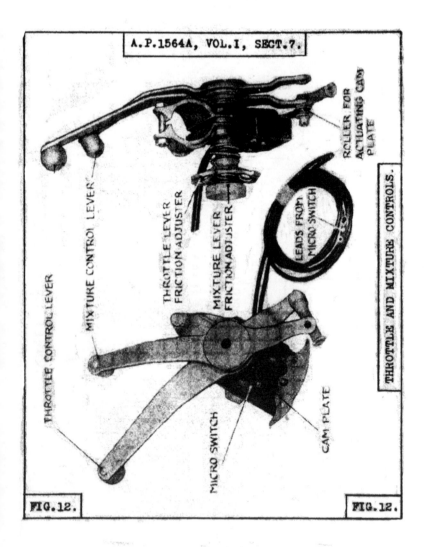

ROLLER FOR ACTUATING CAM PLATE

LEADS FROM MICRO SWITCH

THROTTLE LEVER FRICTION ADJUSTER

MIXTURE LEVER FRICTION ADJUSTER

MIXTURE CONTROL LEVER

THROTTLE CONTROL LEVER

MICRO SWITCH

CAM PLATE

THROTTLE AND MIXTURE CONTROLS.

FIG.12.

FIG.12.

204

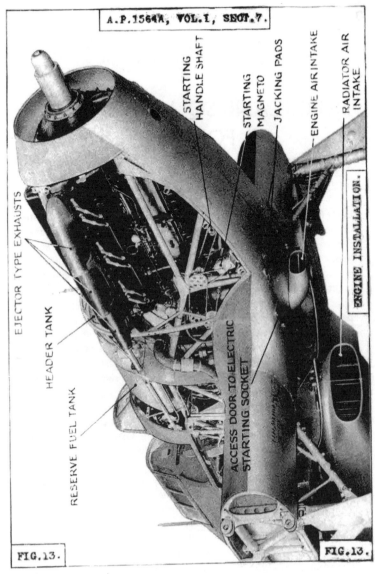

STARTING HANDLE SHAFT

STARTING MAGNETO

JACKING PADS

ENGINE AIR INTAKE

RADIATOR AIR INTAKE

EJECTOR TYPE EXHAUSTS

HEADER TANK

RESERVE FUEL TANK

ACCESS DOOR TO ELECTRIC STARTING SOCKET

ENGINE INSTALLATION.

FIG.13.

FIG.13.

4

HURRICANE SQUADRON DIARY: FORM 540

Every RAF squadron during the Second World War recorded its activities in the 'Operations Record Book' (ORB). This is essentially a diary in two parts: the 'Summary of Events' or 'Form 540', and the 'Detail of Work Carried Out' or 'Form 541'. These records provide historians with essential information – but unfortunately their detail and quality is often inconsistent. The ORB was generally completed by or at the direction of the squadron adjutant, responsible for administration and personnel movements. During the Battle of Britain, of course, squadrons hotly engaged were busy, often far too busy to devote too much time to recording these events; indeed, as the famous Spitfire test pilot Jeffrey Quill once said to me, 'Our minds were not focussed on posterity in 1940!' Nonetheless, most ORBs are packed with clues and information helpful to the would-be researcher.

The following pages are the Form 540s belonging to 242 Squadron for the month of September 1940. This was a Hurricane squadron based in 12 Group, responsible for defending the industrial Midlands and the North, and 11 Group's airfields when Air Vice-Marshal Park's fighters were engaged further forward. This Canadian squadron was commanded, in fact, by none other than the legendary Squadron Leader Douglas Bader – who had lost both legs in a pre-war flying accident. Bader was, of course, a gift to the propagandists of the Ministry Of Information, who widely publicised his inspiring exploits. After the war Bader became a global household name when Paul Brickhill's book Reach for the Sky, concerning his life to date, became a best-seller in 1954, and a box-office hit in the film adaptation in 1956.

During the Battle of Britain, Bader believed that the enemy should be met en masse, not by the 'penny-packet' formations preferred by Air Chief Marshal Dowding, who was desperate to preserve his limited forces. Bader's controversial view, however, was supported by his

Group Commander, Air Vice-Marshal Leigh-Mallory. Consequently on 7 September 1940 – the day on which began the round-the-clock bombing of London, Bader led not one but three squadrons into action for the first time. Thereafter such 'Wing' operations became the common feature of 12 Group patrols, which were more akin to fighter sweeps than controlled interceptions. On 15 September, Bader led a five-squadron wing of sixty fighters into action over London – an incredible sight, heartening the hard-pressed defenders but crushing to the enemy airmen, who believed that Fighter Command was finished. The following pages detail in sum the daily activities of 242 Squadron throughout September 1940. Predictably, the detail is succinct and the drama involved totally understated.

(2043—319) Wt. 42460—3324   21,500   3/39   T.S. 700
(3666—319) Wt. 29760—2642   40,000   9/39   T.S. 700

OPERATIONS

*See instructions for use of this form in K.R. and A.C.I.,
para. 2349, and War Manual; Pt. II., chapter XX., and
notes in R.A.F. Pocket Book.*

No.
of (Unit or Formation)..............

Place.	Date.	Time.	
COLTISHALL.	1-9-40.		F/O H.V. SMITH recalled from le:
			as Intelligence Officer.
		X	Squadron carried out Patrols fr
	2-9-40.	O	Operating from DUXFORD over LON!
			P/O E.A. SUMMERS reported for di
	3-9-40.	✓	Squadron Operating COLTISHALL -
			as Flight Commander.
	4-9-40.	✓	Squadron Operating COLTISHALL -
			and attached No. 5 O.T.U.
	5-9-40.	✓	Squadron Operating COLTISHALL -
	6-9-40.	X	Squadron Operating DUXFORD.
	7-9-40.		Operating from DUXFORD. 11 Ene:
			Signals of Congratulation recei
			of State for Air
			P/O BENZIE reported missing, P/(
			maching badly shot up. Pilot r
	8-9-40.		Squadron operating DUXFORD. Se:
			One flight No. 266 Squadron ope:
			Serviced by our personnel.

Summary of Events.	References to Appendices.

ave on posting to No 85; Squadron, KENLEY

om DUXFORD - No combat.

DON - No combat.

uty as Squadron Intelligence Officer.

Patrols. F/O CHRISTIE posted to No. 66 Squadron

Patrols. P/O CRYDERMAN posted No 242 Squadron

Patrols.

ny Aircraft shot down near NORTH WEALD.

ved from Air Officer Commanding and Secretary

) CROWLEY-MILLING crash landed near CHELMSFORD

eported back to DUXFORD for duty.

rvicing Party despatched to DUXFORD.

rating from our Dispersal Point COLTISHALL.

Place.	Date.	Time.	
COLTISHALL.	9-9-40.		Squadron operating DUXFORD; Squa
			Nos. 242, 310 and 19 Squadrons.
			formation of Enemy Aircraft. Bo
			led the attack and shot down 10.
			No. 19 Squadron 2. One pilot of
			(Sergt. LONSDALE) Baled out and
			Congratulations received from Ai
	10-9-40.		Squadron operating COLTISHALL.
	11-9-40.		Squadron Operating COLTISHALL.
	12-9-40.		Squadron operating DUXFORD. Patr
	13-9-40.		Squadron operating DUXFORD. Patr
	14-9-40.		Squadron operating DUXFORD. Patr
	15-9-40.		Squadron Leader BADER awarded D. Squadron operating DUXFORD. Squa
			302, 310 and 611 Squadrons. Comb
			by Squadron. Another combat in
			This brings the total up to 50 s
			F/Lt. POWELL-SHEDDON admitted Ry
			out and shooting down a Dornier
	18-9-40.		Squadron operating from Duxford
			by Squadron Leader BADER DSO. an
			Messages of Congratulations rece
			Chief of the Air Staff.
	19-9-40.		Squadron at DUXFORD. Carried ou
	20-9-40.		Squadron operating DUXFORD. F/L RAUCEBY, LINCS.

Summary of Events.	References to Appendices.

dron Leader BADER leading Wing consisting of

Patrolling over LONDON encountered large

mbers and Fighters. S/Ldr and No. 242 Squadron

No. 310 (Czech) Squadron shot down 7 and

242 Killed (P/O SCLANDERS). One pilot

returned to Squadron next day unhurt.

r Officer Command and Chief of the Air Staff.

Squadron Leader BADER visited A.O.C. Hucknall.

ols over LONDON and NORTH WEALD.

ols over LONDON and NORTH WEALD.

ols over LONDON and NORTH WEALD.
3.0. F/Lieut. BALL awarded D.F.C.
iron leading Wing composed of Nos. 242, 19,

at over LONDON in morning. 6 Enemy Aircraft shot down.

afternoon. 5 enemy aircraft shot down.

not down since Squadron returned from FRANCE.

e Hospital with dislocated shoulder after baling

and disabling another.

shot down 12 enemy bombers - 12 Group Wing led

l 242 Squadron accounted for

lved from Secretary of State for Air and

; Patrols - No combat - bad weather.

;. POWELL-SHEDDON admitted R.A.F. Hospital

(2043—319) Wt. 42460—3324 21,500 3/39 T.S. **700**
(3666—319) Wt. 29760—2642 40,000 9/39 T.S. **700**

OPERATIONS

*See instructions for use of this form in K.R. and A.C.I.,
para. 2349, and War Manual, Pt. II., chapter XX., and
notes in R.A.F. Pocket Book.*

No.

of (Unit or Formation)...............

Place.	Date.	Time.	
COLTISHALL.	21-9-40.		Squadron went to DUXFORD mid-day
			Two officers P/O DIBNAH and P/O
			NORTHOLT for Flying Duties and S
			Squadron DIGBY.
	22-9-40.		Squadron operating Duxford. Patr
	23-9-40.		Squadron operating Duxford. Patr
			Duty Squadron for week ending 29
	24-9-40.		Squadron operating Duxford. Patr
			Sub. Lt. CORK awarded D.F.C.
	25-9-40.		Squadron available COLTISHALL al
			weather conditions.
	26-9-40.		Squadron available COLTISHALL al
			weather conditions.
			P/O CHYDERMAN reported for duty
	27-9-40.		Squadron operating from DUXFORD
			between CANTERBURY and DOVER. 4
			and 2 Probable J.U. 88's. P/O H
			at MANSTON.
			A/F/Lt, TURNER and P/O STANSFIEL
			Bar to D.F.C.
	28-9-40.		Squadron operating DUXFORD - Pat

RECORD BOOK

R.A.F. Form 540

242 Squadron.

Summary of Events.	References to Appendices.

.

HOMER posted to Squadron from No. 1 Squadron

ergt. Pilot SAVILL, J.E. posted from No. 151

ols carried out with 12 Group Wing but no combat.

ols carried out with 12 Group Wing but no combat.

-9-40.

ols carried out with 12 Group Wing but no combat.

1 day. Unable to go to Duxford owing to bad

1 day. Unable to go to DUXFORD owing to bad

from No. 5 O.T.U. ASTON DOWN.

- Engagement with enemy aircraft (109's)

M.E. 109's shot down; 1 M.E. 109 damaged

OMER reported missing. F/Lt. BALL came down

D awarded D.F.C. and P/O McKNIGHT awarded

rols over SOUTH LONDON, no combat.

Place.	Date.	Time.	
COLTISHALL.	29-9-40.		Bad weather conditions - Squadron
			P/O STANSFIELD posted to No. 229
	30-9-40.		Squadronntook off for DUXFORD 123
			No combat with enemy. Returned to

Summary of Events.	References to Appendices.
available COLTISHALL all day.	
Squadron as Flight Commander.	
0 hours. 12 Group Wing Patrol over LONDON.	
COLTISHALL 1900 hours.	

5

HURRICANE SQUADRON DIARY: FORM 541

The ORB's other form, the 541, is really a squadron logbook, detailing the individual flights of specific aircraft and pilots. Whereas the Form 540 includes diverse information, including postings and other movements, the 541 concentrates exclusively on flying. The following pages are 242 Squadron's Form 541s covering the period 5 September–25 September 1940.

Aircraft Type and No.	Crew.		Duty.	Time Up.	Time Down.
Hurricane.					
P.3048.	F/Lt.	Ball.	Patrol.	0945	1000
P.2961.	P/O.	Brown.	"	"	"
P.3207.	P/O.	Milling.	"	"	"
P.2982.	P/O.	Stansfeld.	"	1055	1205.
P.3715.	P/O.	Campbell.	Patrol	"	"
P.3718.	S/Lt.	Corke.	"	"	"
P.3907.	P/O.	Milling		1145	1205.
P.3087.	P/O.	Brown.	"	"	"
P.2982.	P/O.	Stansfeld.	"	"	"
P.3087.	P/O.	Brown.	"	"	1205.
P.3218.	P/O.	Bush.	"	"	"
P.2884.	S/Lt.	CGardner.	"	"	"
P.3864.	P/O.	Hart.	"	"	"
P.3087.	S/Lt.	Cork.	"	1735.	1825.
V.7203.	P/O.	Latta.	"	0705	0730.
P.3218.	F/Lt.	Powell-Shedden.	"	"	"
P.2967.	P/O.	Sclanders.		"	"
P.3485.	P/O.	Turner.	to Duxford.	0740.	0810.
P.2884.	S/Lt.	Gardner.	"	"	"
P.3054.	P/O.	Bush.	"	"	"
P.4115.	P/O.	Hart.	"	"	"
P.2967.	P/O.	Sclanders.	"	"	"
P.3218.	F/Lt.	Powell-Shedden	"	"	"
V.7203.	P/O.	Latta.	"	"	"
P.3061	S/Ldr.	Bader.	"	"	"
P.3048.	F/Lt.	Ball.	"	"	"
P.2961.	P/O.	MacKnight.	"	"	"
P.3718.	Sgt.	Brimble.	"	"	"
P.3207.	P/O.	Benzie.	"	"	"
P.2962.	P/O.	Brown.	"	"	"
P.3715.	P/O.	Stansfeld.	"	"	"
P.3218.	F/Lt.	Powell-Shedden.	"	0915	1005.
R.4115.	P/O.	Hart.	"	"	"
V7203.	P/O.	Latta.	"	"	"
P.2884.	S/Lt.	Gardner.	"	"	"
P.2967.	P/O.	Sclanders.	"	"	"
P.3485.	P/O.	Turner.	"	"	"
P.3054.	P/O.	Bush.	"	"	"
P.3218.	F/Lt.	Powell-Shedden	"	"	"
V.7203.	P/O.	Latta.	"	1300	1420.
P.2884.	S/Lt.	Gardner.	"	"	"
P.2967.	P/O.	Sclanders.	"	"	"
P.3054.	P/O.	Bush.	"	"	"
R.4115.	P/O.	Hart.	B	"	"

Details of Sortie or Flight.	References.
5th September, XXXX,1940.	

Patrol NORWICH at 15000 ft.   Nothing to report.
visibility fair.

Patrol NORWICH at 15000ft.   No E/A sighted.

Orbit base 20m000 feet, No enemy aircraft sighted.

Aircraft took off on patrol.   Nothing to report.
    6th September, 1940.

Patrol base, weather cloudy, nothing to report.

to operate from DUXFORD.

Patrol North WEALD

Operating from DUXFORD.

Operating from DUXFORD.

DETAIL OF WORK C/

From 1745 hrs. 6 / 9 / 40 to 1120 hrs. 10 / 9 40   By 242 Squadron, Col

Aircraft Type and No.	Crew.	Duty.	Time Up.	Time Down.	
Hurricane.					
P.3218.	F/Lt. Powell-Shedden	Patrol	1745	1905	Patrol North W
V.7203.	P/O. Latta.	"	"	"	visibility.
V.2884.	S/Lt. Gardner.	"	"	"	
P.2967	P/O. Sclanders.	"	"	"	
P.3485.	P/O. Turner.	"	"	"	
P.3054.	P/O. Bush.	"	"	"	
R4115.	P/O. Hart.	"	"	"	Patrol from D
P.3218.	F/Lt. Powell-Shedden	"	"	"	"
V.7203.	P/O. Latta.	"	1940	2010.	Patrol from D
P.2884.	B/Lt. Gardner.	"	"	"	
P.2967.	P/O. Sclanders.	"	"	"	
P.3485.	P/O. Turner.	"	"	"	
P.3054.	P/O. Bush.	"	"	"	
					7th Se
P.3218.	F/Lt. Powell-Shedden	"	0545	0605.	Aircraft took
V.7205.	P/O. Tamblyn.	"	"	"	nothing to re
P.3218.	F/Lt. Powell-Shedden		0700	0735.	Aircraft took
V.7205.	P/O. Tamblyn.	"	"	"	
P.3054.	P/O. Bush.	"	"	"	
P.5090.	P/O. Turner.	"	"	"	
P.2884.	S/Lt. Gardner.	"	"	"	
P.2967.	Sgt. Richardson.	"	"	"	
P.3087.	P/O. Latta.	"	"	"	
P.3207.	S/Lt. Cork.	patrol	1030	1130	Aircraft took
P.3081.	S/Ldr. Bader.	"	"	"	no enemy airc
P.3715.	P/O. Stansfeld.	"	"	"	
P.2982	P/O. Milling.	"	"	"	
P.3718.	Sgt. Longsdale.	"	"	"	
P.2967.	Sgt. Richardson.	"	1630	1820	Operating fro
P.3087.	P/O. Latta.	"	"	"	
P.3218.	F/Lt. Powell-Shedden	"	"	"	
P.5090.	P/O. Turner.	"	"	"	
P.5054.	P/O. Bush.	"	"	"	
V.7205.	P/O. Tamblyn.	"	"	"	
P.2884.	S/Lt. Gardner.	"	"	"	
P.3087.	P/O. Latta.	return	1900	1935	Aircraft retur
V.7205.	P/O. Tamblyn.	"	"	"	
P.2884.	S/Lt. Gardner.	"	"	"	

ARRIED OUT.

[t.ishall........   No. of pages used for day.........................

Remarks.	References.
veald. Weather conditions good, with good No enemy aircraft sighted, or incidents to report.	
uxford, return to base.	
uxford, return to base.	
ptember, 1940. off on patrol, patrolled DEBDEN. Vis good, port, or enemy aircraft sighted. off for operating at DUXFORD.	
	P/o Benzie K/A
off to patrol DEBDEN at 15000 feet, raft sighted, or incidents to report.	
m DUXFORD.	
rned to Base from DUXFORD.	

Aircraft Type and No.		Crew.	Duty.	Time Up.	Time Down.	
Hurricane						
P.3218.	F/Lt.	Powell-Shedden	return	1915	1950.	Aircraft retur
P.3090.	P/O.	Turner.	"	"	"	
P.3054.	P/O.	Bush.	"	"	"	
P.2907.	Sgt.	Richardson.	"	"	"	
P.3207.	S/Lt.	Cork.	Patrol	1630	1745.	AIRCRAFT took
P.3061.	S/Ldr.	Bader.	"	"	"	shot down.
P.3715.	P/O.	Milling.	"	"	"	
P.3718.	Sgt.	Lonsdale.	"	"	"	
P.3048.	F/Lt.	Ball.	"	"	"	one aircraft
						8th Septem
P.3218.	F/Lt.	Powell-Shedden	"	1705	0740.	Aircraft took
P.3090.	S/Lt.	Gardner.	"	"	"	
R.4115.	P/O.	Tamblyn.	"	"	"	
P.4348	P/O.	Turner.	"	"	"	
P.3087.	P/O.	Sclanders.	"	"	"	
P.2967.	Sgt.	Richardson.	"	"	"	
P.3218.	P/O.	Sclanders.	return	1155	1230	Aircraft retur
F.3087.	S/Ldr.	Bader.	"	1840	1915	"
R.4115.	P/O.	Tamblyn.	"	"	"	
P.4348.	P/O.	Turner.	"	"	"	
F.3087.	S/Lt.	Gardner.	"	"	"	
P.2967.	Sgt.	Richardson	"	"	"	
P.3054.	F/Lt.	Powell-Shedden	"	"	"	
						9th Septem
P.3218.	Sgt.	Brimble.	Patrol	0655	0730.	Aircraft took o
R.4115	P/O.	Tamblyn.	Duxford	1800	1825	Operating from
F.3054.	P/O.	Bush.	"	"	"	
P.3218.	F/Lt.	Powell-Shedden	"	1700	1845	
P.3090.	S/Ldr.	Bader.	"	"	1810.	
P.3087.	P/O.	Sclanders.	"	"	"	P/O. Sclanders
P.2967.	Sgt.	Richardson.	"	"	1820	
P.3485.	P/O.	Latta.	"	"	1825.	
P.2961.	P/O.	McKnight.	"	1730	1850	Patrol NORTH W
P.3048.	F/Lt.	Ball.	"	"	"	"
P.2851.	Sgt.	Lonsdale.	"	"	"	Sgt. Lonsdale
P.2982.	P/O.	Brown.	"	"	1815.	
						10th Septemb
P.3054.	P/O.	Bush.	Patrol	0920	0935	Aircraft took
P.3054.	P/O.	Bush.	"	1040	1155	Aircraft patro
R.4115.	P/O.	Tamblyn.	"	"	"	nothing to rep
V.7203.	P/O.	Latta.	"	"	"	
P.3048.	P/O.	Campbell.	"	1035	1055	Orbit base. N
P.2982.	P/O.	McKnight.	"	"	"	
P.3207.	Sgt.	Brimble.	"	1120	1150.	Aircraft patro
P.3048.	P/O.	Campbell.	"	"	"	
P.2982.	P/O.	McKnight.	"	"	"	
P.3207.	Sgt.	Brimble.	"	"	"	

Remarks.	References.

ned from DUXFORD. Nothing to report-vis good

: off to patrol NORTH WEALD. 8 enemy a/c
visibility good.

took off on patrol. Nothing to report.
ber, 1940.
: off for operations at DUXFORD. Vis.Good.

ned to base. No incidents to report.

ber, 1940.

ff on patrol. Nothing to report. Vis good.
Duxford.

 shot down.

ELD. aircraft shot down 4 enemy aircraft.

baled out.   Pilot safe.

er, 1940.
off on patrol.   Nothing to report.
lled between COLTISHALL and NORWICH.
ort. Weather cloudy.

o enemy aircraft sighted.

lled COLTISHALL to NORWICH. Nothing to report.

Aircraft Type and No.	Crew		Duty	Time Up.	Time Down.	
Hurricane.						
V.7467.	S/Ldr.	Bader.	Patrol	1745	1945.	Aircraft
P.3515.	S/Lt.	Cork.	"	"	"	sighted
V.6578.	F/Lt.	Ball.	"	"	"	
P.3048.	P/O.	Milling.	"	"	"	
P.2961.	P/O.	Campbell.	"	"	"	
P.3207.	Sgt.	Brimble.	"	"	"	
V.7467.	S/Ldr.	Bader.	patrol. to Duxford	1125	1255	Patrolle Number n
V.6576.	F/Lt.	Ball.	"	"	"	F/Lt. Ba
P.2 2.	P/O.	Stansfeld.	"	"	"	"
V.t /5.	P/O.	Campbell.	"	"	"	
P.3515.	S/Lt.	Cork.	"	"	"	
P.4355.	P/O.	Turner.	"	"	1300	
V.6578.	F/Lt.	Powell-Shedden	"	"		"
V.7203.	P/O.	Latta.	"	"	"	
P.3054.	P/O.	Hart.	"	"	1255	"
P.2884.	Sgt.	Richardson.	"	"	"	
R.4115.	P/O.	Tamblyn.	"	"		
V.7467.	S/Ldr.	Bader.	"	1430	1525	Patrol c
P.2982.	P/O.	Stansfeld.	"	"	"	visibili
V.6575.	P/O.	Campbell.	"	"	"	
P.3515.	S/Lt.	Cork.	"	"	"	
P.3048.	P/O.	Milling.	"	"	"	
P.2884.	S/Lt.	Powell-Shedden	"	"	"	Aircraft
P.4355.	P/O.	Turner.	"	"	"	
V.7205.	P/O.	Latta.	"	"	1505.	
P.3054.	P/O.	Hart.	"	"	1510.	
V.7467.	S/Ldr.	Bader.	DUXFORD	0810	0925.	Patrolle
B.3048.	F/Lt.	Ball.	"	"	"	weather
P.2982.	P/O.	Stansfeld.	"	"	"	
P.3515.	S/Lt.	Cork.	"	"	"	
P.3718.	Sgt.	Brimble.	"	"	"	
P.3207.	P/O.	Hart.	"	"	"	
V.6575.	P/O.	Milling.	"	"	"	
V.7303.	P/O.	Latta.	"	"	0910.	
R.4115.	P/O.	Tamblyn.	"	"		
P.3218.	S/Lt.	Gardner.	"	"	0925.	
P.2967.	P/O.	Turner.	"	"	"	
P.3218.	P/O.	Turner.	"	1500	1615.	Patroll
P.2967.	S/Lt.	Gardner.	"	"	"	weather
R.4115.	P/O.	Tamblyn.	"	"	"	
V.7203.	P/O.	Latta.	"	"	"	
P.3054.	P/O.	Bush.	"	"	"	
V.6578.	P/O.	Hart.	"	"	"	
V.7467.	S/Ldr.	Bader.	"	1515	1640.	Patrol c
P.2961.	P/O.	McKnight.	"	"	"	
P.3718.	P/O.	Campbell.	"	"	"	

Remarks.	References.

. patrolled NORTHXXX WEALD. No enemy aircraft
or incidents to report. Weather remaining cloudy.

15th September, 1940.

d on the way nto DUXFORD. enemy aircraft shot down,
ot Known. (5 E/A down ?)
11 crashed. landed safely.

arried out enemy machines shot down. No, not known.
ty ggod.

crashed, F/Lt. XXXX Powell-Shedden safe.

16th September, =1940.

i on the way to DUXFORD. Nothing to report,
cloudy.

17th September, 1940.

carried out no enemy droraft encountered.
cloudy. poor visibility.

urried out. Nothing to report or incidents to report.

OPERATIONS REC

DETAIL OF WORK CA

From 1515 hrs 17 / 9 / 40 to 1105 hrs 23 / 9 / 40   By XXX   242 Squadrn.

Aircraft Type and No.	Crew.		Duty.	Time Up.	Time Down.	
Hurricane.						
P.29"?.	P/O.	Brown.	Patrol.	1515	1645.	Patrol. noth in
P.5 5..	P/O.	Milling.	"	"	"	
P.3247.	F/Lt.	Ball.	"	"	"	
						18th Se
V.7467.	S/Ldr.	Bader,	"	0930	1045.	NORTH WEALD pa
P.3048.	F/Lt.	Ball.	"	"	"	
P.2982.	P/O.	Milling,	"	"	"	
P.3718.	Sgt.	Brimble.	"	"	"	
PL3207.	P/O.	Brown,	"	"	"	
V.6575.	P/O.	Campbell.	"	"	"	
P.2961.	P/O.	McKnight.	"	"	X	
V.7467.	S/Ldr.	Bader.	"	1200	1315.	NORTH WEALD pa
P.3048.	F/Lt.	Ball.	"	"	"	
P.2982.	P/O.	Milling.	"	"	"	
P.3718.	Sgt.	Brimble.	"	"	"	
P.3207.	P/O.	Brown.	"	"	"	
V.6575.	P/O.	Campbell.	"	"	"	
P.2961.	P/O.	McKnight.	"	"	"	
V.6575.	S/Lt.	Gardner.	"	1250	1400	Patrolled NORT
P.3215.	P/O.	Hart.	"	"	"	
P.3434.	P/O.	Turner.	"	"	"	
R.411b.	P/O.	Tamblyn.	"	"	"	
V.7205.	Sgt.	Richardson.	"	"	"	
P.3054.	P/O.	Bush.	"	"	"	
V.7467.	S/Ldr.	Bader.	"	1600	1640.	NORTH WEALD pa
P.3048.	F/Lt.	Ball.	"	"	"	
P.2982.	P/O.	Milling.	"	"	"	
P.3718.	Sgt.	Brimble.	"	"	1645.	
P.3207.	P/O.	Brown.	"	"	"	
V.6575.	P/O.	Campbell.	"	"	"	
P.2961.	P/O.	McKnight.	"	"	"	
V.6575.	S/Lt.	Gardner.	"	1615	1750.	Patrol carried
R.411b.	P/O.	Tamblyn.	"	"	1750.	
P.3434.	P/O.	Turner.	"	"	"	
P.3215.	P/O.	Hart.	"	"	"	
P.3054.	P/O.	Bush.	"	"	"	

ORD BOOK.

IRRIED OUT.

..COLTISHALL. No. of pages used for day.......................

Remarks.	References.
ig to report.	
)ptember, 1940.	
.trolled. Nothing to report. vis good.	
.trolled. Nothing to report. vis good.	
H WEALD No enemy aircraft sighted. Vis good.	
trolled eleven enemy aircraft shot down.	
out. No ▮▮▮▮▮ incidents to report.	

Aircraft Type and No.	Crew.		Duty.	Time Up.	Time Down.	
Hurricane						No operational
						20th Se;
P.3034.	P/O.	Turner.	Patrol	1135	1240.	Operating from
P.2306.	B/O.	Hart.	"	"	"	
V.6578.	P/O.	Latta.	"	"	"	
P.3054.	P/O.	Bush.	"	"	"	
V.6740.	S/Lt.	Gardner	"	"	"	
P.2967.	P/O.	McKnight.	"	"	"	
P.3218.	P/O.	Tamblyn.	"	"	"	
V.7467.	S/Ldr.	Bader.	XXXX	1135	1250	Patrol carried
P.3048.	F/Lt.	Ball.	"	"	"	
V.6575.	P/O.	Campbell.	"	"	"	
P.3207.	P/O.	Brown.	"	"	"	
P.37 8.	P/O.	Milling.	"	"	"	
			"			21st
V.6578	Sgt.	Richardson.	"	1810	1925	Aircraft took
P.3034.	P/O.	Turner.	"	"	"	weather cloudy
R.4115.	P/O.	Tamblyn.	"	"	"	
V.6740.	S/Lt.	Gardner.	"	"	"	
P.3054.	P/O.	Bush.	"	"	"	
V.7205	P/O.	Latta.	"	"	"	
						22nd S
V.7467.	S/Ldr.	Bader.	Patrol	1030	1100	Aircraft took
V.6578.	F/Lt.	Ball.	" "	"	" "	to report.
P.2982.	P/O.	Stansfeld.	"	"	"	
V.6575.	P/O.	Campbell.	"	"	"	
P.3515.	S/Lt.	Cork.	"	"	"	
V.6540.	S/Lt.	Gardner.	"	1040	1115	Too operated fro
P.3034.	P/O.	Turner.	"	"	"	
V.6578.	Sgt.	Richardson.	"	"	"	
V.7203.	P/O.	Latta.	"	"	"	
R.4115.	P/O.	Tamblyn.	"	"	"	
P.3060.	P/O.	Bush.	"	"	"	
						23rd Se
P.2982.	P/O.	Stansfeld.	"	0940	1105.	Operating from
V.7467.	S/Lr	Bader.	"	"	"	aircraft sight
P.3515.	S/Lt.	Cork.	"	"	"	
V.6575.	P/O.	Campbell	"	"	"	
V.6576.	F/Lt.	Ball.	"	"	"	
P.3207.	P/O.	Brown.	"	"	"	
P.3054.	P/O.	Bush.	"	"	1105	
V.7203.	P/O.	Latta.	"	"	"	
P.3034.	P/O.	Turner.	"	"	"	
V.6740.	S/Lt.	Gardner.	"	"	"	
V.6578.	Sgt.	Richardson.	"	"	"	
R.4115.	P/O.	Tamblyn.	"	"	"	

Remarks.	References.

flying. carried out on 19th Sept.1940.

ptember, 1940.

DUXFORD. Nothing to report. weather cloudy.

out. Nothing to report.

September, 1940.

off on patrol, Nothing to report.
r.

eptember, 1940.

off on patrol on way to DUXFORD. No incidents.

m DUXFORD. weather cloudy..

ptember, 1940.

DUXFORD. Nothing to report, no enemy
ed. Weather cloudy, with poor visibility.

OPERATIONS REC

DETAIL OF WORK C/

From 0820 hrs 24 /.9 / 40 to 0955 hrs. 28 /9 40.   By No. 242 Squadron,

Aircraft Type and No.	Crew.		Duty.	Time Up.	Time Down.	
Hurricane,						
V. 7.67.	S/Ldr.	Bader.	patrol	0820	0955.	To DUXFORD for
P. 3058.	P/O.	Milling.	"	"	"	to report. Vi:
V. 6576.	F/Lt.	Ball.	"	"	"	
P. 3467.	P/O.	McKnight.	"	"	0945.	
P. 3207.	P/O.	Brown.	"	"	0955	
V. 6575.	P/O.	Campbell.	"	— "	0910.	
V. 7467.	S/Ldr.	Bader.	"	1145	1245.	Patrolled DUXF(
P. 3048.	P/O.	Milling.	"	"	"	
V. 6576.	F/Lt.	Ball.	"	"	"	Patrolled NORTH
P. 3467.	P/O.	McKnight.	"	"	"	
P. 3207.	P/O.	Brown.	"	"	"	
V. 6575.	P/O.	Campbell.	"	"	"	
R. 2967.	Sgt.	Saville.	"	"	"	
P. 3034.	P/O.	Turner.	"	"	"	
P. 2806.	P/O.	Hart.	"	"	"	
V. 7640.	S/Lt.	Gardner.	"	"	"	
V. 7205.	P/O.	Homer.	"	"	"	
R. 4115.	P/O.	Tamblyn.	"	"	"	
						25th Se⌐
						No operational
						26th Sep
						No operational
						27th Sep
P. 3034.	P/O.	Turner	"	0925	1050.	Operating from
P. 2806.	P/O.	Hart.	"	"	"	
R. 4115.	P/O.	Tamblyn.	"	"	"	
V. 7205.	P/O.	Latta.	"	"	"	
R. 3054.	P/O.	Bush.	"	"	"	
P. 2967.	P/O.	Homer.	"	"	"	

ORD BOOK.

___

RRIED OUT.

Coltishall.   No. of pages used for day.........................

Remarks.	References.
operations, and patrol on way; ̄ Nothing sibility poor.	
RD area, nothing to report.	
I WEALD.	
tember, 1940.	
flying carried out owing to very bad weather.	
tember, 1940.	
flying carried out owing to very bad weather.	
tember, 1940.	
DUXFORD. Patrolled DOVER and DUMGENESS	

6

COMBAT REPORTS

After every Battle of Britain combat, pilots recorded details of their engagement on Fighter Command Form 'F'. This was either filled out immediately upon landing and by hand, or dictated to the Intelligence Officer. Reporting on combats in this way was very important, providing information on enemy and friendly casualties, tactics and aircraft. The great thing about reading combat reports is that these are not fiction but actual aerial combat – recorded by the pilot who thumbed the gun button.

The following reports are typical of those submitted by Battle of Britain Hurricane pilots. Firstly we have 242 Squadron's Form 'F' for their engagement over Hatfield on 30 August 1940 – significant as the action which convinced Squadron Leader Bader that mass-fighter tactics would achieve greater execution (he was wrong, in fact; see *Douglas Bader* by this author, Amberley, 2013). In this report, the 242 Squadron 'Spy', Flight Lieutenant A. Maybaum, has extracted the relevant detail from various Hurricane pilots to produce an overview of the battle. This was then sent to both 12 Group Headquarters at Hucknall and Fighter Command Headquarters at Bentley Priory. Intelligence officers would then sift through reams of such reports to reconstruct the action – in much the same way as historians use these documents today. The second report is a similar document concerning the same engagement, summarising the combats of Northolt's Hurricane-equipped 1 Squadron. The reference to 'a Hurricane of "LE" squadron' in Pilot Officer Matthews' report refers to an aircraft of Bader's 242 Squadron.

A good example of a detailed individual combat report is our third document, this being Squadron Leader Bader's description of his claims for one Me 109 destroyed and another probably destroyed over Canterbury on 27 September 1940. Our final report is that of 501 Squadron's Sergeant Tony Pickering, a VR pilot who flew Hurricanes with this AAF squadron during the Battle of Britain, relating his claim for one

Me 109 destroyed over Cranbrook on 29 October 1940. 501 Squadron, in fact, fought in France before remaining in the front line throughout the entire Battle of Britain – a unique achievement. It also suffered the highest number of casualties – nineteen pilots killed.

From: No. 13 Group,

To: Headquarters, FIGHTER COMMAND.

(A) Sector Serial No.   J2
(B) Serial No. of Order detailing Flt. or Sqdn to patrol
(C) Date,   30.8.40
(D) Flight   Squadron 242
(E) Number of Enemy Aircraft   70 - 100
(F) Type of Enemy Aircraft,   Me. 110 and He. 111
(G) Time attack was delivered.   1700
(H) Place attack was delivered. Hatfield   - N. Weald.
(J) Height of enemy,   12,000 feet.
(K) Enemy Casualties.   (Destroyed 7 Me. 110, & 5 He. 111)(probable,
                            3 Me. 110.)   (Damaged.. Nil.)

(L) Our Casualties - Aircraft.   NIL
(M)   Personnel   NIL
(N) (i) Searchlights   N/A.
    (ii) Anti-Aircraft   NO.
(P) Range at which fire was opened in each attack on the enemy together
    with estimated length of burst.
                        See below.

(R) GENERAL REPORT.
Sqdn 242 were ordered at 1623 from Duxford to patrol North Weald at
15,000 feet on a vector 190 degrees just north of North Weald. They
received a vector of 340 degrees. 3 aircraft were noticed to the
right of the formation, so the Squadron Leader detached Blue Section
to investigate. Green Leader then drew attention to a large enemy
formation on their left so the rest of the Sqdn turned and saw a
vast number of aeroplanes flying in an easterly direction. These
were recognised to be from 70 to 100 E/A, twin engined in tight
formation stepped up at about 12,000 feet after which there was a
gap of 1000 feet, then another swarm of twin engined machines stepped
up from about 15,000 to 20,000 feet. Green section were ordered
to attack the top of the lower formation; Red and Yellow sections
were ordered to get into line astern. It seemed impossible to order any
formation attack. The Squadron leader dived straight into the middle
of the formation closely followed by Red 2 and Red 3; the packed
formation broke up and a dog fight ensued. S/Ldr. Bader saw 3 Me.
110's do climbing turns to the left and 3 to the right. Their tactics
appeared to be to climb in turns until they were nearly stalling
above the tail of S/L Bader's a/c. S/Ldr. Bader fired a short burst
into the Me. 110 at practically point blank range and the E/A burst
into flames and disintegrated almost immediately. S/Ldr. Bader then
continued his zoom and saw another Me. 110 below and so turned in behind
it and got a very easy shot at about 100 to 150 yards range.
After the E/A had received S/Ldr Bader's first burst of from 2 to 4
seconds, the enemy pilot avoided further action by putting the stick
violently backwards and forwards.

S/Ldr. Bader got another burst in and saw pieces of the enemy's
starboard wing fly off; then the whole starboard wing went on fire
and E/A went down burning in a spiral dive. S/Ldr. Bader then saw
in his mirror another Me. 110; he did a quick turn and noticed 5 or 6
white streams coming out of forward firing guns; the E/A immediately
put his nose down and was lost but was subsequently seen far below.

S/Ldr. Bader saw nothing around him, called Duxford and was told to
land. Weather was hazy for reflector sights. Plain glass was used.
Span 50 feet range 250 yards. No cine camera was carried. R/T
was satisfactory.

No hit sustained on own aircraft. Fired 960 rounds with no stoppages.
Landed Duxford 1720.
                    over...

Red 2 P/O W.C.McKnight went into attack with S/Ldr. Bader; he got behind an Me. 110 and opened fire at 100 yards, the E/A burst into flames and crashed to the ground. Next he attacked an He. 111, formation carrying out a beam attack on nearest one; E/A rolled over on back port engine caught fire and finally crashed to the ground. P/O McKnight was then being attacked by a Me. 110 but succeeded in getting behind and followed E/A from 10,000 feet to 1,000 feet. P/O McKnight opened fire at about approx 30 yards; E/A's starboard engine stopped; the port engine caught fire and E/A crashed in flames alongside a large reservoir.
No rear fire was noticed from first 2 enemy but last machine used a large amount but with no effect.
E/A had usual camouflage. Reflector sight, 60 feet span 250 yards range, no slip stream affect felt on astern attacks. Deflection allowed on beam attack, no hits sustained and R/T OK, no cine camera carried. 2640 rounds fired.

Red 3. P/O Crowley - Milling also went into attack with Red 1 and 2. Seeing an He. 111 break away from formation he made an astern attack giving a 5 secs burst. The enemy did not avoid action, but rear gun fire was experienced. Starboard engine of E/A started to smoke then E/A made dive to ground. At this particular moment a Me. 110 was commencing an attack so did not observe He. 111 crash though P/O Hart confirms seeing this a/c going down in flames. Landed North Weald 1725 and returned Duxford 1740. No slipstream was felt reflector sight used, span 60 feet range 230 yards, no hits sustained, R/T satisfactory. No cine camera carried. All rounds were used with no stoppages.

Yellow 1 F/Lt. G.E.Ball sighted an He. 111 diving and turning and gave him a third of his ammunition.
F/O Stansfield was also attacking this a/c which went down with engines alight and went down on aerodrome full of cars. F/Lt. Ball then attacked an Me. 110 making a port attack finishing with stern attack. One engine stopped dead and no return fire was experienced, all ammunition used, no stoppages reflector sights. span 60 feet range 250 R/T was satisfactory. No cine camera was carried. The sun was behind in both attacks. Yellow 2 F/Lt. R.L.R.L.Cork, Royal Navy saw a Me. 110 which he attacked in company with several others and which he saw going down, he broke away and saw another Me. 110 flying East, made a beam attack noticing port engine in flames. E/A did a stalled turn and dived to ground. E/A made no evasive tactics except in countering some rear fire from first E/A but which ceased very quickly. E/A were painted dark green and swastikas stood out clearly, allowed deflection on beam attack, reflector sight used, span 60 feet, 250 yards range. No hits sustained, R/T worked satisfactorily. No cine camera carried. 2000 rounds used, no stoppages. Yellow 3, Sgt. Lonsdale attacked an He. 111 which had broken away from its formation. After a prolonged burst of fire from quarter attack, E/A circled and crashed in flames, made no evasive tactics, landed Duxford 1750. rounds used 2410. 1 stoppage owing to rear cover unlocked used plenty of deflection.
Reflector sights. Span 60 feet range, 250 yards, no hits sustained R/T worked satisfactorily. No cine camera carried. Green 1 F/O Christie was with his section attacking a higher formation of E/A when he sighted an He.111 and 3 Me. 110. He carried out an head on attack on 1 Me. 110. E/A dived to port. He then attacked from astern, damaging starboard motor, then gave him 2 quarter attacks. Finally causing E/A to dive from 2000 feet crashing into a green house 500 yards west of Welsh Harp Lake. 1 short burst from rear gunner but no effect. All ammunition used, no stoppages. Reflector sight 50 feet. span;250 yards range; No cine camera carried. P/O Hart witnessed combat.
Green 3 P/O Hart saw 3 He. 111's below him and started to dive on them. He saw Yellow 1 attacking the last one and so attacked the second which went into a steep dive. He was about to follow the first E/A started a right hand turn. He turned inside E/A and gave him

over:....

all his ammunition. E/A plunged downwards in flames and crashed in
a field. White Leader. P/O Stansfield saw a straggler, an He. 111
He made 3 attacks all from port receiving a small amount of rear fire
but which very quickly ceased. E/A starboard motor stopped, a/c
started to dive and crashed in an aerodrome full of cars expended
all his ammunition. No stoppages.
Reflector sights used. No cine camera carried.
Landed Duxford 1725. F/Lt. Ball also attacked this E/A

White 2 Sgt. G.W.Brimble was flying at the rear of the sqdn and
after E/A formation had been broken saw an He. 111 which he gave
a burst of 3 secs. P/O Stansfield was also attacking the a/c and
he followed it to the ground.
White 2 then broke away and saw below him an Me.110 doing a gentle
turn to port. He made a quarter attack opening fire for 3 secs at 250
yards. E/A immediately burst into flames and crashed to the ground.
On rejoining his leader he saw another Me. 110 commencing an attack
on his a/c from the front. He opened fire finally making a
quarter attack noticing the glass in front of E/A splinter and
machine going into a violent dive. He did not see a/c crash as
another Me. 110 was on his tai, but felt certain that the pilot
was dead. He received little return fire from E/A and no evasive
tactics were made. Rounds used 720, no stoppages. Deflection
allowed on quarter attacks. Reflector sights. Span 60 feet.
Range 250 yards. No hits sustained and no cine camera carried.
R/T worked satisfactorily. Landed Duxford approx. 1730.

     Sgd. A. Maybaum,   F/Lt. Sector Intelligence Officer,
                              COLTISHALL.

R. 1645 hrs. 1.9.40.
FG/S. 17570/INT.

FCOR/634/40.   FORM "F"   S E C R E T+

FIGHTER COMMAND COMBAT REPORT.

To: FIGHTER COMMAND.

From No. 11 Group.

30. 8. 40. Intelligence Patrol Report.

11 Hurricanes No. 1 Squadron left Northolt at 1631 hours - Landed Northolt 1730 to 1745 hours. When North of London they sighted 6 a/c and when preparing to attack recognised them as Blenheims. Shortly afterwards an Enemy formation consisting of 30 to 40 bombers, protected by a similar number of fighters in no standard formation from 12,000 to 25,000 ft. were seen. The attack which followed was carried out individually by the pilots.

Sgt. Merchant reports:
"I was No. 2 of Red Section, and upon sighting enemy followed my Section Leader in line astern. After attacking a Do. 17 which was in Company with another E/A, a Me. 110. dived on me from astern. Breaking away I shook him off, and then saw ahead a single Heinkel 111 K. Climbing and going ahead, I attacked from the beam. On the second attack the Port engine stopped. At this moment a Hurricane from another Squadron dived from the rear of the He. 111 and got in a burst. Again attacking from the front I got in a long burst, and a man jumped by "chute". A further two parachutists jumped after about one minute as I put in another burst. The aircraft dived down and crashed in the middle of a road near a Cemetary to the East of Southend. Rounds fired 300 from each gun".

P/O Birch reports: "I was Blue 2. I attacked a Heinkel 111 at 10,000 ft. From in front port quarter I got in two bursts and saw short burst of black smoke and bits come from Port engine. It continued in flight with white smoke coming from this engine and loosing height towards Thames Estuary, but I was unable to gain on it, so returned to base.".

P/O Hancock reports:

"I was Blue 3. After making a false attack on 6 Blenheims, I pursued the main body of enemy aircraft. One He. 111 was lagging behind. I gained height and prepared to attack it. Before doing so however, a Spitfire did an astern attack of about 5 sec. duration. I then went in and fired several long bursts at each engine in turn. I observed smoke, oil and flames coming from each engine. I did not follow the aircraft to the ground as a Vic of Me. 110 appeared to be attacking me. I evaded them and returned to base."

Sgt. Clowes reports. "I was Yellow One. I sighted Enemy and reported to Garter. 15 leading Bombers fairly close at 11,000 ft. with twenty to thirty stragglers up to 15,000 ft and a larger number of Me. 110's (50 to 60) up to 15, to 25,000 ft. in no standard formation. I looped up to one Me. 110 and gave him a short burst which caused the starboard engine to omit a strong streak of white smoke. I then made an astern attack on three He. 111's at 12,000 ft. The first He.111 omitted smoke and some flames. The second the perspex exploded, and I made a head on attack on a Do. 17 at 10,000 ft with no apparent results. My range in each attack was about 250 yds and bursts about two seconds each. I then returned to base".

P/O Mann reports:

'I was Yellow three. After the false attack on the Blenheims I broke away to follow the C.O. I gave the alarm on sighting 30 Bombers and 20 Me. 110's immediately above us. I followed a Me. 110 and gave three bursts about 3 secs each one on each engine, and one on fuselage. Port engine was damaged and smoking. He returned my fire, probably cannon. E/A took evasive action and I broke away, and followed another ME 110, and gave it two bursts on Port engine, which started smoking fairly heavily. My ammunition gave out and so I returned to base.

over...

FOCR/634/40.

P/O Matthews reports :-

" I was Red 1. I followed the C.O. Section 27 Blenheims, and before engaging broke section away to left towards about forty e/a. I was attacked by Me. 110's at 12,000 ft. They were in turn attacked by Hurricanes. I saw a straggling He. 111 and fired all my ammunition into it from astern. Starboard engine packed up. I broke away when I had finished my ammunition and a Hurricane of No. 56 Sqdn came in to finish it off. I did not see the result. Rear Gunner fired the whole time until I broke off."

S/L Pemberton reports that while attacking an E/A in company with a Hurricane of "L.E." Squadron, the rear gunner continued to fire when within a few seconds of hitting the ground. This e/a which fell near Epping, will be claimed by that Hurricane.

As a result of the Sortie, one He. 111 was destroyed, one He. 111 was probably destroyed, 3 He. 111's and 3 Me. 110's damaged.

FO/S. 17570/INT.
23.9.40.

A. Sector Serial No....J1.
B. Serial Number of order detailing Flight or Squadron to patrol...25
C. Date...27.9.40.
D. Leader...Squadron 242.
E. Number of enemy aircraft... Approx.20.-30.
F. Type of enemy aircraft..... Me.109.
G. Time attack was delivered...Between 12:0 1230 hours.
H. Place attack was delivered..Dover-Dungeness-Canterbury area.
J. Height of enemy.............Approx.17-20,000 feet.
K. Enemy Casualties............1 Destroyed, 1 Probable.
L. Our Casualties-Aircraft..... --
M. Our Casualties-Personnel.... --
N(i)Searchlights (Did they illuminate enemy; if not, were they in front
        or behind target?).....Not applicable.
N(ii)A.A. Guns (Did shell bursts assist pilot intercepting the enemy?)...No.
P. Range at which fire was opened in each attack delivered on the enemy
        together with estimated length of burst...A number of 2 second bursts
                                            at close range.

R. GENERAL REPORT

        12 Group Wing were ordered off to patrol around London - Wing consisted
of 242, 310 (Hurricanes) and 19,616 (Spitfires). Heard over the R/T that
enemy formations were reported S.E. of Estuary so patrolled South of
E stuary. Eventually sighted what seemed to be enemy aircraft circling
around near Dover - Canterbury at about 18-20,000 feet. The wing was at
23,000 feet. On approaching I discovered what appeared to be a number
of Me.109's just milling around. No formation attack was possible or
desirable so I manoeuvred the wing up sun from enemy who did not see us
and then ordered the wing to break up and attack as they liked. I chose
an Me.109 which was passing underneath me and turned behind and above him
and gave him a short 2 seconds burst with the immediate result that he
became enveloped in thick white smoke turned over slowly and dived
vertically. I did not follow it down and as it was the first 109 shot
down, it was seen by P/O Cowley-Milling (Red 3) P/O Bush (Blue 2) and F/Lt.
Turner (Blue 1) in fact almost the whole Squadron. I also had my camera
gun in action which will give further confirmation. A second 109 passed
in front and below me and I turned in behind him and I got in a short
squirt and he took evasive action by rolling on to his back and diving
down. I did the same but pulled out short and cut him off on the climb and
had a long chase after him finally getting near enough for a short long
distance squirt (400) yards, this caused a puff of white smoke from him
and slowed him down perceptibly and I managed to close up. I gave him
more short bursts, one missed him completely but the others hit and besides
white vapour the last squirt caused black smoke from the port side of his
fuselage and my aeroplane and windscreen was covered with oil from his
aeroplane. His propeller stopped dead and the last I saw of him was
gliding down quietly and apparently under full control, with his engine
dead and his aeroplane smoking in the Channel. As I was on the Coast
myself and out of ammunition and we were both by this time at about 10,000
feet I decided discretion was required and I dived to ground level into
the haze and went back to Gravesend and landed, rearmed and refueled and
lunched with 66 Squadron. This last combat finished on the Coast between
Dover and Ramsgate. This Me.109 was a definite write-off but can only be
considered a probable because the pilot was O.K., obviously and although
he was bound to land in the Channel from 10,000 feet he might have been
picked up by his own people. A camera gun record was taken of this fight
also.

        On the way back I saw the burning wreckage of an Me.109 on the ground
just South of Canterbury.

        12 Group Wing as a whole did well, because in a complete shambles with

                                                        Cont...

fighters it is difficult to get a continued attack and with everyone
manoeuvring in a small space and the enemy aircraft really running
away the chances are less than when a bomber formation is attacked
further inland. The 2nd. 109 I attacked fired back at me with a
cannon situated just under the starboard wing close in to the fuselage.
I took careful note of this and it was quite ineffective. The enemy
did not seem to be working to any plan and I had no enemy aircraft
on my tail the whole time.

Visibility was good with a rather fortunate cloud layer at about
25,000 feet although only about 6/10ths it was in the right position
to afford some protection to the Wing while patrolling Dungeness-
Dover. I do not think that enemy saw us at all until we arrived amongst
them. It is considered essential that the Squadrons comprising the
Wing should be re-equipped as soon as possible (1) with V.H.F. (2)
with Hurricanes 11 and Spitfires 11 for altitude performance which
is vitally important.

                              Signed.
                                    D. R. S. Bader
                                                   S/LDR.
                              O/C
                                  242 Squadron.

COMBAT REPORT

Sector ....rial No............(A)..................................

IIN 40 K28 28

Serial No. of Order detailing
Flight or Squadron to Patrol.(B)...............................
Date.......29.10.40.........(C).................................

                          Flight "B"
     Flight, Squadron, Type Squadron 501 Squadron
     of Aircraft.........(D) Aircraft Hurricanes
Number of enemy aircraft....(E).........One.......................
Type of enemy aircraft......(F).........M.E.109..................

Time attack was delivered...(G).........17.15...................
Place attack was delivered..(H).........Greenbrook..............
Height of enemy............(J).........10,000 ft...............
Enemy casualties...........(K).........1 M.E.109 destroyed.......
Our casualties...(1)Aircraft(L).........Nil....................
         (2)Personnel(M).........Nil.....................
Searchlights on target
  ahead or behind,,,,,,,,,,(N)1.................................
A.A. Guns-Did they assist....(N)2..............................

Range at which fire was opened, 1st burst 300 yards. 4 secs,5bursts
and estimated lengths of bursts(P)..150 yards. 2 secs...........
No. of rounds fired....................2,400....................

Pilots name and position in section Sgt. T.G.Pickering.. Yellow 4.........

General Report...............(R)

      We were vectored onto 2 waves of enemy aircraft at 23,000 feet
which seemed to be engaged by spitfires. I heeled off after one
M.E.109 but he easily out dived me and I lost him before I could
get within range. I circled around for ten minutes at 10,000 ft
looking for he Squadron when I saw 2 J.U.88's at 12,000 feet
going east over Tonbridge. I climbed to attack but could not
get within 800 yards and they were steadily drawing away from me,
I then saw on my Starboard side and about a mile in front an
aircraft which proved to be an M.E.109, I closed in to 300 yards
and saw it was yellow with large black crosses on the upper
surface of the wings. I immediately opened fire from dead astern
and he went into a dive turning and twisting to evade my fire. I
followed him down firing short bursts all the time and when he
was at about 500 feet diving towards the ground I gave him my
last burst which set fire to his starboard petrol tank and he
dived into the ground at the corner of a wood and immediately
blew up. The pilot did not bale out. The aircraft crashed at
Ham Street approximately 15 miles North West of Dungeness.

                  Signed... T.G. Pickering Sgt.

7

AIRCRAFT RECOGNITION

Aircraft recognition was a big interest during the Second World War among civilians on the Home Front – not least schoolboys! However, for fighter pilots this was essential knowledge which could mean the split-second difference between life and death. Crew rooms on airfields throughout the world were awash with aircraft models and recognition handbooks. Playing cards were a novel way of brushing up on aircraft recognition – these four cards showing the Hawker Hurricane Mk I in plan views are from a deck called 'War Planes: A Card Game For Aircraft Spotters', published early in the Second World War by Temple Press and costing all of three shillings (15p).

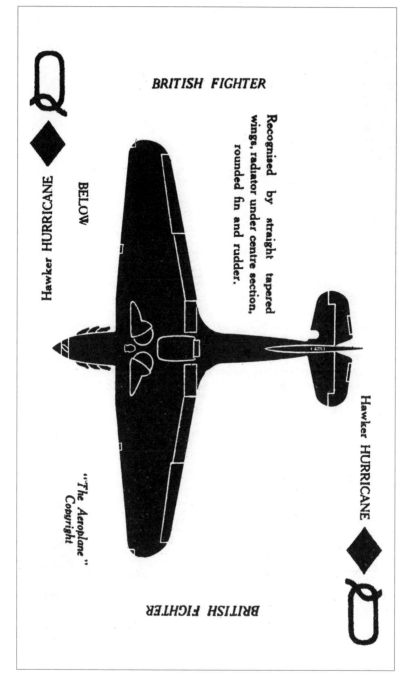

BRITISH FIGHTER

Recognised by straight tapered wings, radiator under centre section, rounded fin and rudder.

BELOW

Hawker HURRICANE

Hawker HURRICANE

"The Aeroplane"
Copyright

BRITISH FIGHTER

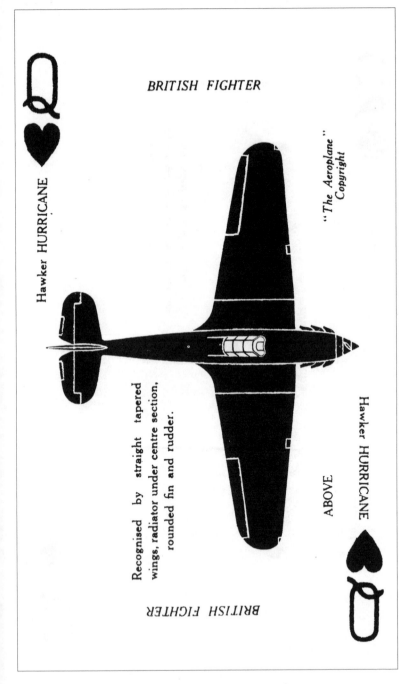

BRITISH FIGHTER

Hawker HURRICANE

"*The Aeroplane*"
Copyright

Recognised by straight tapered wings, radiator under centre section, rounded fin and rudder.

ABOVE

Hawker HURRICANE

BRITISH FIGHTER

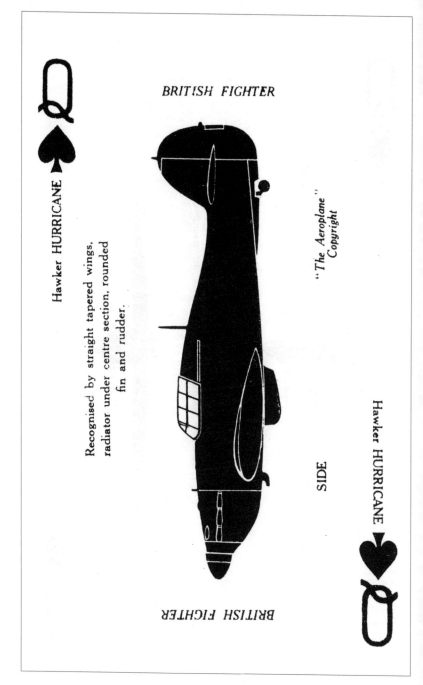

BRITISH FIGHTER

Hawker HURRICANE

Recognised by straight tapered wings, radiator under centre section, rounded fin and rudder.

"The Aeroplane" Copyright

SIDE

Hawker HURRICANE

BRITISH FIGHTER

BRITISH FIGHTER

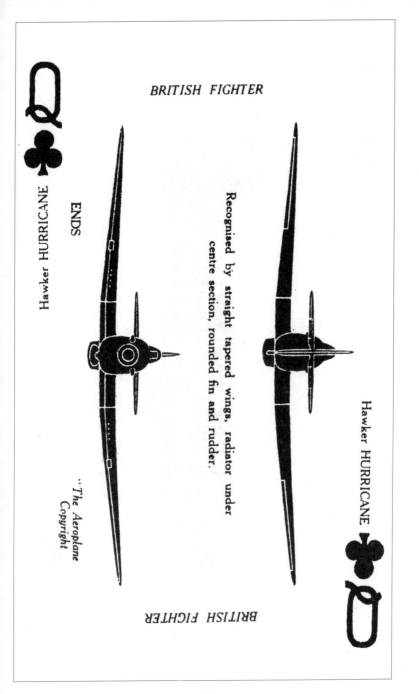

Recognised by straight tapered wings, radiator under centre section, rounded fin and rudder.

Hawker HURRICANE

ENDS

Hawker HURRICANE

"The Aeroplane Copyright

BRITISH FIGHTER

ACKNOWLEDGEMENTS

Like my *Spitfire Manual* this book was not actually my idea but that of my publisher, Jonathan Reeve, of Amberley Publishing.

All of the Hurricane pilots quoted herein were friends of mine; sadly all are now deceased, but their foresight to help me record their wartime experiences will leave a lasting legacy – long after my own exit to that great Sector Station in the sky.

OTHER BOOKS BY DILIP SARKAR
(IN ORDER OF PUBLICATION)

Spitfire Voices: Life as a Spitfire Pilot in the Words of the Veterans
How the Spitfire Won the Battle of Britain
Spitfire Ace of Aces: The True Wartime Story of Johnnie Johnson
The Sinking of HMS Royal Oak
Douglas Bader
Spitfire: The Photographic Biography

Also available from Amberley Publishing

SPITFIRE
A PHOTOGRAPHIC BIOGRAPHY

DILIP SARKAR

Also available from Amberley Publishing

Also available from Amberley Publishing

How to fly the legendary fighter plane in combat using the manuals and instructions supplied by the RAF during the Second World War

'A Must' *INTERCOM: THE AIRCREW ASSOCIATION*

An amazing array of leaflets, books and manuals were issued by the War Office during the Second World War to aid pilots in flying the Supermarine Spitfire, here for the first time they are collated into a single book with the original 1940s setting. An introduction is supplied by expert aviation historian Dilip Sarkar. Other sections include aircraft recognition, how to act as an RAF officer, bailing out etc.

£9.99 Paperback
40 illustrations
264 pages
978-1-84868-436-2

Also available as an ebook
Available from all good bookshops or to order direct
Please call **01453-847-800**
www.amberleybooks.com

Also available from Amberley Publishing

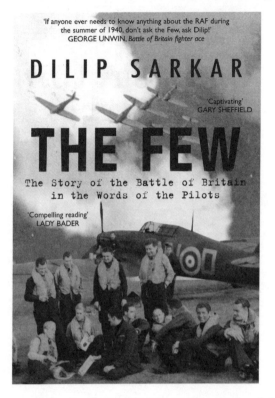

'If anyone ever needs to know anything about the RAF during the summer of 1940, don't ask the Few, ask Dilip!'
GEORGE UNWIN, *Battle of Britain fighter ace*

DILIP SARKAR

'Captivating'
GARY SHEFFIELD

THE FEW

The Story of the Battle of Britain in the Words of the Pilots

'Compelling reading'
LADY BADER

The history of the Battle of Britain in the words of the pilots

'Over the last 30 years Dilip Sarkar has sought out and interviewed or corresponded with numerous survivors worldwide. Many of these were not famous combatants, but those who formed the unsung backbone of Fighter Command in 1940. Without Dilip's patient recording and collation of their memories, these survivors would not have left behind a permanent record.' LADY BADER
'A well-researched detailed chronicle of the Battle of Britain'. HUGH SEBAG MONTEFIORE

£9.99 Paperback
129 photographs
320 pages
978-1-4456-0701-6

Also available as an ebook
Available from all good bookshops or to order direct
Please call **01453-847-800**
www.amberleybooks.com

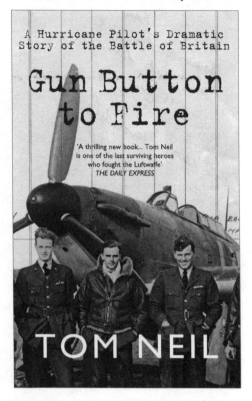